STATE AND POLITICS

DELEUZE AND GUATTARI ON MARX

SEMIOTEXT(E) FOREIGN AGENTS SERIES

© Presses Univertaires de France, 2013. 6, avenue Reille, 75014 Paris.
© This edition 2016 by Semiotext(e)

Published by Semiotext(e)
PO BOX 629. South Pasadena, CA 91031
www.semiotexte.com

Special thanks to John Ebert.

Cover art by Ben G. Fodor, EUR Roma (from the series I.V.N.), 2007.

Design by Hedi El Kholti

ISBN: 978-1-58435-176-4
Distributed by The MIT Press, Cambridge, Mass. and London, England
Printed in the United States of America

STATE AND POLITICS

DELEUZE AND GUATTARI ON MARX

Guillaume Sibertin-Blanc

Translated by Ames Hodges

Contents

Introduction

The political thought of Deleuze and Guattari is largely neglected. It is either deferred through a so-called micropolitical approach, or called on as a speculative supplement to other contemporary thinkers like Foucault, Negri, or Rancière, who do fine on their own. Sometimes, it is simply omitted in favor of bizarre extrapolations from political implications found in metaphysical, noetic, or ontological statements in Deleuze's work without accounting for any of his assertions on the key signifiers that have polarized and divided modern political thought. It would be poor form to call for a discursive police to return all statements belonging to the domains of "metaphysics," "aesthetics," or "politics" behind their borders, especially when trying to do justice to two authors who endeavored to blur the boundaries between them. Yet when this decoding of discourse, in the name of a micropolitics of subjectivity, eschatology of the multitude, or plundering the *sans-parts*, leads not to restating the macro-political problems but acting as if they miraculously disappeared, then this omission deserves reflection.

Most obviously, this oversight allows one to pass over in silence the nonetheless massive fact that the joint work of Deleuze and Guattari gives rise, in a direct, explicit, and identifiable manner in perfectly circumscribable texts, to the work of re-elaborating a certain number of nodal problems of contemporary political thought: the State-form; the question of sovereignty; the relationships between economic processes and the relationship between violence and law; the historical rise of national formations and the recombinations that they initiated between the concepts of people, minority, autonomy, and sovereignty; the relationships between economic processes and structures of social and State power; the question of war; the entanglements between geo-economy and geopolitics, and more. One part that contributes to such a patent omission is the persistent repression, within philosophical studies, of the theoretical, political, and institutional trajectory of Félix Guattari and his effects on Deleuze's work.[1] This repression cannot be explained only by disciplinary frontiers and the play of unequal recognition in both the academic and analytical fields between the two authors. More profoundly—at least in the angle of approach proposed here in a reading that focuses primarily on the two volumes of *Capitalism and Schizophrenia*[2]—it is a question of how this repression is intensified by another, no less persistent repression: repression of the contexts in which the political positions of their times were defined, in theory and practice, where the means specific to conceptual work were supposed to take action. Whether we like it or not, most of the problems that Deleuze and Guattari faced in the field of political thought, and to which they proposed variously critical and inventive reworkings, came to them from specific discursive formations, the first of which is Marxism, whose theoretical language and political grammar still greatly polarize the modes of utterance, representation, and problematization of resistance and liberation struggles. Deleuze and Guattari, however, and in another way Foucault, wanted to find an *alternative* to Marxism, an alternative that required no little endurance to find in the play of substitutions from Nietzsche to Marx, from the "philosophy of difference" to the driving negativity of "Hegelian-Marxism," from the micropolitics of subjectivity to the dialectics of heteronomy and split identities. This operation, which appeared at the turn of the 1960s–1970s, and was sometimes validated by the authors themselves in somewhat awkward declarations in terms of what was stated in their work, was systematized in the reception of the 1980s–1990s, while the alternatives of Nietzsche-Marx, Difference-Dialectic, and others became the object of academic exercises with increasingly intangible theoretical and political stakes.

In this case it is better to follow the working hypothesis recently proposed by Isabelle Garo in a book dedicated to this philosophical and political sequence,[3] and that gives timely support to other attempts in recent years to give a symptomatic reading of French philosophy in the decades after the Second World War. This approach reinserts their thought into the highly problematic field of ideological and political decompositions and recompositions of the 1960s and 1970s, where the relationship with Marxists was central (even and perhaps especially when it was only alluded to or oblique).[4] It contributes to accounting for the "crisis" that Marxism underwent, but without forgetting that Marxism itself often pronounced this same diagnosis, that the diagnosis is even in some ways coextensive with its history, inseparable from its transformations through the organizations and mass movements that appropriated it, and from its divisions in contact with the contexts and struggles that called on it. The context that interests me the most here requires us to account for the fact that if there was a crisis, it was inseparable from a complex movement involving the history of the labor movement and its organizations in Western Europe, the rise of new forms of struggle made possible by the structures of the social State (even when these struggles targeted it), but also the major tendency towards depoliticization that took place in the decade after

May 68.[5] On the one hand, this tendency aggravated the division within the communist movement between political practice and theoretical practice, making the critical or even dissident self-referentiality of Marxism increasingly difficult (*Marxist* critiques of Marxism). On the other, it could trigger a compensatory "over-politicization" of the philosophical field with inevitably ambivalent effects: opening a space for experimentation with a "politics of philosophy" that implied the invention of new modes of problematizing Marxist critique (including the critique of political economy) *in part outside its language*, but at the price of simultaneously ratifying a growing abandonment of strategic, organizational, and political-ideological problems, and at the risk of trading this politics of philosophy for depoliticized political practice.[6]

While I fully agree with the framework of reflection proposed by Isabelle Garo, although we arrive at different and even diametrically opposed conclusions, I infer that the same working hypothesis leaves open the possibility of contrasting interpretations—of texts, of the ambivalences of their contextual meaning, of the diverging appropriations performed later, and of their potential, alternative reactivations today—and therefore a space for agreement and debate to which the following pages hope to contribute. In attempting to identify a divergence that relates to the main theme proposed here, it can be found in the meaning given to this reading "in context." Resituating the theoretical co-production of Deleuze and Guattari in the historical, social, political, and intellectual context that made it possible, and shedding light in return on the forms and objectives they gave to their intervention, means first, in taking distance from their statements, to give ourselves the means to question their operativeness, hypothetical analyzers of what we have inherited from this context where the continuities and cuts, the identifications and dis-identifications are hard to perceive. However, by looking more specifically at the period that separates the two tomes of *Capitalism and Schizophrenia*, I will ask what is diffracted from a *fusion of several contexts*, which both thwart the sequencing of a univocal chronology of the period and singularly complexify the perspective we can receive from it in the present.[7] The difficulty can be expressed in terms of a chiasmus. On the one hand, these two works can be read as signs of an historical transition, one on which they give perspective through their very differences, through a series of displacements from the first to the second volume that need to be identified. It is strange that they have been read as a philosophical interpretation of capitalism that took the Fordist period as the definitive end of its contradictions, renouncing the program of a critique of political economy, and idealizing instead in the period of self-centered growth of Western countries as a political-economic system finally free of its systemic crises and class conflicts, capable of neutralizing in advance any constitution of a counter-hegemony capable of calling it into question globally. The hypothesis of capital as "global axiomatics" starting in 1972 reveals on the contrary and all too explicitly the crisis of this "Keynesian-Fordist" sequence while calling for a new systemic critique of capitalist power on a global scale. It justifies a theory of the State-form manifestly constructed as an operation of *dis-idealization* of the Keynesian social-capitalist State. It also carries out a rereading of the Marxist corpus polarized throughout by the problem of "immanent limits" (*immanenten Schranken*) of expanded accumulation and the drop in the rate of profit (a tendency that has grown since the end of the 1960s), by the crises of overproduction and the new economic and monetary forms that they were taking, by the transformations, through the twists and turns of the Cold War and national liberation struggles, of structures of the international division of labor, of unequal exchange, and of the "postcolonial" modes of exploitation and domination. Moreover, and to symbolically retain dates that have nothing symbolic in themselves, from the oil crisis and the deregulation of the exchange market by abandoning gold conversion (one year after the publication of *Anti-Oedipus*), to the "financial coup-d'état" carried out by the American central bank by lifting restrictions on the mobility of capital and freeing the mechanisms of financial globalization for three decades to come[8] (one year before *A Thousand Plateaus*), the analyses of Deleuze and Guattari record, through the work of a conceptual retranslation of the program of a critique of political economy, the attacks on neoliberalism already developing its enterprise of dismantling the compromise of class after the Second World War, and combining new forms of "interior peripheralization" and the reactivation of predatory techniques of primitive accumulation in the "center" of globalized capitalism.[9]

Yet the question is not simply to reevaluate the clairvoyance of these two authors regarding the future of the capitalist form found during their time. It is much more surprising that these large trends were reactivated within Deleuze and Guattari's thought, either explicitly as thematization, often indirectly through motifs or cases presented, the problems posed by the systematization of the nation-State form on the European continent after the First World War, the correlated "invention" of the status of minority as a "permanent institution" (Hannah Arendt), the chain of economic, financial, and political crises, and the exacerbation of class racism and xenophobia on a massive scale, the paroxistic fusion of sovereignties with the forces of nationalism and imperialism, the repression of communist organizations and the failure of the labor movement to counter European fascism, the completion of the "fascist solution" in a global war machine. Such that the political thought of Deleuze and Guattari is penetrated by a troubling after-effect: as if the changes in capitalism for which their analyses bring the most destructive and "aneconomic" vectors back to the fore, had the correlate of making the specter of the European context between the World Wars "return" to the 1970s as well, forming the most significant tropism of Deleuze and Guattari's macropolitical thought. The question would then be to examine the extent to which this context, which in some ways "anachronizes" this thought in relation to its time, still contributes to addressing our own, paradoxically because of this anachronism itself.

The trajectory that I propose through *Capitalism and Schizophrenia* aims to shed light on this "between the wars tropism": its central thread is the question of the place of violence in political space, and more precisely, that of the ways in which it can be pushed to extremes where political confrontations shift into an *impolitical* dimension of violence that nullifies the very possibility of conflict. For Deleuze and Guattari, these paths are irreducibly multiple, and refer to a pluralist philosophy of forms of power, calling each time on specific dialectics of politicization and "impoliticization," or distinct modalities of illimitation of violence in the becoming of antagonisms. The three principal ways analyzed correspond to the outline of the book: I/ State power, to which I attach, using the expression "archi-violence," Deleuze and Guattari's concept of an illimitation of sovereign violence inscribed in the State-form and the structure of its "apparatuses"; II/ the power of war, which through the term "exo-violence" refers to the becoming-unlimited of an extrinsic war machine that States can only ever partially appropriate, and to which they can even subordinate their own power; III/ capitalist power, with which I associate under the expression "endo-violence" a way to illimit violence carried specifically by the dynamics of a world-economy destroying all exteriority or "exogeneity." Step by step, it will be a way to draw an overall portrait of the lines of ascension to extreme violence, allowing us to read the macropolitics of Deleuze and Guattari as a theory of the plurality of genealogical ways to destroy politics.

At the same time, these three moments correspond to what Deleuze and Guattari themselves presented as working *hypotheses*: the hypothesis of an "*Urstaat*," the hypothesis of a "war machine," the hypothesis of capital functioning as an "axiomatic." For this reason, I endeavor, on the one hand, to redraw the terrain of dialogues and polemics on which these hypotheses were developed, and the conceptual arrangement that allows them to be situated in relation to each other. This terrain and this arrangement find their unifying expression, or at least the one with the most consistent balance, in the table of "machinic processes" established in the 12th and 13th of the *Thousand Plateaus*, and for which the synoptic summary is given on pages 435–437.[10] This explains in part the selection, and therefore the points of focus and blind spots of the reading I propose, as well as the interlocutor it privileges: historical materialism (which also implies critical questioners of historical materialism, as we will see for example in the place occupied by Pierre Clastres in Deleuze and Guattari's theory of the State). It explains in any case the choice of the expression "historico-machinic materialism" to refer to the macropolitics of Deleuze and Guattari under its philosophical, epistemological, and political expectations. Like any label, this one runs the risk of simplification. I hope that it is seen as the counterpart to the position it attempts to signify and offer up for further discussion. By also taking into account this hypothetical value of the concepts of "*Urstaat*," "nomadic war machine," and "capitalist axiomatic," in the margins of the reading, I initiate a series of confrontations with other contemporary authors, like Étienne Balibar and David Harvey, or "untimely" ones, in particular Clausewitz and Carl Schmitt, by trying to imagine the context of the debate in which this triple hypothesis deserves to be considered. The essential work remains to be done; here, I will only attempt to set the stage and lay down some groundwork.

This book collects the results of my doctoral research at the Université Lille 3 between 2002 and 2006 under the direction of Pierre Macherey. Some texts have already appeared in *Deleuze et l'Anti-Œdipe. La production du désir* (PUF 2010), of which this work is the continuation. The first part on Deleuze and Guattari's theory of the State was the object of a previous synthesis in *Revista de Antropologia Social dos Alunos do PPGAS—UFSCar* (São Carlos 2011), also published in English and Turkish in *Monokl* (Istanbul 2012). The second part drew on two previous pieces on the theme of the "war machine" that have been reworked and combined here: "Mécanismes guerriers et généalogie de la guerre: l'hypothèse de la 'machine de guerre' de Deleuze et Guattari," and "The War Machine, the Formula and the Hypothesis: Deleuze and Guattari as Readers of Clausewitz," that appeared respectively in the review *Asterion* in September 2005 and in the volume *Deleuze and War* coordinated by Brad Evans and Laura Guillaume for *Theory and Event* (Johns Hopkins University Press). The conclusive theses of the third part were first sketched out in "Deleuze et les minorités: quelle 'politique'?" in *Cités* 40, 2009, translated into English as "Politicising Deleuzian Thought, or Minority's Position Within Marxism," in Dhruv Jain (ed.), *Deleuze Studies*, Edinburgh University Press, vol. 3, suppl, December 2009; and in "D'une conjuncture l'autre: Guattari et Deleuze après-coup," *Actuel Marx*, 52: *Deleuze/Guattari*, 2nd semester 2012.

This book is dedicated to Pierre Macherey, in recognition and fidelity.

PART ONE

ARCHI-VIOLENCE:
PRESUPPOSITION OF THE STATE

1

Historical Materialism and Schizoanalysis of the Form-State

In the joint works of Deleuze and Guattari, the question of the State first emerges in a trope that is enigmatic to say the least, and in the context of a no less disconcerting argument. In 1972, in Chapter III of *Anti-Oedipus*, at the heart of a vast genealogy of morality and capitalism, there is a study of a "despotic" social machine and its corresponding State: "despotic," "Asian," "original State," *Urstaat*, "cerebral ideality" and objective paradigm, ideal "model of everything the State wants to be and desires."[1] Playing on old, "orientalist" imagery borrowed from the accounts of missionaries, travelers in the Levant, and guests of the Great Mughals, these expressions recreate an ambiguity that we often find in *Anti-Oedipus* and that can be found in all of Deleuze and Guattari's reflections on the State, like a zone of undecidability between two regimes of utterance. Are we dealing with an analysis of historical positivity, or is it a question of having us glimpse and feel, using the resources of writing and the image, the way that history is desired, constitutively hallucinated under a desiring investment which, according to the principle thesis of "schizoanalysis" is part of its objective determination just as much as its social or structural positivity? Are we reading a continuation of Marx's *Pre-Capitalist Forms of Production*, or a variation on Freud's *Moses and Monotheism*? A rewriting of Engels'

Origin of the Family, Private Property, and the State or a new variation on *Totem and Taboo*? Since the superposing of palimpsests, the multiplication of sources and interlocutors, the embedding of argumentative styles, and hypotyposis make the choice between these alternatives undecidable, we already have a clue as to the objective of the *Urstaat* hypothesis and of the analysis of its becoming in the history of social formations: the refusal to separate the level of distinct "subjective" or "psychical" desire from historical objectivity; substituting a relationship of co-constitution and co-production of historical reality by social formations and desiring formations for relationships of internalization and projection that presuppose the reciprocal exteriority of terms. This hypothesis opens a *theory of the State-form* that aims to identify its modes of efficacy and efficiency simultaneously in social production and unconscious production. This form therefore combines an apparatus of power and a trans-individual position of desire, a complex institutional system and a system of collective subjectivation.

The problem lies with understanding the articulation of these two aspects at the point of interference between an anthropological and historical approach to the State in the material becoming of societies and a shizoanalytical approach of the *Urstaat* as a group fantasy:[2] "model of everything the State wants to be and desires," but also the desire of the *subjects* of the State, subjectivation of a "desire of the desire of the State."[3] First there is a return to the question of sovereignty, which Deleuze and Guattari propose to formulate so that it allows thinking the type of subjection implied by the constitution of a sovereign power in its indissolubly socio-institutional and unconscious dimensions. Tying the question of the institutional and symbolic organizations supporting the representation of this power to a study of the forms of collectivization of demands, representations, and affects exercised by its authority, their analysis of the State phenomenon situates itself in a debate with Reichian Freudo-Marxism and the Freud of *Group Psychology and the Analysis of the Ego*, but in the wake of Spinoza's *Theological-Political Treatise*. It finds its culmination in the construction of the concept of an "original State," the operator of a *seizure of power* in the trans-individual productions of the unconscious, which reorganizes the fantasy scenarios in which collective identifications are regulated and the modes of subjectivation of social individuals. From there, from this operator, the effects of *après-coup* or the constant "returns" through history make intelligible what seems to constitute the rock of irrationality that both legal and political sciences as well as sociological and psychological approaches to State power run up against: the paroxystic or "ultra-institutional" forms that State violence takes when it manifestly exceeds any social, economic or political functionality of the State's repressive power, no less than the subjective intentionality of its agents or representatives. This archi-violence is what, for them, comes to explain the thesis of an inherent paranoia in the State-form.

Deleuze and Guattari by no means intend to psychologize the State phenomenon or substitute an applied psychoanalysis of political phenomena for a historical and materialist decoding of State apparatuses and the transformations of State power in dialectics of social relationships and collective struggle. In accordance with an immanent concept of desire, the State does not become a "complex" within desire without desire itself, according to the main schizoanalytic thesis becoming a production that is immanent to economic and political relationships and to the collective, historical-global identifications that support them. The *sui generis* Freudian-Marxism of *Anti-Oedipus*—a strange Lacanian-Althusserianism in point of fact—is still *Marxism*.[4] A heterodoxical Marxism, to be sure, but precisely in the sense that its fundamental theoretical decisions concerning the theory of the State are determined by the difficulties inherited from this theoretical-political movement, and for which Deleuze and Guattari attempt to shift/displace the terms. For this reason, I will begin by showing that a materialist recasting of the theory of the State and the aporia associated with it is the basis on which our authors problematize a State-form *in excess* of its own material apparatuses (Chap. 1). This debate will also shed light on the reason why a theory of the *State as fantasy*, which imposes in return a *fantasmatic moment of the theory* of the State, and therefore a limit-moment of theoretical writing itself. This torsion does not propose abandoning a clarification of the State's functions in the social body; on the contrary, it redirects the examination, under the conditions of modern nations, of the place of the State in the mode of production and accumulation of capital. From Chapter III of *Anti-Oedipus* in 1972 to the 12th and 13th of *A Thousand Plateaus* in 1980, the hypothesis of the *Urstaat* comes to be articulated with a new concept of the *State apparatus* ("apparatus of capture") (Chap. 2). This first part will retrace some of the sectors of this trajectory to indicate how, at the intersection of the materialist-historical approach to the State phenomenon and the schizoanalytical hypothesis of the *Urstaat*, the question of violence or economies of violence implied by the State apparatus and power is reworked/resituated.

Aporia in the Origin of the State: Impossible Genesis and Untraceable Beginning

The singularity of Deleuze and Guattari's theory of the State comes first from the fact that it is based on a questioning of the very possibility of making the State the object of a "theory," in the sense of a conceptual practice that masters, at least rightfully, its own operations of intelligibility. This is apparent, both in *Anti-Oedipus* and the 13th Plateau ("7000 B.C.: Apparatus of Capture"), in the fact that this theory takes a profoundly aporetical form. The aporia appears in different ways that are interconnected while interacting each time with specific interlocutors. First, it touches on the anthropological-historical problem of the *origin of the State* and proceeds to a deconstruction of this problem itself, by means of a dialogue with ethnological and archaeological disciplines that each resituates in its own way the problem of the conditions of emergence of a separate apparatus of power within social formations that did not contain it. Yet this dialogue leads the simply empirical resolution of the problem of origin to a dual impasse: the genesis of the State-form there is revealed to be impossible, and its historical beginning cannot be ascribed. The problem of the origin of the State runs up against an unresolvable "mystery," one which, as Pierre Clastres noted, has the pitfall of the always tautological allure of genetic or evolutionary explanations of crossing the State threshold. The aporia of the origin of the State then moves to a philosophical and speculative level: it focuses on the *materiality* of the State, and more precisely, on the impossibility of identifying the State-form with its material apparatuses. On the one hand, Deleuze and Guattari maintain the need to account for the State from the socioeconomic conditions that are the only ones to explain the disparity between its concrete historical formations, and the plurality of ways in which it is transformed through the becoming of societies. On the other hand, the aporia of evolutionist explanations of the appearance of the State require problematizing the *efficacy* of the movement through which the State-form seems to presuppose itself and "produce," on its own, the material conditions of its own institutional apparatuses. While the aporia of the origin, on the level of anthropological and historical positivity, first stumbles against an "apparent mystery" that makes the State inexplicable in its genesis or its emergence, it then falters, on the level of philosophical decisions, in the undecidable relationship between the idealist and materialist concept of the State; in other words the two antinomical ways of thinking the effectiveness of this "appearance" itself, two antinomical ways to understand the *Darstellung* or the "apparent objective movement" of the State.

Let us turn briefly to the first of these two aporias. Deconstructing the problem of the origin of the State first passes through the economic anthropology of Marshall Sahlins on the "Domestic mode of production,"[5] and a re-reading of the Clastres and his anthropological-political thesis on the "mechanisms of conjuration" through which lineal societies, due to a "premonition" or implicit sociological intention, block the development of an organ of power separate from the social body in advance.[6] Economic or political attempts at an evolutionist interpretation of the formation of the State are invalidated by the impossibility of explaining the appearance of a monopolist State reserve and apparatus from the development of productive forces or a differentiation of the political functions of primitive institutions. While Marx and Gordon Childe suppose the prior development of the productive forces of communes to make the constitution of a State reserve possible, anthropologists object that a large number of so-called primitive societies show an active concern directly connected to their infrastructure to avoid both this type of development of the technical forces and means of production as well as this political differentiation. Far from betraying the weight of an atavistic tradition, or the impotence expressed by chronic penury and for which compensation would require a laborious search for sustenance, this concern displays a form of "abundance" in societies of refusal: refusal of work, refusal of over-work. The lack of surplus is by no means the result of an inability to develop technological equipment or surmount environmental obstacles. On the contrary, it is a positive object, given social value and expressed as such both subjectively, by the fact that the groups attach no sense of constraint or difficulty to their activities and display "confidence" in natural prodigality, and quantitatively, in the irregularity and strict limitation of time consecrated to productive activity. At the same time, the technical innovations imported by the whites are used not to increase production for an equal work time, but to reduce work time for equal production, and the surplus obtained without overwork is immediately expended, consumed for political or religious purposes, "during feasts, invitations, visits from strangers, etc."[7] Accommodating this situation with the theoretical fiction of "primitive communes" as a basis of historical evolution, the infrastructural determination that is supposed to make the State possible under the generic determination of a *stock*, then becomes problematic. Materially, this State necessarily presupposes the development of productive forces conditioning the reproduction of an unproductive apparatus by constituting excess production to be capitalized by this "separate" apparatus, allowing it to maintain its personnel (administrators, priests…), its aristocratic court, and its specialized bodies (warriors, craftspeople, and merchants), and eliciting a differentiation of social relationships and political functions in conformity with the monopolizing appropriation of overproduction. Yet how can the establishment of this mode of production and accumulation be considered diachronically, if we start with the conditions of "domestic production" that render it impossible: as Sahlins states, "production for consumption" without excess work and without surplus?

For his part, Clastres draws from it the thesis that this blocking of an evolutionist explanation can only be removed by a political differentiation prior to the development of the economic foundation, under the conditions of an autonomization of coercive power that is capable of exercising itself unilaterally on the social field from which it results, and to "unblock" social productivity by making productive activities enter a regime of production unfettered by the collective evaluation of the group's immediate needs. In this sense, "the economy" *presupposes* the State: there must be a political differentiation that is able to hypostatize a body of power raised to a position of exteriority in relation to the codes and mechanisms of production of the life of the group, in order for production to be able as such to take on a collective "desirability," and for a development of forces and means of production to be able to be valorized socially. Thus the poorly named "stateless" societies are instead characterized by institutional mechanisms that ward off the State: societies "refusing the State" no less than "refusing economy," writes Clastres in analyzing the *Tupi* institutions of chiefdom and warfare, carrying out in political terms a reversal that is equivalent to the one Sahlins performs in economic terms. The absence of a State in primitive societies is freed from a negative or limiting explanation. It is not the result of weakness or a lack of organization or differentiation, but can be explained on the contrary by a social and institutional strategy that neutralizes the formation of this type of power apparatus autonomized in relation to the social body. In return, the question of the historical appearance of the State from its "protohistory" seems all the more caught in an impasse: each time, as Clastres states, it encounters the irreducible "mystery" of the origin of the State.

Far from seeking to resolve this aporia, Deleuze and Guattari take Clastres' formulation and strengthen it, or make it even more radical. For Clastres, the "mystery of the origin" remains relative to an evolutionist set of problems. At the same time as he establishes the formal and more or less transcendental impossibility of the appearance of the State from stateless societies, he maintains the general format of a passage from the latter to the former, from the self-sufficiency of primitive communes to the great Leviathan. The first make the second impossible, and yet the second must come from the first… In Clastres, there is therefore a curious evolutionism without evolution, a genesis without development that makes the State necessarily emerge all at once, the mystery without reason of "an emergence all the more miraculous and monstrous."[8] Neutralizing this outline is what motivates the archaeological research of Deleuze and Guattari, which is paradoxically put in the service of a suspension of chronological succession. We will see in what way it comes from a *topological* approach to the State phenomenon. First, however, how do they approach the evolutionist presuppositions that persist even in an anthropologist who constantly assailed these same presuppositions? By pushing them to the limit: "Archaeology discovers it everywhere, often lost in oblivion, *at the horizon of all systems or States*—not only in Asia, but also in Africa, America, Greece, Rome. Immemorial *Urstaat*, dating as far back as Neolithic times, and *perhaps farther still* […] the origin of these Neolithic States *is still being pushed back in time* […] the existence of *near-*Paleolithic empires is conjectured."[9] Pushing "back in time" is not what is important here, rather the dynamic that *it is constantly being done*. It is not a question of contesting the perfectly legitimate search for a *de facto* beginning (there must have been a *first* State that appeared somewhere at some point), but of critiquing the tendency of archaeological research to take it to its virtual limit (*no matter how old* the traces of the State discovered, they still seem to refer to another, prior State formation), and therefore to the limit on an *untraceable* humanity, as if the State was precisely the first socio-anthropological body to leave a trace.[10] Thus when archaeologists, excavating the vestiges of proto-urban forms that continue to reach farther back in time, periodically make conjectures that make their emergence reach the threshold of the Neolithic era itself, and hypothesize "near-Paleolithic" empires, the problem is no longer merely *de facto*—a simple quantity of time pushing back the chronological threshold of the appearance of the State—and becomes a qualitative and *de juris* problem. Short-circuiting the evolutionary format that had the appearance of cities and the first State structures preceded by the prerequisites of sedentism, technological evolution, and agricultural accumulation, these conjectures tend to portray the emergence of the State phenomenon as contemporary with the Neolithic revolution and even as a condition for sedentism by precipitating simultaneously the appearance of an agrarian civilization and crossing the urban threshold. Referring to the hypotheses elicited by the digs in the famous Anatolian site of Çatalhöyük, Fernand Braudel challenged the standard idea that assumed the countryside "necessarily preceded towns in time": "It is of course frequently the case that the advance 'of the rural milieu, by the progress of production, permits the town to appear.' But the town is not always a secondary development. Jane Jacobs, in a persuasive book argues that the town appears at least simultaneously with rural settlement, if not before it. Thus in the sixth millennium BC, Jericho and Çatalhöyük in Asia Minor were already towns, creating countrysides around them that could be called advanced or modern. They could do so to the extent, presumably, that the surrounding land was an empty, uninhabited space, in which fields could be established virtually anywhere. This situation may have occurred again in Europe in the eleventh century."[11] In short, at the horizon of civilization, the *Stock*-form seems to emerge as a presupposition by the mode of production that nonetheless conditions it materially. What occupies this horizon, at the limit of historical, ethnological and archaeological positivities is precisely what Deleuze and Guattari call the *Urstaat*: "We are always brought back to the idea of a State that comes into the world fully formed and rises up in a single stroke, the unconditioned *Urstaat*"—unconditioned because it is up to it to produce its own conditions, or in Hegelian terms, to *pose its own presuppositions*.[12]

The Movement of Self-Presupposition of the *Urstaat*: Antinomic History of the State-Form

It would be imprecise to see this as a renouncement of the requisites of historical materialism. The aporia of impossible identification of the State-form to the materiality of its apparatuses explains on the contrary the central importance occupied by the categories of the Asiatic mode of production and Asian State in Deleuze and Guattari's theory of the State *because of* the very difficulties that they pose for Marxism, and that these authors intended to resolve, not by eliminating these categories but by giving them an unprecedented scope while transforming their conceptual meaning. Yet we would be just as wrong in assuming the irony (albeit not without humor) of the reference to Hegel (one of the few positive references Deleuze concedes to him) that the thematization of State apparatuses as apparatuses of capture came to him in 1980. The Hegelian logic of reflection, determining the objective movement of the concept as negation of the given conditions, and as *posing of its own presuppositions*, provides the most rigorous exposition of the structure of "presupposition to self" or self-presupposition in which the State-form consists.[13] It is even in this sense that *A Thousand Plateaus* defines the State as a "form of interiority," a form against which evolutionist postulates constantly stumble when seeking factors of development in the distinct social, economic, or military causes of the State-form itself:

> States always have the same composition; if there is even one truth in the political philosophy of Hegel, it is that every State carries within itself the essential moments of its existence. [...]That is why theses on the origin of the State are always tautological. At times, exogenous factors, tied to war and the war machine, are invoked; at times endogenous factors, thought to engender private property, money, etc.; and at times specific factors, thought to determine the formation of "public functions." All three of these theses are found in Engels, in relation to a conception of the diversity of the roads to Domination. But they beg the question. War produces the State only if at least one of the two parts is a preexistent State; and the organization of war is a State factor only if that organization is a part of the State. [...]Similarly, private property presupposes State public property, it slips through its net; and money presupposes taxation. It is even more difficult to see how public functions could have existed before the State they imply. We are always brought back to the idea of a State that comes into the world fully formed and rises up in a single stroke, the unconditioned Urstaat.[14]

This problem, however, is not external to Marxist theories of the State: it was present, but under a symptomatically polemical form, in the appearance of a singular "Asiatic mode of production" (AMP) that continued to create difficulties, even within historical materialism. Introduced succinctly by Marx and reworked by Engels in *The Origin of the Family, Private Property and the State*, the AMP category only gained renewed interest after the Stalinist period during which it was proscribed. Historians, anthropologists, and sinologists reopened the debates that had been suspended when Stalin's theory of stages was made official and then revived by the contemporary problem of the "transition to socialism."[15] Wasn't the AMP a weak hypothesis that Marx finally abandoned after reading Morgan, as Plekhanov argued in *Fundamental Problems of Marxism*? Or is it a mode of production in its own right? Or is it, according to the thesis issuing from the debates organized in 1931 in Leningrad, a "quasi-feudal" formation of transition between a primitive communist mode and the ancient mode of slavery? Or could it be, according to the interpretation established by *Dialectical and Historical Materialism* that was dominant among Soviet orientalists under Stalinism, an embryonic form of an ancient mode of production "stuck" at a "primitive phase of the evolution of slavery"? Political resonances can also be felt in these theoretical problems, particularly in the controversy raised by Karl Wittfogel's study, *Oriental Despotism*, which appeared in France in 1964, and which had ideological-political proposals that rendered its theoretical propositions unreadable for many.[16] Wittfogel took up the question of AMP by combining the construction historically informed by an ideal-type paradigm ("hydraulic States") and an approach comparing this model to contemporary State formations. With the aim of renewing the understanding of this mode of production by identifying the functions of its bureaucratic power apparatus, this study introduced a series of tensions into the presuppositions of classical Marxism. It led to considering the State apparatus not as a dominant authority guaranteeing externally the conditions of appropriation of the surplus of social work, but as a power of organization that is directly economic and socializing of work that internally conditions the relationships of production that make the surplus possible.[17] Initiator of major monumental, hydraulic, and urban projects; agent of the monetization of income and exchanges through taxes and credits; creator of commercial markets under the control of public powers; initiator of planning in embryonic or developed form, the Asiatic or tributary State organizes surplus labor and conditions the surplus production that it simultaneously appropriates. Referring the Asiatic mode of production to the imposing apparatus of bureaucratic power that frames it, Wittfogel's study opened an awkward perspective in relation to the instrumentalist conception of the State (as an "instrument" in the hands of a dominant class), as it presented a mode of domination and exploitation of the labor force by a State apparatus that produced its own dominant class or rather its political-religious domination of castes.[18] Thus Wittfogel's work was not only an invitation to a comparative evaluation of bureaucratic power in despotic imperial formations and in the modern history of capitalist States, it took direct aim at Soviet bureaucracy and did not fail to elicit passionate critiques from the defenders of the planned economy by giving State Marxism an embarrassing filiation. "One may recall the insults addressed to Wittfogel for having raised this simple question: wasn't the category of the Oriental despotic State challenged for reasons having to do with its special paradigmatic status as a horizon for modern socialist States?"[19] It nonetheless leaves open the problem of understanding what this "paradigmatic" status consists of and the nature of this "horizon."

This problem imposes a shift from the evolutionist understanding of the three types of social formations presented in succession in Chapter III of *Anti-Oedipus*. Under the rehabilitation of the categories of Ferguson, Montesquieu, and British anthropology of the nineteenth century, "savages," "barbarians," and "civilized men," a law of three states seems to be developed on first reading, juxtaposed like stages on a linear axis of evolutionary chronology. Yet the differences in the conceptual status and the logical value of the three categories respectively put into play ("territorial" social machines or lineal, "despotic," and capitalist) prevent their identification with evolutionary stages or with the ideal-types of comparative sociology. The "primitive" type is an ideal-type for which the unity comes from reason, theoretically subsuming a plurality of really heterogeneous societies (and thus only comparable in an extrinsic manner). The capitalist type has not only the theoretical but the historical unity of a *singular universal* in the sense of an absolutely singular process of universalization historically contingent on its singularity (the expanded reproduction of the capitalist relationship of production and the correlative expansion of its social and geographic base).[20] Deleuze and Guattari, however, give the "despotic" type a unity of an entirely different nature: *real unity*, omnipresent, currently or virtually, in every social field, not only in the so-called Asiatic or tributary formations, which simply present "the purest conditions,"[21] but also in stateless societies, and in modern societies themselves, and everywhere under the paradoxical form of the return of an origin that never took place.[22] From that point, it is impossible to say that the relationship of this type to the two others is one of evolution, or even simple periodization. Anchoring the hypothesis of the *Urstaat* in the theory of the Asiatic mode of production produces this paradoxical effect of imposing the conceptual construction, not of a paradigm of the State, but a paradigmatic moment of every State: a moment of abstraction, ideality, and transcendence as an objective dimension of every historical State. This dimension is designated by the notion of an *Urstaat*, which is never given as such but is struck with "latency, like the Freudian *Urszene*," and yet always and already given by concrete historical States, in other words, always *presupposed* by them. At play here is not only the fixation of a trans-historical invariant but the elucidation of the temporal structure that this invariance takes in historical formulations: a structure of forgetting—disappearance or latency—and return that makes each concrete State appear to be the re-actualization, under variable historical conditions, of an abstract paradigm that forms its preexisting horizon.[23] The problem is no longer one of chronological anteriority but a scission of time that defines the relationship of the State to its own historicity—an "extra" of the State-form in relationship to its concrete historical reality—such that each State appears in the re-actualization of a latent and presupposed original State already required by its own historical beginning, still at the horizon of its later historical evolutions, developing an eternalizing effect that is one with its objective being in the history of societies.

This split temporality that makes each State appear as always-already-there and yet always reborn, re-actualizing an Origin that never occurred and that nonetheless conditions the opening to History, of which it will appear after the fact to be the real "subject,"[24] has the effect of making the alternative between materialist and idealist conceptions of the historicity of the State into an aporetical one. With the idealist conception making the concept of the self-movement of the State the genetic principle of its own temporality, and the materialist conception reducing State transformations to forms of historicity produced by heterogeneous social relationships, the two constantly refer to each other in a circular manner. If the State produces the historicity in which it develops or if it is inscribed in a historicity that is not derived from it and of which it is at no moment the subject, then we encounter the same paradox of a historicity in which the State break remains unassignable. Everything takes place then as if, in the theory of the State, the alternative between Hegelian idealism and Marxist materialism became undecidable, as if the structure of presupposition to itself in which the State-form consists as such made this philosophical break impossible to locate. Must we then speak of a materiality *of the ideality of the State* or of a State-form for which the "objective movement" was to idealize its material conditions? These expressions merely circumvent the difficulty at the risk of obscuring the stakes of this aporia in thinking the State-form. More crucial, to my mind, is the *enunciative break* that inscribes this aporia in the chain of Deleuze and Guattari's discourse:

> The State was not formed in progressive stages; it appears fully armed, a master stroke executed all at once; the primordial Urstaat, the eternal model of everything the State wants to be and desires. "Asiatic" production, with the State that expresses or constitutes its objective movement, is not a distinct formation; it is the basic formation, on the horizon throughout history. [...] the primordial despotic state is not a historical break like any other. Of all the institutions, it is perhaps the only one to appear fully armed in the brain of those who institute it, "the artists with a look of bronze." That is why Marxism didn't quite know what to make of it: it has no place in the famous five stages: primitive communism, ancient city-states, feudalism, capitalism, and socialism. It is not one formation among others, nor is it the transition from one formation to another. It appears to be set back at a remove from what it transects and from what it resects, as though it were giving evidence of another dimension, a cerebral ideality that is added to, superimposed on the material evolution of societies, a regulating idea or principle of reflection (terror) that organizes the parts and the flows into a whole.[25]

The emergence at this moment in the enunciation of schizo-analysis of the ravaging Nietzschean figure of creators of empires, founding "like fate, without cause, reason, consideration or pretext," imposing their new configuration like "an inescapable fate that nothing could ward off, which occasioned no struggle,"[26] is a precise marker of this dual aporetical blockage and of the problem of the origin of the State (or, which amounts to the same thing, of its genesis from stateless societies), and the problem of the materiality of the State (or of the identity of the State-form with its apparatuses). The fact that this figure comes precisely as an *interruption* of historical enunciation, and in a form for which the quasi-hallucinogenic appearance cannot be overlooked, is very important. As if what thinking of the State could not obtain except at the limit of historical States, as at the limit of its own discursiveness, could only come to it from an outside interrupting the theoretical perception of the State phenomenon, emerging from a radical exteriority, in a transfixed vision. The effects of paradoxical unintelligibility that can be produced by this twist to the understanding of State power through which Deleuze and Guattari strive to give place to this *atheoretical* break in their own discourse should be examined. First, let me announce the positive program to which the aporetical chain that we have followed until now leads. A program of both conceptual (for thinking the State-form) and epistemological (for the concrete analysis of State forms in history) expansion which we can trace in the shifts in Deleuze and Guattari's thought between *Anti-Oedipus* and *A Thousand Plateaus*.

Neither Concept nor Apparatus: the State-Form as an Original Fantasy and Delirium of the Idea

The antinomy between idealist and materialist conceptions of the State expresses a dual impossibility: the development of material conditions of the State presupposes the existence of the State-form but the latter cannot identify with the self-movement of its idea without being unable to locate its emergence in time. It therefore requires first of all a more complex understanding of the State-form, in order to account for its "excess," an excess which is itself double: on its own materiality (its apparatuses), and on its own ideality (its Idea or self-movement of its concept):

a) First its excess on the materiality of its apparatuses, in which the State-form cannot posit itself without presupposing itself in a primary "cerebral ideality": to go to the heart of the matter, this first aspect touches on the question of the temporality of the State-form itself, both "always-already there" and "emerging all at once 'once and for all.'" This question is most developed in the examination of the *semiotic composition of the State-form*. Begun in *Anti-Oedipus* in the development of the concept of "overcoding,"[27] this analysis reaches a point of systematization in the description of the operation of "capture," leading to an understanding, in terms of the material constitution of State apparatuses, of why the accumulation of stock takes the objective form of a movement of self-constitution of a body of power that appropriates a monopoly on what it contributes to "producing." One could already object that a semiotic genesis is no better than a socio-economic one, and that a semio-genesis falls back into the evolutionist aporia mentioned earlier. This would be true if semiotics was just one social structure among others. However semiotics or "collective regimes of signs" are spatio-temporal arrangements that configure space-time, according to Deleuze and Guattari. They do not aim to assign lines of causality or determination according to a given course of time but to make intelligible the temporal structures of anticipation of what does not yet exist and that nevertheless is still effective, and of recurring action on what has already taken place. We will see how the analysis of the capture of the State, a semiotic operation of the State monopoly, allows a return to Clastres' thesis of the mechanisms of anticipation-conjuration, by removing it from the formally evolutionary framework in which Clastres remained caught and by giving it an unprecedented theoretical yield.

b) In terms of the second excess indicated above—the excess of the State-form as to its own ideality or the self-movement of its concept (its "form of interiority")—it leads us to confront the structure of self-supposition with the *always overdetermined character of the State-form*, which comes from being always caught up in relationships of coexistence with *other power formations* that escape the challenge of its form of interiority. The most systematic conceptual underpinnings for the analysis of this overdetermination can be seen in the 13th Plateau with the *topology of "machinic processes"* or processes of "power" (capture, anticipation-warding-off, nomadism, polarization, englobing), on which the modes of production are said to depend.[28] It is elaborated through an analysis of the theories of world-economy developed by Fernand Braudel and redeveloped in theories of dependency that draw attention to the relationships that State powers maintain with other heterogeneous power formations: ancient empires, the "multinational" empires of the modern age, lineal societies without a State, banking and commercial urban powers, but also (and making it a specific power formation is of course one of the major theoretical inventions of Deleuze and Guattari) the powers known as the "war machine" of nomadic formations. The thesis of overdetermination of the State-form therefore forces a break with evolutionist readings (connecting social formations along a linear axis) as well as functionalist ones (which relate, for example, the development of the modern State with the rise of a bourgeois class that is incapable of overcoming its internal divisions in any other way than in the form of the nation-State). On the contrary, this thesis implies that the State-form never exists in its pure state, but is always tangled in complexes of hetero-geneous powers that confer unavoidably ambivalent political significations on the State, its apparatuses, and its modes of domination. This conceptual disposition finally organizes a diagnosis by Deleuze and Guattari of State reality in the geopolitical and geo-economic axioms of accumulation of capital, and their evaluation of the ways to confront the associated domination and subjugation.[29] This conceptual apparatus also will allow us to shed light on the question raised in 1972: how, in the modern world, capitalist societies "breathe new life into the *Urstaat* in the states of things," resuscitating the extreme, paranoid violence of an original State, which has become the sign of a "civilization" taking itself as the object of its madness?

c) In fact, before examining these two lines where Deleuze and Guattari deploy their thinking about the State, I would note that the theoretical program of the 12th and 13th Plateaus is not made dis-tinct from an additional, difficult task. Because it would serve no purpose, except to give fictive autonomy to a speculative philosophy of the State, to isolate a distinct State-form, calling for a thematiza-tion that denotes its intransigence in relation to its material implementations and in relation to its process of intelligibility itself, if we did not ask how this dual excess *is brought about*. To put it another way, how docs the State-form *compensate for* its own gap, the difference with its material apparatus and with its concept, through an operation that cannot be material or conceptual in itself? Herein lies the abovementioned importance of the break that marks thought of the State-form in the chain of theoretical discourse, as an indica-tion towards a first supplement in the properly fantastical element of the *Urstaat*: fantasy of an original State as fantasy *originating* the State. Yet if we ask how this fantasy makes its return *into* history, then the fantasy supplement is not enough, and it necessarily takes on a second form. The problem is not only to understand the functioning of self-presupposition, its material and semiotic operations, and its overdetermination by other, coexisting power formations. It is also to understand how States can be led to "deal" with the impossibility of closing their structure, or the impossibility of presupposing themselves without presupposing that which escapes their form of interiority ("decoded flows"), or even that which can destroy it ("war machine"). As objective movement of the State-form, the structure of self-presupposition thus has the drawback that everything that does not appear to presuppose the State appears to it as a threatening escape, challenge, or aggression. The State-form can only compensate for the impossibility of organic closure through a supplement that is no longer fantasy in the strict sense, but literally *mad*: no longer the State-form as original fantasy, retrospectively projecting the State as the presupposition of its own material conditions of historical emergence (the *unconditioned* State), but the State-form as delirium of the Idea, "cerebral ideality added on to the material evolution of societies," principle of reflection (terror) that organizes parts and flows into a whole," and which can only escape its totalization in the figure of an absolute "outside," where its "Idea" is inverted (as *absolute* State). This mad dynamic does not come from political psychology; it belongs to the State-form. Its structure of self-supposition can only be closed by being forced and can only force this closure by paradoxically including that which escapes it, at the expense of a foreclosure such that that which cannot be inscribed within it can only come to be by emerging from a threatening, persecutory, or deadly exterior. Fantasy of the Origin and delirium of the Idea, original fantasy and paranoid projection: this is the double supplement of the State-form that is one with its material and conceptual implementations, and that State rationality does not recognize, even though it is fully part of its efficacy.

Starting in *Anti-Oedipus*, this thesis of a paranoid vector structurally inscribed in the State-form drives the cross-reading that Deleuze and Guattari perform of the category of "natural or divine presupposition" that Marx introduced in *Pre-Capitalist Economic Formations* and the Africanist anthropology of sacred kingdoms that inspired Elias Canetti to notice the paranoid valences of rituals surrounding the "body of the despot."[30] It is a way to rework, in anthropological-historical material, the problem that had already preoccupied Walter Benjamin, Wilhelm Reich, and Georges Bataille, and that has more recently been taken up by authors like Jacques Derrida and Étienne Balibar: the problem of institutional violence.[31] Or more precisely (to borrow one of the latter's expressions), the problem of the forms of "ultra-institutional" violence, the excess of State violence over its political, social, or economic functions, referring to a "cruelty" of this Institution of institutions that is the State, which is not to be confused with the psychology of its agents or its representatives, and for which Deleuze and Guattari seek the "clinical" model in paranoia. The Sultan Mohammed Tughluq, who has just risen to the throne, receives an offensive letter from the inhabitants of Delhi... the response must be equal to the insult: he casts out its entire population, deporting them to Daulatabad, then relocates his palace there and has the city razed: "A person of my confidence told me that the Sultan climbed onto the roof of his palace one night, and seeing Delhi where there was no fire, smoke, or light to be seen, said: 'Now my heart is calm and my anger assuaged.'"[32] The problem, however, is that there is always one letter too many, an undesirable message escaping control, a decoded sign (offense) slipping between the links of the State's overcoding. The paranoiac structure inscribed in the State-form is not capture or overcoding. It is overcoding *and the impossibility of overcoding*: not only the structure of self-presupposition but the impossibility of closing this self-presupposition without including that which escapes it, which "flees" its supposition, and challenges its closure. The consequences still must be determined: from this point of view, *the generic factor of decompensation of State paranoia is the same as the historicization of the State-form*:

The archaic State does not overcode without also freeing a large quantity of decoded flows that escape from it. [...] the overcoding of the archaic State itself makes possible and gives rise to new flows that escape from it. The State does not create large-scale works without a flow of independent labor escaping its bureaucracy (notably in the mines and in metallurgy). It does not create the monetary form of tax without flows of money escaping, and nourishing or bringing into being other powers (notably in commerce and banking). And above all, it does not create a system of public property without a flow of private appropriation growing up beside it, then beginning to pass beyond its grasp; this private property does not itself issue from the archaic system but is constituted on the margins, all the more necessarily and inevitably, slipping through the net of overcoding.[33]

2

Capture: For a Concept of Primitive Accumulation of State Power

State Capture and the Analysis of Social Formations: the Fundamental Concepts of Historico-Machinic Materialism

We must now look at the historicization of the State-form: it places us immediately at the heart of the theory of "capture" developed in the 13th Plateau and the redefinition of State apparatuses as *apparatuses of capture*. It involves what I see as the most decisive shift from *Anti-Oedipus* to *A Thousand Plateaus*, both in terms of the reflection on the State-form and in dealing with the problems left by historical materialism. This shift touches on the previously mentioned problem of *overdetermination of the State-form*, which is developed as follows in the 12th Plateau:

> We are compelled to say that there has always been a State, quite perfect, quite complete. [...] It is hard to imagine primitive societies that would not have been in contact with imperial States, at the periphery or in poorly controlled areas. But of greater importance is the inverse hypothesis: that the State itself has always been in a relation with an outside and is inconceivable independent of that relationship. The law of the State is not the law of All or Nothing (State societies or counter-State societies)

but that of interior and exterior. The State is sovereignty. But sovereignty only reigns over what it is capable of internalizing, of appropriating locally.[1]

Here, above all, the concepts available for thinking this "outside" of the State are called into question. We can recall that the conceptual apparatus of 1972, which is echoed in the passage quoted at the end of the preceding chapter, gave this outside the generic figure of "decoded flows," passing through every social formation, and against which social socio-institutional strategies (coding, overcoding, recoding, and axiomatization) are differentiated to inhibit, counter-invest, and connect their vectors of upheaval or destruction.[2] Retrospectively constructed in function of capitalist "civilization," the universal history of *Anti-Oedipus* was concerned with perverting historical teleology by underlining the contingencies, the destructions, and finally the *Impossible* (the "unnamable") that had to be produced so that a social formation could come to make this generalized decoding, which signified the death of all previous social formations, its immanent "motor." This explains the importance attributed to Marxist analyses of expanded accumulation of capital, singularly that of the crises of overproduction of Book III of *Capital* and the concept of "immanent limit" that Marx introduced there. Whereas non-capitalist formations encountered decoded flows as an extrinsic, accidental, "real limit," capitalist formations made it their *internal* limit, a structural limit that they continuously destroy to rediscover on a new scale. No matter what Deleuze and Guattari said about it, decoding flows of production and circulation occupied a function of driving negativity in *Anti-Oedipus*, even if this negativity was not considered to be universally "internal" (non-capitalist formations deferring it on the contrary as only an external and accidental possibility), and implying neither "negation of negation" nor "surpassing" but either the pure destruction of social codes (when decoding is imposed on non-capitalist formations "from the outside," through colonization and imperialism), or its critical expansion, in and through systemic crises (when it is constantly displaced "from the inside," as the immanent limit pushed back to a constantly expanding scale).[3]

The major shift carried out by *A Thousand Plateaus* comes from this "outside" being thought as crossing an unprecedented *threshold of categorization*, in function of which the concept of *overcoding* is profoundly reworked in the concept of *capture*. The stakes are both philosophical and epistemological. The idea of an underlying decoding of material and semiotic flows does not disappear; but instead of being assigned retrospectively as a generic process of universal history, this tendency is pursued in a differentiated way that can be indexed in geographic and historical positivities to the *social formations* that "deal with" these flows. The first effect of this shift concerns the type of historicity engaged by the analysis. The register of universal history (as history of the contingent universalization of capitalist singularity), in its dual function of critical ironization of teleologies, and blurring of theoretical and libidinal investments of the historical Real, cedes its place to an approach in terms of "global history," which borrows less from the speculative and fastasmatic register of universal history than from the geo-history of "system-worlds." Less from Condorcet, Comte, or Hegel, than from Fernand Braudel, Andre Gunder Frank, and Samir Amin. It is then less a question of making a determination about the paradigmatic moment of the State-form than of accounting for its modes of presence in social formations (including in societies said to be without or against the State), which in turn imposes a reevaluation of the relationships of coexistence of heterogeneous formations of power that encounter, condition, and confront

Statified social formations. For this reason, the threshold of categorization of what Deleuze and Guattari would soon call a "geophilosophy"—and that will be defined just as well as the conceptual framework of an *historical-machinic materialism* to the extent that the conditions of analysis of the modes of production and of social formations are redefined there[4]—is crossed in a double gesture, both *typological and topological*:

> We define social formations by machinic processes and not by modes of production (these on the contrary depend on the processes). Thus primitive societies are defined by mechanisms of prevention-anticipation; State societies are defined by apparatuses of capture; urban societies, by instruments of polarization; nomadic societies, by war machines; and finally international, or rather ecumenical, organizations are defined by the encompassment of heterogeneous social formations. But precisely because these processes are variables of coexistence that are the object of a social topology, the various corresponding formations are coexistent. And they coexist in two fashions, extrinsically and intrinsically. Primitive societies cannot ward off the formation of an empire or State without anticipating it, and they cannot anticipate it without its already being there, forming part of their horizon. And States cannot effect a capture unless what is captured coexists, resists in primitive societies, or escapes under new forms, as towns or war machines[…]. There is not only an external coexistence of formations but also an intrinsic coexistence of machinic processes. Each process can also function at a "power" other than its own; it can be taken up by a power corresponding to another process. The State as apparatus of capture has a power of appropriation; but this power does not consist solely in capturing all that it can, all that is possible, of a matter defined as phylum. The

apparatus of capture also appropriates the war machine, the instruments of polarization, and the anticipation-prevention mechanisms. This is to say, conversely, that anticipation-prevention mechanisms have a high power of transference: they are at work not only in primitive societies, but move into the towns that ward off the State-form, into the States that ward off capitalism, into capitalism itself, insofar as it wards off and repels its own limits. [...] Similarly, war machines have a power of metamorphosis, which of course allows them to be captured by States, but also to resist that capture and rise up again in other forms, with other "objects" besides war [...].Each process can switch over to other powers, but also subordinate other processes to its own power.[5]

The State can be thought here, no longer in relationship with an exterior considered indistinctly, but as a function of a plurality of essentially or formally distinct processes, which in each case determines the way in which the same geohistorical field divides "interior" and "exterior," circumscribes the form of interiority of capture, and maps its milieus of exteriority—peripheries, semi-peripheries, *interlands* etc. As these processes are qualitatively heterogeneous, Deleuze and Guattari draw up both the typology (according to the five machinic categories: anticipation-warding off, capture, war machine or smooth space, polarization, englobing), and the topology (these five machinic processes determining not sociological or historical invariants, but on the contrary variables of coexistence of corresponding forms of power). It is therefore both a categorical table of social formations and a map of the composition of power between the social formations and within each one. And under this dual aspect, Deleuze and Guattari's thinking about social formations attains a remarkably integrative exposition of the speculative decisions of their philosophy and of the conceptual instruments that they propose to analyze geographical and historical positivities concretely. This categorization of "machinic processes" is supported by thinking about power, Spinozist thinking if you will, which produces three main effects corresponding to a) an ontology of affirmation, b) a logic of attributes, and c) a physics of existent modes and their "limits":

a) Most obviously, it disqualifies the analysis of social forms in terms of deficiency, loss, or privation, betraying the weight of an implicit Statification of social theory which makes the State the norm for any form of collective life. The speculative idea that Deleuze attaches to his Spinozism, which would have all reality be determined as a position of power, affirmation of a perfection ("quantity of reality") *under a determined power*, invariably has the critical effect of dismissing the theoretical pretensions of categories of privation. In the elementary schema where their mystification is revealed, these claims are supported by a circle: starting with a norm of existence or intelligibility which is supposed to establish what things should be to be what they are, a thing is related to this supposed model rather than to its own mode of being, to explain finally that it is truly what it is through the perfections that can be judged to be missing in comparison to this model. These theoretical claims are immediately caught in the mirror of the State-form and its structure of self-presupposition: it is in relation to a State, in function of a supposed State, that the litany of "societies without" unfolds—not only "without State," but "without history," "without writing," "without territory," "without religion." It is a singularly Statified thought that each time seeks the lack and assigns privations everywhere. Yet this circle is cut by the access to social formations by the forms of power affirmed in them.

b) Second, the double typological and topological articulation of historico-machinic categories avoids the confusion, of which

Clastres himself was the victim, between the *formal exteriority* of forms of power and the *substantial independence* of corresponding social formations. Formal exteriority meaning qualitative heterogeneity, heterogeneity of essence, between machinic processes. However, like the Spinozist logic of Attributes, each one of which is infinite in its genre and self-explanatory, and for which the real multiplicity does not introduce any diversity in the substance, historico-machinic materialism promotes a "logic of coessential positivities and coexisting affirmations."[6] If the attributes of a geohistorical Real are called "machinic processes," it is precisely because there is a *real* distinction between the processes (each one comprising the full positivity of a form of power that does not define itself in comparison to others and does not lack what belongs to another) that this real distinction is not the foundation of any substantial independence between the social formations where they are affirmed. On the contrary, it inscribes them in the same single plane of immanence of which the different qualities of power are the rules or the variables of coexistence, which is shown in the principle of multiplicity indissociably external and internal postulated by historico-machinic materialism. On the one hand, no social formation is an autarkic reality to the point that the relationships of "extrinsic coexistence" or interaction that they maintain with other social formations can be neglected, *in that these relationships of extrinsic coexistence are always efficient within each formation* (for example, the relationships of interaction between mechanisms of anticipation-warding off and State capture must already be analyzed within Stateless societies). Yet these relationships of extrinsic coexistence are only effectively determinant to the extent that they refer to relationships of *intrinsic coexistence* between forms of power themselves. In other words, every social formation is not ruled by *one* form of power (and one machinic process) but is composed of a plurality of processes which, in relationships of interaction and conflict (extrinsic coexistence) change their nature by entering into relationships of subordination and domination (thus the power of the war machine changes nature when it is "appropriated" by the State;[7] State capture itself changes when it is subordinated to a power of ecumenical inclusion like the global capitalist market).[8] This is why, we should note in passing, every social formation encounters its own *reproduction* as a problem, far from the balance of a structure that is supposedly, principally simple; this is also why the analyses of the Plateau "Apparatuses of Capture" make massive use (although commentators are loath to admit it) of an Althusserian type of conceptuality, in terms of multiplicity "with a dominant" or of "overdetermined" complexity.

The Clastrian thesis of mechanisms of anticipation-warding off therefore sees its stakes for the theory of the State considerably changed, at the same time as its conceptual functioning and the extent of its operation. As the form of power dominating the mechanisms of reproduction of lineal or segmentary societies, anticipation-warding off goes not only against crossing the *State threshold* (in function of a power apparatus separate from the social group), but also and distinctly against crossing the *urban threshold* (in function of a polarization of circuits of exchange by markets exceeding the limits imposed by the codes of alliances between groups), and also against crossing the *nomadic threshold* (in function of war mechanisms becoming autonomous in relation to institutions of alliance, chiefdom, or shamanism, etc.).[9] However, the inverse consequence is just as important. According to the relationships of "intrinsic coexistence" between forms of power, urban formations can in turn integrate mechanisms of anticipation-warding off under their power of polarization (as dominant machinic process), warding off, for example, the crystallization of a State power. And the State itself, as Deleuze and Guattari suggest, can *appropriate* for itself the "mechanisms of anticipation-warding off" of lineal societies, when it must in turn confront processes that exceed its own power: for example to inhibit the rise of urban formations that tend to avoid State territorial control by connecting directly to banking and commercial flows that escape its apparatuses of power; or to channel processes of "ecumenical enveloping" that traverse heterogeneous social formations (sometimes even by grafting themselves on a network of cities and appropriating its power of polarization): "for example, commercial organization of the 'multinational' type, or industrial complexes, or even religious formations like Christianity, Islam, certain prophetic or messianic movements, etc."[10]

When Deleuze and Guattari take up the question of the rise of banking and merchant cities starting in the 14th and 15th centuries, which is crucial for the "primitive accumulation" of capital, the variables of coexistence of State power and urban power are determined in function of these differential thresholds of power, according to whether the former appropriates the mechanisms of anticipation-warding off to inhibit the latter, and whether it directly appropriates its instruments of polarization, capturing the urban dynamics while subordinating them.[11] Like Fernand Braudel, it must be said both that the State organizes *its* urban spaces and submits them to its bureaucratic control, and that there is a history specific to cities when they develop in the decoding margins of States, break free of their control, and invent practices and institutions that would have been inconceivable in a system overcoded by a State apparatus (the "city power invents the idea of *magistrates*, very different from the State *bureaucrats*"). The problem is therefore not only the great diversity of cities in different regions and time periods, but first the heterogeneity of the processes of power under which the urban phenomenon is determined. No more than *circulation* is enough to determine the State city (what is determinant is the overcoding inscription of what circulates, inseparable from the master-signifier of the sovereign and his writing machine, as in the Mycenaean city),[12] the market is therefore not enough to make a mercantile city. The market-city is not defined by the market as such but as a mechanism to polarize circulations,[13] which drains the surrounding towns of their local markets, "swallows" them, and allows the city to "detach" from its territory by cutting itself off from its surrounding companions to connect directly to other urban centers, even distant ones, in a city-to-city network. Precisely, cities, in their commercial, maritime, and banking activities, develop a power of deterritorialization far superior to the one a State can handle, since the State cannot be separated from the territorial inscription of its power.[14] So much so, that even when States are able to appropriate the inventions of the cities that States were unable to produce themselves, this capture does not take place without tension or conflict, nor without a mistrust that leads Braudel to speak of a premonition similar to the one Clastres attributed to societies without a State: "As soon as the State was solidly in place, it disciplined the cities, violently or not, with an instinctive determination wherever we turn our eyes throughout Europe."[15] The history of conflicts between free cities and State apparatuses can be understood as the history of conflicts *for* prerogatives, economic interests, and appropriations of power; yet it is determined *through* vectors of power; it is by the degrees of power, by the differential thresholds of decoding and deterritorialization that they command, and by their antagonistic relationships, that the lines of force of a social formation become tied or untied in the becoming of its historical-political field.

c) It leads to the third major effect of the categorical threshold crossed by historico-machinic materialism in the 13th Plateau: a recasting of the concept of *limit of power*, as a category that is both structural and processual, and that is essential to the analysis of social formations. *Anti-Oedipus* already explicitly focused on this problem by distinguishing the position of a *real* limit within each social machine (decoding as it is warded off by social codes, and which can only arise as extrinsic destruction), of a *relative* limit (decoding as an internal factor of crisis and development, a limit that is only destroyed by being reproduced on a larger scale in the system), or an *absolute* limit (schizophrenic decoding of sociolibidinal production) and an *internalized* limit (Oedipal subjectivation).[16] However the concept of limit becomes a fully consistent category both philosophically and epistemologically, from the moment when it is determined by the concept of power, and by the typology that differentiates its qualitative forms. To the questions: What is a social formation capable of, what can it tolerate or bear, in function of its internal relationships, its codes, its institutions, its semiotics, and its collective practices? What on the contrary are the processes that exceed its conditions of reproduction, or call them into question?—it is no longer enough to respond by a universal decoding of flows, precisely because the concept of limit is *pluralized* by the categorization of forms of power. The limit of what can be anticipated-warded off (in a segmentary or lineal society) does not function in the same way as the limit of what can be polarized (in an urban formation), or as the limit of what can be captured (in a State formation) or deployed in a "smooth space" (in a "nomadic formation"). As a first illustration, let us return to the two cases that were largely developed in the 13th Plateau: predominantly anticipation-warding off societies, which integrate their own limit in a *serial* and *ordinal* economy; and predominantly capture societies, which impose an *ensemblist* and *cardinal* functioning of the limit.[17]

Return to the Question of "Societies Without a State": Anticipation-Warding Off and Stock-Form

The articulation of different processes of power is the concrete object of historico-machinic materialism, analyzing the vectors that it defines in a historical field, vectors that work its representations and its practices and collective utterances, the institutions and economies, the political rationalities, and the modes of subjectivation. The binary opposition between societies with State/societies without State becomes insufficient. Societies without State cannot simply *without* State (as if they were missing something), or even *against* State (as if they were warding off its future appearance), but also have to be worked by processes of Statificaiton (of "capture"), that constitute the positive internal object on which their mechanisms of anticipation-warding off operate. The vectors of are either actualized, effected, or remain warded off as virtual. Yet it cannot be said that this virtual has no effect; on the contrary, since it is under this modality that State capture can be the object of anticipation by positive institutional mechanisms (in accordance with Clastres' thesis). What they ward off is not current: that which they "anticipate." Yet that which is not current already has reality: that for which they can ward it off, in other words, act on what is not yet current. The question of the contingency of crossing the State threshold is now rephrased. One must say at the same time that "primitive peoples have always existed only as vestiges"[18] and that the emergence of the State in any geohistorical configuration remains contingent, since "it is not at all in the same way that the State appears in existence, and that it preexists in the capacity of a warded-off limit."[19] It therefore seems that the very categories of necessary and contingent have to be "topologized" such that in a movement that differentiates "interior" and "exterior," the "same" phenomenon can be said to be really contingent following one vector, and really necessary following the opposite vector (which the first one inhibits or contradicts). It is like a circle of becoming-necessary of the contingent (anticipation: existence in vestiges) and of the becoming-contingent of the necessary (warding-off: the inexplicable "mystery"). From there comes the objective undecidability that was already suggested in *Anti-Oedipus*, combining a Spinozism of death as extrinsic accident and a Freudism of death as endogenous tendency in the tension of an astonishing formula: *death comes from the outside by force of rising from the inside*.[20]

In 1980, in particular, the new conceptual arrangement allows for a positive determination of the all-too vague "premonition" to which Clastres referred, like a type of social intentionality that is not only implicit but necessarily empty of content, since primitive society, as Luc de Heusch later noted, is supposed to "resist with all its strength a form of political organization of which it has not yet experienced the dangers, situating itself in a sort of future perfect tense."[21] This premonition does not only refer to a "political philosophy" that would be the unconscious impulse of primitive social subjectivity. It expresses the tensions internal to societies against the State, between the vectors of Statification and the counter-tendencies that inhibit them. "And in primitive societies there are as many tendencies that 'seek' the State, as many vectors working in the direction of the State, as there are movements within the State or outside it that tend to stray from it or guard themselves against it, or else to stimulate its evolution, or else already to abolish it: everything coexists, in perpetual interaction."[22] It is no longer a question of explaining how to pass from one to the other, but also not to carve out a substantial independence that would render this passage unthinkable. The problem becomes: why doesn't the State *appear* everywhere, since it is in a sense always already there? And inversely, how do societies against the State resist, not only the State alongside them or elsewhere, but already inside them, under the threshold of crystallization in autonomous institutions of constraint, regulation, and deduction? In short, where are they aiming their warding-off mechanisms?

Extending the political anthropology of Clastres, but also the reflections of Lévi-Strauss on "dualist organizations" and the work of Africanists like Luc de Heusch, *Anti-Oedipus* and then the 5th and 9th Plateaus ("On Several Regimes of Signs" and "Micropolitics and Segmentarity"), identify a number of these vectors of stratification, touching on the emergence of ancestralness as a sign of power (warded off by the disjunctive articulation and relative autonomy of practices of alliance in relation to the genealogical language of filiation), the fusion of various centers of power (warded off by the frequently observed division between "political" power and sacred power, between chief and shaman, or between the head of a lineage and guardian of the land),[23] and in the final analysis the "sense of debt" and the inseparable anthropological, cosmological, and economic-political significations of its circulation. These vectors share the indication made towards the concentration of a separate power, corroborating Clastres' thesis that only a *political* change (through a transformation of indigenous semiotics, symbols, and cosmology) could explain the freeing of an economy, in the sense of a system of production determined by a condition of accumulation. When taken up in the 13th Plateau ("7000 B.C.: Apparatus of Capture"), the terms of the problem are noticeably shifted. A reinterpretation of Marx's "trinitarian formula" of capital, in a highly organically composed image, highlights the semiotic operations implied by a *preliminary capitalization of State* (Stock-form). In diverting the standard alternative between an ideo- or semio-logical explanation (by degradation of the symbolic function, or a transformation of intellectual and perceptive pragmatics) and a materialist explanation (by a development of the productive forces and a transformation of the corresponding social relationships), Deleuze and Guattari attempt to determine the State threshold at the level of modes of encoding the material conditions of existence. The vectors of Statification already let themselves be determined in the practical-cognitive arrangement, in ideational, practical, and perceptive treatment of the material worked, logically coming before the institutional, economic, and symbolic bonds of caste or class inequalities. It is therefore significant that among the basic apparatuses of the State, there are no repressive or ideological ones. "The fundamental aspects of the State apparatus [are] territoriality, work or public works, taxation,"[24] and the apparatuses of capture that correspond to them: Rent, Profit, and Taxes, in accordance with the three faces of the conceptual character of the Despot, in Marx's Asian paradigm and in the idealtype of Wittfogel's hydraulic states: eminent Owner of the land as an inalienable public property, Entrepreneur of the first surplus labor in major works, Master of foreign trade and agent of monetizing the economy. Rent, Profit, Tax are precisely the forms of material constitution of a Stock, as the organic form of the existence of a State as a material apparatus, on which the repressive and ideological powers themselves depend. Therefore, it is not a problem of political economy but of State economy, or *Statification of an economy in general.* Thus these three forms are less defined by institutional bodies or economic and legal arrangements than by processes of inscription and objectivation specific to the land, productive activities, and exchanges.

Following a basic outline, differential rent implies, at a minimum, the possibility of comparing different territories exploited simultaneously, or different, successive exploitations of a single territory, using a common measure of production. Profit from work implies, at a minimum, the possibility of comparing different activities under the relationship of an expenditure (of force, of time...) as the common measure. A tax on a piece of merchandise or a transaction implies the possibility of comparing goods or services, not only in function of a market standard, but with the measure of an "objective price" determined in a market. In short, Deleuze and Guattari begin their argument by remarking that these three suppositions are precisely blocked by primitive social codes, which are constantly, on the contrary, heterogenizing the invested territories, activities, and transactions. Depending on the material being worked, the circumstances and their complex qualifications, the extra-economic significations, and the forms of expression of the activities, the practices, like their spatiotemporal contexts are maintained in a qualitative heterogeneity that prevents the appearance of a surface of anthropological inscription that is capable of homogenizing the territories, activities, exchanges, and entities exchanged. This does not mean that there is no metric power for comparison: the surface of inscription neutralizes in advance the condition of possibility of any comparison, in other words, the homogeneity on which the commensurability of the related terms relies.[25]

The question from the start—determining the threshold of emergence of a Stock-form—therefore becomes a dual question, since it cannot receive the same response in one system or the other, or to put it in a different way, since from one system to the other, the meaning of the term "threshold" itself has to change. To say that the three forms of Rent, Profit, and Tax are warded off in primitive societies, and only figure as such in a position that can be determined as a *limit*, one must still account for the fact that this limit *is precisely not invested as such*, and does not have to be. The danger, in fact, is always the same: attributing to societies a calculation to resolve a problem that does not belong to them, and that they only pose once it has been imposed on them from the outside (generally with the calculation supposed to allow them to "deal" with it).[26] Thus it is not enough to say that societies without State limit the exploitation of territories (in relation to a presumed, given measurement of land production), that they limit work (in relation to a presumed, given productivity, as a measure of the force or time expended in production activities), or that they limit exchanges (in relation to a presumed, given quantitative measurement of accumulated goods). One has to say that they ward off the possibility of this triple measurement, albeit in a determinable relationship with it. What they ward off is *the very possibility* of having to encounter it, as a fact or as a problem. "Primitive" productive activity does not limit itself simply to avoiding the production of *more* than required by the needs of the group, or to exchanging *more* goods than prescribed by debts of alliance; it limits itself to avoiding the possibility of this differentiation establishing itself. In all rigor, we will therefore say both that it does not "limit" itself (except from the external point of view of the State thinker who already presupposes what is in question): it only gives an anticipatory evaluation of the limit in function of which the arrangement can be reproduced *before* the limit is occupied and becomes a problem.

From here comes the idea that, in the processes of anticipation-warding off, the limit does not determine a *principle of differentiation* (between lands or their production, between productivities, between "necessary" and surplus labor, etc.), but functions in itself as a *differential relationship* ("limit" / "threshold"). This differential conception of the limit finds its technical model in a reinterpretation of marginalist *logic* (leaving aside, as our authors insist, the weakness of marginalism in economic terms), to formalize a cycle of simple reproduction without an effect of accumulation. In other words, a serial and ordinal logic such that, in a cycle of exchange, each service is proportioned, not to a stock to expend or replenish (according to an economic principle of accumulation), nor even to a counter-service to which response is given, but to the internal differential, between the limit as "last" exchange before beginning the cycle again and the limit as "*threshold*" where the cycle can no longer be reproduced without changing its structure, calling into question the evaluation of the "*last*" as reason for the series, and potentially opening an expanded or virtually unlimited accumulation. Following this logical outline, the limit/threshold differential, as reason for the series or rule for serializing services, functions as a principle of ordinal distribution: each term is not related to the preceding and following term by direct comparison but by its relationship to the limit that proportions it. The corresponding machinic process is precisely called "anticipation-warding off" (and not only warding off as in Clastres' work), to indicate this differential relationship. The State threshold is *warded off*; but what is *anticipated*, under the threshold, is the limit at which the cycle can be closed and begin again in a simple reproduction, in other words, *without having to anticipate the threshold itself*. We will see how even "primitive war," which Clastres made one of the principal devices for warding off the State, only effectively wards off the capturing of a monopoly on violence to the extent that war is inscribed in such a *marginalist economy of violence*, in other words a serial and ordinal treatment of its limitation (on the contrary, the question of knowing how the State thinks its own limitation of violence will find itself surely changed).

The material condition of the State threshold (stock) is thus defined not simply by an empirically observable "excess" but by a change in the function of the limit in the new system. More precisely, beyond the limit, the *threshold* must be occupied and take on a new meaning at the same time as the limit simultaneously takes on a new function. From a descriptive point of view, as Deleuze and Guattari summarize, it is necessary that "the force of serial iteration [be] superseded by a power of symmetry, reflection, and global comparison," which submits all things to a formal homogeneity that makes them commensurable and directly comparable between themselves. The limit becomes precisely the operator of this direct comparison and provides a principle of differentiation between the necessary and the stockable excess: "it no longer designates the end point of a self-fulfilling movement but the center of symmetry for two movements, one of which is descending and the other ascending." The singular determination of the "threshold" in the new ensemble therefore becomes essential. It is no longer the external border of the system, "after" the limit ordering the practical series; it is on the contrary internalized in the system and constitutes its basis, the principle of a *cardinal set* of which it determines the *zero degree*. The abstract model of differential rent already suggests this, where "the worst land (or the poorest exploitation) bears no rent, but it makes it so that the other soils do bear rent, 'produce' it in a comparative way."[27] However, the threshold does not only characterize part of the whole (the least fertile land); it is more the paradigmatic moment of homogenization of the whole of the new surface of inscription, by preliminary de-qualification of primitive territorialities that make its apprehension and global appropriation possible. It is like a preliminary *tabula rasa*, such that it is all the same to say that all territories are equivalent and that the land itself is not "worth" anything (land is an idea of the city), but that a set of values will be "produced" by the comparison of territories between each other (differential rent) and *under the presupposition of a point of global appropriation* (eminent owner) operating a distribution of territories that includes in the calculation of value the worst land (absolute or monopoly rent).[28]

The same is true of activities. According to the Asian paradigm, the new threshold of the system is determined in State entrepreneurship: in the labor expended in monumental construction as socially non-consumable works. What in Marxist terms would be called surplus labor is also the zero degree of the new system of productive activities. Directly in the place where the surplus labor is organized, in major hydraulic, monumental, and urban public works, a global appropriation of activities can occur, transforming the regime of inscription of all productive activities, where a socialization and cooperation of tasks are invented that make them comparable to each other, where an entire scriptural and actuarial technology of quantification of the collective forces expended is put in place. Surplus labor therefore does not come "after" labor, as a surplus to a supposedly necessary labor (for the satisfaction of needs or to reproduce the labor force expended), as an actuarial meaning of their difference would lead one to believe, or a merely empirical distinction between labor for consumption and labor as a duty or tribute. The first distinction is not between necessary and surplus labor but between continuously varied activity and the surplus labor-labor system that constitutes the labor-form as a whole. "[E]ven when they are distinct and separate, there is no labor that is not predicated on surplus labor," from which it is deduced and which it presupposes like the direct comparison between activities presupposes the monopolistic appropriation of these activities: "It is only in this context that one may speak of labor value, and of an evaluation bearing on the quantity of social labor."[29] State capture of activities is analytically included in the idea of abstract labor.

Can we find an analogous logical schema in the third requisite of the Stock-form: in the element of exchange and commerce? Beyond the limit that maintains "primitive" exchanges in a qualitative heterogeneity, in virtue of a principle of non-commensurability that integrates services into codes of alliance expressed in terms of gifts and debts and not in terms of equalization and comparison of exchange values,[30] how can the *threshold* be determined for which exchange ceases to express social relationships of alliance directly, and becomes a derived function of an accumulation, a practice conditioned by the use and reconstitution of a stock?[31] For Deleuze and Guattari, determination of this threshold relates to fiscal capture: taxes as an apparatus of capture that materially condition the maintaining of a bureaucracy, a body of civil servants, specialized professions, and judicial and military institutions. Yet how can taxes be determined as a *zero degree of exchange* (instead of the correlate or even the effect of a market economy): no longer the limit anticipated-warded off by primitive exchange, but on the contrary the basis of a new system that changes the meaning and the function of the limits of the exchangeable and the unexchangeable?

By reversing two long-held prejudices in economic history and anthropology: the history of taxes would follow the evolution of rent, corresponding to a prior monetization of the economy, which would lead from rent in labor and in nature to a pecuniary rent. As for this monetization itself, it would come from the development of merchant exchanges and the demands of commerce between distant groups. Against this, Deleuze and Guattari look at examples that are all the more significant in that, by referring to later situations that diverge from the paradigmatic-despotic pole of the State apparatus in favor of a dominant class that distinguishes itself from it and uses it for the sake of its interests and its private property, they nonetheless still bear witness to a process that archaic empires were familiar with independently of the problem of private property. Thus the reform of the tyrant Cypselos in Corinth, according to the study by Edouard Will that already inspired Foucault in 1970 to analyze the ritual, political, and religious functions rather than the market functions of the monetary institution,[32] sheds light on the mechanism through which "taxes on the aristocrats and the distribution of money to the poor are a way to bring money back to the rich" by making the regime of debt unilateral and larger. In this strange State parody of gift/counter-gift—*zero degree of exchange* or euphemism of the State when it claims to reestablish itself by abolishing "small debts"—the monetary institution and function reveal themselves to be immediately determined in a cycle that only opens a system of merchant exchange because it makes the debt relationship infinite: "(1) a portion of the land belonging to the hereditary aristocracy was confiscated and distributed to the poor peasants; (2) but at the same time a metallic stock was constituted, through seizure of the property of proscribed persons; (3) this money itself was distributed to the poor, but in order for them to give it to the old owners as an indemnity; (4) the old owners from then on paid their taxes in money, so as to ensure a circulation or turnover of the currency, and an equivalence between money, goods, and services."[33]

The exemplarity of Edouard Will's study was to show that taxes, when they pass through a monetary form, are indivisible from a control of money, its issuance, and its distribution by an apparatus of power. And this distribution takes place under conditions such that an *indebtedness in principle* is the result, which is translated on the one hand by a return to State money, and on the other by an equivalency between money with goods and services that becomes inaccessible outside this monetary circulation. The order of both logical and historical reasons is not: development of commerce —> necessity of a general equivalent of the exchange value and appearance of a monetary standard —> transformation of modes of State deduction occurring in money and no longer in nature. On the contrary, it is: constitution of a stock of metal —> creation of a system of circulation where rents, goods, and services are made equivalent and where issuance of this stock can function as money —> effective circulation of exchange values monetized in systemic conditions of State control, and monetary circulation, and commercial exchanges. Taxes are the original form of money, the basic condition for a monetized market. It is one of the applications of the conceptual axiom encountered previously: social formations are defined "by *machinic processes* and not by modes of production (these on the contrary depend on the processes)." Moreover: "It is not the State that presupposes a mode of production; quite the opposite, it is the State that makes production a 'mode.'"[34] Our authors draw the conclusion in *A Thousand Plateaus*: it is through other machinic processes, under other forms of power relating through coexistence, conditioning, and conflict with the State power of capture that money is placed at the service of new signs of commercial power (in formations of urban polarization, in formations of ecumenical englobing, and even in nomad formations, in function of their role in long-distance commerce *between* State or imperial formations), in banking and merchant enterprises that are relatively autonomous in relation to State overcoding or even capable of diverting the State regime of infinite debt to serve other powers. However, the monetary form, as a general equivalent of exchange values *does not come* from this history, which is constantly, on the contrary, betraying the operation of power and not exchange on which it is based. "[M]oney does not begin by serving the needs of commerce, or at least it has no autonomous mercantile model," and when it begins to take on a role in merchant exchanges, it is less as ex-merchandise raised to the rank of form of expression of all exchange values than as an economic-political instrument of subjecting merchants to the State.[35] Money comes from taxes and first under conditions where, through money, the State constitutes a market domain that is immediately, in its very structure, appropriated in a monopolistic way, submitted to its control, and used to make the State debt infinite.

Here we find the *double bind* of capture: not only relative comparison and monopolistic appropriation, but most importantly, the *presupposition of monopolistic appropriation* structurally included in the field of the comparable. Money is the instrument or the means of comparison of exchange values expressed in objective prices. Yet it is only this way to the extent that it comes from taxes, which carries out the homogenization of money, goods, and services, in other words, which produces the context for general equivalency (which money, as *means* of comparative measurement of equivalents, expresses and presupposes but does not produce itself) and makes direct comparison and differential deduction possible. In this sense, taxes constitute the "threshold" of exchange or the zero degree of the new system. Tax deduction carries out an excess component of exchange value, which is represented in the actuarial objectivity of the price system as additional fiscal value; however, the surplus also constitutes the basic element that allows the objectification of prices. Taxes therefore constitute in reality less an additional element to previously determinable prices than "the first layer of an 'objective' price, the monetary magnet to which the other elements—price, rent, and profit—add on and adhere, converging in the same apparatus of capture."[36] As we saw with surplus labor, appropriation relates to a difference or an excess, but the excess does not come "after" the "normal" limit. On the contrary, it determines internally the constitution of the standard in which it is thus always already understood, such that *"the mechanism of capture contributes from the outset to the constitution of the aggregate upon which the capture is effectuated."*[37]

This analysis of the Stock-form and its process of capture thus sheds a materialist light on the structure of self-presupposition (and on Marx's "natural or divine presupposition"). It no longer characterizes the State-form considered globally; it depends on the semiotic functioning of State material apparatuses in their respective dimensions, and their convergent action. It depends on mechanisms in their convergent action. It depends on mechanisms, in the technologies of thought and collective practice, of *inscription* of bodies and territories, goods, and signs, actions and circulations. If the State always seems to presuppose itself, like an "idea" always-already required by the appearance of its material apparatuses, it is in the constitution of these apparatuses: differential rent *presupposes an absolute rent*, productive labor *presupposes a surplus labor*, the monetary market *presupposes taxes*. The State does not renounce a capture of material flows: people and land, goods and signs. However this capture does not only consist of an economic or juridical appropriation *of* these things. It first means *constitution of a mode of objectification, tracking, and identification* of these things such as the State deduction and appropriation appear objectively inscribed in their very "nature." If it is true, as Foucault noted, that power cannot be analyzed only as a negative operation, as a system of privation, deduction, or constraint, it must be said that State power limits itself even less to deducting and appropriating in that it begins by constituting the space within which deductions can take place, its subtraction therefore appearing objectively inscribed in the very structure of social phenomena. Deduction and constraint are only a moment in the double bind of capture—and it is a fleeting moment… The State contributes to producing social objectivity such that it will necessarily be submitted to its control and appropriation, gaining an absolute necessity in this circular closure, within this objectivity where its constraint is incorporated and even erased as such in the anonymous normality of the order of things. One can therefore understand how the structure of self-presupposition determines a very singular functioning of the *monopoly*. If State monopolies (not only "legitimate physical vio-lence" but taxation, territorial borders, and ultimate standards of residence, etc.) are not like any other monopolistic phenomena, but the paradigm of any monopoly, it is because the monopoly does not appear like a possibility outside the relationship between the monopolizer and the thing but as an internal property of the thing, a destination internal to the thing. In this sense, the monopoly has a fetishistic structure. It is the primary effect of the "apparent objective movement" of the State-form. As a State fetish, the fact of monopoly is the most basic fetishism.

Capture and Sovereignty: State Economy and Anti-Economy of Violence

The definition of the State by the monopoly on legitimate physical violence is inscribed in a circle that bears witness to an already "Sta-tified" thinking of the State and its relationship with violence. Indeed, this monopoly is over violence that only the State can exer-cise. When one specifies that the violence is legitimate, the precision is more analytic than synthetic; one is not adding a restrictive clause to the monopoly of State power but locking a tautological circle in which monopolization and legitimization refer to each other and reinforce each other. The monopoly on "legitimate violence" would be a contradiction in terms as untenable as the law of the strongest in Rousseau. Inversely, how can State violence be contested except by linking the critique of its legitimization and that of its monopo-lization, by translating one into the other the right to its delegitimization and the fact of its counter-violence?

This situation seems to hold essentially under modern condi-tions, in the relationship with the "Rule of law" (*État de droit*). For

Deleuze and Guattari, it is inscribed in the for-State as such, to the extent that it determines the nodal problem of sovereign authority: the problem of State articulation (both institutionalizable and monopolizable) of violence and law that modern States are only rediscovering in function of new dialectics of legitimization and delegitimization of State power, and in function of the conflictual articulation that they bring together between processes of capture and other powers. This problem can be elucidated in light of the *sui generis* functioning of the *limit* of social formations proceeding predominantly by capture (State formation) by contrast with the ordinal and serial economy of the limit implied by mechanisms of anticipation-warding off. Two very distinct ways of dealing with violence, of "economizing" it, which does not mean exercising it less, but in two qualitatively or structurally distinct manners of limiting it *by having its limitation function in the way it is exercised*.

Stock-form and Sovereignty-form are the two heads of State capture. Like the first, the second calls for a structural determination and not only a juridical determination of the State monopoly. For that reason, Deleuze and Guattari return to Dumézil's classic analyses of the "trifunctional ideology" of the Indo-Europeans: not so much to return to the myths themselves as to draw out an intellectual structure in the myths that is perfectly contemporary in the social and political sciences, which rediscovers on the juridical-political level the evolutionist aporia previously brought out in economic terms.[38] This is apparent in sociology and legal history in the weight of the scientific myth of an evolution in social violence in the sense of a specialization of its exercise within an institution reserved for it, and that its progressive monopolization would orient towards a rationalization of its rules, its means, and a specialization of its ends according to a trend towards the self-limitation of State violence in the institution of the rule of law. In its juridicist version, no less than in its economist or politicist versions, this evolutionist schema supposes that the problem of the origin of the State is resolved and represses at the same time the aporetical nature of this resolution. It therefore denies equally the objective functioning of State tautology, the permanence of its structure in the history of States, and the chronic violence of its specific effects. Yet it is precisely this evolutionary myth and this denegation that mythology is constantly staging. The leitmotiv of political science of a *legalization of violence by the State* even belongs to the basal structure of the "function of sovereignty" as Dumézil reveals it. Whether it is in its archaic mythological expressions or in its later rewritings, the same duality of the sovereign function places face-to-face, sometimes in a relationship of complementarity, sometimes of opposition, and sometimes even of evolution, the figure of a terrible sovereign, magical-religious power proceeding by "ties" or "magical capture," and the figure of a pacified and pacificator sovereign, a jurist power operating by rules and with respect for obligations, agent of a "civilization" of violence of which the first pole was exempt: Varuna and Mitra, Jupiter and Mars, Romulus and Numa, etc. Yet this ideological structure in which the law reveals itself, no matter what the ambivalence of their relationship, inseparable from a sovereign gesture of the magical-religious type of which the historians of the archaic pre-law constantly renounce the traces, shakes the idea of a simple evolution that would lead us from an age dominated by the symbolic efficiency of a power to that of a positivism satisfied with the value of obligation that formality grants the rule. The second pole of sovereignty, the juridical and civic pole, opposes the first pole in vain, and substitutes for the sovereign violence of the "combining god" the pacifying sovereignty of the rule and its commitments to justice; it necessarily presupposes this first violence without which it would never find the possibility of establishing itself. It presupposes it to be already done in the very moment it represses it; even more, it presupposes the permanent effect of this violence in the very place where it supplants this violence.[39] The reason is that the legal codification of violence, its limitation under the conditions of the rules of law, *presupposes* a prior operation of *destruction of the social significations of violence*. It assumes that violence ceases to appear as a social fact. Without this "decoding" that breaks the immediate collective meanings of violence, it could never become the object of a relatively autonomous, normative utterance—like a legal utterance—in relation to the set of social practices and heterogeneous normative sources connected to them. The legal codification of violence presupposes a sovereign decoding of violence, a desocialization of violence such that it ceases to appear as a mode of social relations, as a dimension constitutive of social relationships that can be codified, regulated, and ritualized as such.

This non-juridical codification of violence is what Clastres displays emblematically when analyzing the highly constrained and ritualized functioning of the Guayaki institutions of combat. The functioning must be called economic, in other words, integrated in a *social economy of violence*, to the extent that it inscribes warrior violence—the very one that the Empire constantly hopes to break to impose the *Pax Incaica*—in a system of apparent reciprocity (blows are exchanged like exchanging women, goods, and signs), the dynamic disequilibrium of which wards off the threshold that would turn the series of blows given and taken into a system of accumulation of blows won and lost, in other words into a capitalization of the exercise of warrior violence for the sole profit of an individual or a group to the detriment of others, making an embryonic form of the place of State-like power based on superiority of force or prestige in weaponry. In the terms of Deleuze and Guattari for the process of warding-conjuration, societies without State proceed from a *segmentary and serial* economy of violence, and it is expressed in social objectivity in the form of a "blow for blow," an apparent exchange without accumulation of victories and defeats. Exchange or reciprocity only belong to the apparent objective movement: in the underlying arrangement of anticipation-warding off, each blow given is proportionate, not directly to a blow received but to the place it occupies in the series of other blows given, in function of the anticipation of an ultimate blow (threshold of the series) which would break the reproduction of the cycle, or in other words would compromise the social structure and modes of institutionalization of violence connected to the reproduction of this structure.[40] What is anticipated, with each blow, is the differential between a "*final* blow," as the limit from which the cycle can begin again or a new series opened, and the "*ultimate* blow" as a threshold that would place reproduction of the social arrangement in danger. The nature of the blows can be very different, but the main thing is the characters that integrate them into a social economy of violence: their serialization; the differential between the limit and the threshold, or "last" and "ultimate"; the play of this differential as reason for the series, constituting the rule of proportion and limitation for each of its terms; the evaluation that constitutes this differential and invests it disjunctively, by disconnecting the limit to be anticipated and the threshold to be warded off, and which thus ensures the cyclical reproduction of the underlying social arrangement; the highly ritualized and codified character of the exercise of violence that results from it; and finally the "apparent objective movement" that violence takes in social objectivity, the movement of an exchange between blows given and received, without the possibility of rising to the extremes but with the possibility of errors in anticipation, incorrect evaluations that would take what was already the threshold for the limit: irreversible destruction and collapse as the ultimate accident.

We understand that, for Deleuze and Guattari, there is no possible evolution from this social economy of violence to State violence: the latter presupposes a radically *aneconomic* moment that supplants the primitive blow-for-blow and destroys its very logic. Original State violence is first aneconomic in the special form of *illimitation* which it precedes, not only in the sense that it transgresses the limit of ordinal series, but in the sense that, beyond the limit, it invests their threshold, which the State does not occupy without changing its meaning and function radically. What was warded off as the threshold of destruction of the group becomes invested in a positive way. What had the value of "ultimate" in the series of lineages becomes the "first" in the instauration of the State. What made the limit function as an operator of reiteration in a cyclical reproduction cedes to a unique act, a single blow, or to use the expression that recurs in the 13th Plateau, the violence of a State emerging at once, which "made a move 'once and for all.'"[41] "[T]he State apparatus makes the mutilation, and even death, come first. It needs them pre-accomplished, for people to be born that way, crippled and zombielike."[42] It is therefore less a "first" as a qualitative element in a series than a zero degree of violence, the threshold of a cardinal set in which all types of violence start by being "placed in common," in other words de-qualified and homogenized, made equivalent between each other by their shared lack of social signification, which is the condition for re-differentiating them under the rule of law according to a new distributive rule proper to State power and its own conflicts.

It would therefore not be precise to think of this threshold of violence carried out "once and for all," as simply outside the law. It does not form an absolute exteriority. It is on the contrary the zero degree *of the law itself*, an internal threshold that cannot be formulated legally but which opens the way for formulating the rule of law. This is the precise sense in which Deleuze and Guattari find in it the form of the *nexum*. For good reason, this form of archaic Roman law has constantly been the object of debate and divergent interpretations between legal historians, given that it seems impossible to reduce it to any category of duty and obligation. The *nexum* was supposedly a legal act that bound without contract, condition, or agreement between parties yet in a unilateral way without transfer of title or alienation, its force of obligation related solely to the word of the lender or donor as expression of a "power" inseparable from a religious or magical symbolic efficacy.[43] When Dumézil suggests reinterpreting this pre- or "quasi-legal" form in light of the mythical figure of the Binder God, he wants to emphasize the singularity of this "bond" which produces an obligation such that there is no resulting symmetry between a right and a duty: a bond that properly speaking does not bind. Capture does not bind the binder and the bound in the still rough outline of reciprocity, in the framework of which it would have to negotiate its own reproduction and the perpetuation of its effect. The Binder God, "terrifying emperor and magician" emerges on the battlefield, paralyzes his adversaries with a single look, and makes all of the warring forces present subject to him in their paralysis. Like Varuna or Romulus, "one is therefore not surprised to see Ódinn himself intervene in battles, without fighting much, and particularly by casting over the army he has condemned a paralyzing fear, word for word binding, the 'army bind.'"[44] As the legal historian Louis Gernet notes, the *nexum* does not constitute a relationship of duty or obligation, but it causes one to undergo a radical and instantaneous "change of state" like the modes of efficacy of religious-magical symbols in the archaic "prelaw."[45] As the myth states: it immobilizes, paralyzes, petrifies. Mythology does not only bring the narrative illustration of a legal form that remained singularly enigmatic for legal theory. Myths on the contrary theorize what is included in the internal scenography of the law and its relationships without being able to be represented in them: the fixation of its scene.

This connection implies a very special violence that can scarcely be called violent, since it makes any resistance impossible. Establishing a relationship of the most unilateral servitude, its very asymmetry ends any possibility of combat in the relation of a non-relation.[46] This violence is not a force applied to an adverse force, on or against a force that might offer a riposte, oppose it, or escape, but a violence that destroys the relationship of forces, therefore immobilizing all violence. In this aneconomic sense, it is also "originary," illustrating one last time the "tautology of the origin" of the State, or the objectively tautological dimension imprinted on the State-form by its own movement of self-presupposition. It imposes thoughts of a first violence, not in a supposedly similar time that would distribute a before and an after, but as a *permanent dimension* of the type of social space that it establishes (a social peace necessarily represented in the form of an *absolute* peace since all violence is "once and for all" deprived of any social signification)[47] but in which it has no *Darstellung* or no objective appearance. As such, one must say both that it has always-already taken place and that it has never taken "place": always presupposed, but as if foreclosed—which cannot take place "inside." State pacification of the social domain passes necessarily through a first violence but it is as if erased in its effect and only appears "mythologically," retro-projected in the figure of an original violence that, *at the limit*, never occurred (whence the recourse to Dumézil).

In this way, as Deleuze and Guattari describe it, the *structural* (and not evolutionary) *relationship* between the two poles of sovereignty is illuminated. The main thing, when "passing" from the first to the second, relates less to a progression, a pacification, or a civilization of violence than a very singular economy of violence that is determined in the circular relationship between the two, as the overall structure of State sovereignty: it is a violence that constantly oscillates between its two erasures of social perception. On one side, the magical violence of the Binder Lord is a violence that it is impossible to resist, a violence done all at once, invincibly—therefore at the limit of non-violence, since it negates any possible riposte or counter-violence. As for the other pole, the just and pacifying Sovereign, it makes violence impossible through another trick: by incorporating it in the rules of the city, and making it proportional to the demands of the *polis*, by making it a practice that is also policed itself, in virtue of a supposedly acquired technique of the political community to limit its own use of violence. The convergence of the magical *threshold* and the legal *limit* thus takes on the structure of the previously mentioned *double bind*, for which the two pincers are, on the one hand, a violence that has always-already/never occurred, and that makes all non-State violence appear as a threat to the "peace" established by this unsituatable violence as a challenge to the Binding Lord exposed to its punishment; on the other, a legally codified violence that makes all non-State violence appear as a first infraction to which the sanction of violence only responds in the second place. And not one *or* the other, but one and the other, in varying proportions, such that any resurgent violence is always subject to a dual interpretation: violence defying the original *nexum* and calling on paranoid sovereign vengeance in reprisal; violence breaking the rule of law and calling for the sanction of justice in the name of civil peace. The *double punishment*, far from being an exception, is inscribed as a necessary effect internal to this structure. Originary and always second, never having taken place and always legitimate when it occurs, State violence always wins. What becomes unlimited is the separation, the distance, the incommensurability that separates State violence from all other violence, between "pacifying" violence and all of the "violent" violence. It is clear that this incommensurability carries the possibility of an extreme violence.

Thus we return, on the level of the intellectual construction of the relationship between violence and law in what could be called the State monopolization of sovereignty, to the structure of the State monopoly brought out in the analysis of the Stock-form. It is therefore easier to understand, to conclude, the reinterpretation on which it results from the idea of "original" or "primitive accumulation" of capital, which Marx introduced in Book 1 of *Capital* to resolve a "mystery" that is formally analogous to the mystery of self-presupposition enveloped by the State-form. This reinterpretation plays on two levels; in fact, one by analogical extension, the other by structural and historical articulation; and from one to the other, the problem of a historico-machinic materialism is reopened in terms of the concrete analytical stakes of its categories.

What interests Deleuze and Guattari is the special relationship Marx describes between State power, its use of violence, and law, along with their transformation in the historical establishment of the capitalist mode of production. The process of primitive accumulation of capital, historically preceding and conditioning its characteristic social relationship, implies a specific action of the State and law that is not opposed to the "use of brutal force" but on the contrary promotes it. The expropriation of small farmers, the privatization of common goods, anti-vagrancy laws and repression, wage compression laws, forced involvement in the circuit of debt, colonization… not one of the methods goes without the exploitation of all "the power of the State, the concentrated and organized force of society."[48] However, at the same time as the new relationship of production is being put in place and capital increasingly subsumes social relations and functions, this violence stops appearing in its brutal form, is interiorized in this relationship as it is systematized, while the capitalist mode of production is articulated with a system of legality that suits it.[49] Such that, "[f]rom a standpoint within the capitalist mode of production, it is very difficult to say who is the thief and who the victim, or even where the violence resides. That is because the worker is born entirely naked and the capitalist objectively 'clothed,' an independent owner. That which gave the worker and the capitalist this form eludes us because it operated in other modes of production."[50] There is a process of monopolization of the force of physical repression by the rule of law, but not in the sense where this repressive force would come to bear on a preexisting field of application, such as a state of nature that had to be domesticated. The monopolization of repressive force in a system of legality is in a relationship of reciprocal presupposition with a system of social relationships that a repressive violence that was first a-legal or paralegal allowed to be formed, before erasing itself and integrating itself in them. This is precisely the form of the operation of capture analyzed in the Stock-form, which allows an expansion of Marx's analysis: "For the fact remains that there is a primitive accumulation that, far from deriving from the agricultural mode of production, precedes it: as a general rule, there is primitive accumulation whenever an apparatus of capture is mounted, with that very particular kind of violence that creates or contributes to the creation of that which it is directed against, and thus presupposes itself."[51]

Yet the connection between these two analyses, first in an analogical extension, also sheds light on the way that the economy of State violence analyzed above is internalized in the modern rule of law, *by the very movement through which it is integrated in the process of accumulation of capital.* From one of these two phases of history distinguished by Marx to the other, the power of the State does not apparently recede at all. On the contrary, it undergoes a complex transformation of its economy, bearing simultaneously on the nature and the role of its repressive violence, and on their relationship to changes of the legal apparatus.[52] In primitive accumulation, liberation of the two basic factors of an economic structure dominated by the law of value and the accumulation of capital (the formation of a capital-wealth as power of independent investment; the formation of a "naked" labor force) does not occur without a *brutal, massive,* and *continuous* intervention of the State's illegal or a-legal power.[53] Moreover, this intervention is necessary to *force* the combination of these two factors. Yet as soon as this combination "takes root," and the new relationships of production contribute to producing the conditions of their own reproduction, there follows, not a disappearance of State violence, but a dual transformation of its economy: a *transformation by incorporation* of direct violence in social relationships of production, and in the legal relationships that guarantee them under the authority of a State. This violence thus becomes structural and tends to be materialized in the "normal" order of social relationships, with as little awareness as for the changing of seasons, and no longer having to show itself brutally, as Marx noted, except in exceptional cases (particularly when these social relationships appear threatened, as a preventive counter-violence).[54]—But also a *transformation by displacement* of the unincorporated remainder of this violence in the repressive apparatus of this new rule of law, in which it no longer appears as direct violence but as the force of law reacting to all direct violence, as the police of "legal violence" exercised against criminals.

From one phase to the other, from the primitive accumulation of capital (under precapitalist modes of production) to accumulation proper (within the new economic structure), from the violent legality of the precapitalist State to the legitimate violence of the capitalist rule of law, it is clear that State power loses none of its repressive power. What is important, on the one hand, is the manner in which the two poles of sovereign violence find ways to operate *differentially* and *distributively*, depending on the internal contradictions of modern States: States responsible for developing within their national framework the relationships of production required by an expanded process of accumulation and reproduction that itself passes through a global division of labor and through a transnationalization of movements of capital; responsible for placing themselves at the service of giving value to capital, and for managing its systemic losses of equilibrium and its crises, by negotiating for better or worse the social repercussions in function of the degree of socialization of their political, economic, and legal apparatuses, the unequal play of inclusion and exclusion in their populations, and the corresponding degrees of collective resistance. What is important correlatively is the unequal play of the exercise of massive, direct violence on the lines of force of the world-economy where, as a *constant* of reproduction expanded to capital on the global scale, and following the position of States in the international division of labor and the integration of their internal market in the global market, the mechanisms of primitive accumulation of capital are replayed: its procession of proletarization of people and spoliation of collective resources, destruction of non-capitalist social relationships and forced socialization in the relationships of capital, submission of socio-anthropological logics of collective territorialities to contradictory logics of mobility and fixation of the force of labor, etc.[55]

Marxist analysis does not simply allow Deleuze and Guattari to reintroduce their analysis of the State-form into a historical perspective that at first appeared suspended; it substantiates, on the contrary, the field of analysis within which the theory of the State-form found its meaning from the start: the "historico-machinic" field of analysis of new forms of distribution of the two poles of State violence (its distributive-integrated pole, its "magic"-paranoiac pole), when State capture itself is submitted to the forms of power of other machinic processes like the processes of urban polarization dominated by capitalist "city-worlds," and the processes of "envelopment" of the capitalist global formation itself. The question still remains to analyze how, in function of the current relationships between these machinic processes, States rework their three apparatuses of capture: their modes of arranging territories, and determining norms of residency and land exploitation; their ways of determining the conditions and norms of overwork, and to intervene in the tendency to impose the labor-form on all human activity; their banking and monetary practices, and their ways of articulating their fiscal capture with an economy of infinite debt that has become the instrument of power of the formation of capitalist englobing.

PART TWO

EXO-VIOLENCE:
HYPOTHESIS OF THE WAR MACHINE

3

Nomadology: Hypothesis of the War Machine

This second part deals with one of the five categories of power encountered in the typology of historico-machinic processes in the 13th Plateau: the category of the "nomad war machine," which designates a process that is qualitatively distinct from the first two that have already been examined (anticipation-warding off and its "mechanisms," and capture and its "apparatuses"). This new category raises complex issues. Established in counterpoint to the State-form, it oversees a critique of State reason, asserting a *heteronomy of State power* that questions its structure of self-pre-supposition. This critique, however, takes on different meanings: theoretical, historical, and political. For this reason, not only the category itself in a fixed terminal formulation must be examined but also the different moments of its elaboration *as a working hypothesis*,[1] passing each time through specific empirical and theoretical singularities (anthropological, mythological, and historical) that each offer potential views of its philosophical and analytical-concrete stakes. Since each moment of the assembly of the hypothesis comes from an operation of disassembly of the self-presupposition of the State-form, I will provisionally distinguish moments here, before returning to an overview of the trajectory (Chapter 3), then return to what Deleuze and Guattari in the 12th

Plateau called the systematic exposition of "the hypothesis as a whole" (Chapter 4).

a) Assembly of the hypothesis begins with the articulation implied by the State-form between war and sovereignty, and proceeds to critique it by positing a heteronomy of the power of war in the face of sovereign power. The absence of any power of war in the State-form analyzed in the first part will not have escaped you. Among the three apparatuses of material State capture, none of them has a directly military function. Between the two poles of the ideological-political function of sovereignty, the magical-religious power of the *nexum* and the legal power of the rule of law, neither has any particularly war-like attributes. Significantly, these attributes are carried, in the 12th Plateau, by mythological figures that are not only distinct from but openly antagonistic to the sovereign function, raised up as living provocations to its power and its law. The superposition of Dumézil's analyses consecrated to this insolent singularity of the warrior function in the "trifunctional ideology," and Clastres' ethnological analyses on the role of "primitive war" in sovereignty's mechanisms of anticipation-warding off, finds a new theoretical efficacy.[2] A dual efficacy, in fact. First, it remobilizes historico-machinic conceptuality in favor of a conceptually mastered relativism: it helps expose the way war changes its form and meaning, not according to "societies," "cultures," or even according to a particular social or cultural function (when, for example, war is taken as a variation of economic or symbolic exchange, its degraded form, or the negative form of an exchange that has become impossible between two groups), but according to the dominant and subordinate machinic processes within a determined field of coexistence. This movement then opens onto the *position* of the hypothesis for itself, enriching historico-machinic materialism with a new category: either the supposition that the power of war not only changes its form and meaning according to the dominant or subordinate machinic processes but itself constitutes a category of power *sui generis*, defined as an autonomous machinic process. Deleuze and Guattari find its anthropological-historical establishment to be typical in the large formations of nomadic breeders and warriors in the steppes of central Asia—which does not mean that it is reduced to them, no more than the process of anticipation-warding off is solely identified with American Indian anthropology or the process of capture with the "Asian State."

b) Elaboration of the hypothesis, secondly, engages a questioning of the modes of territorialization of State power, in other words the modes of production of the space in which the State exercises its power to capture: it asserts a heteronomy of State territoriality. We will see on this occasion that, among the three fundamental State apparatuses, State territorialization has the privilege of functioning as an empiric-transcendental doublet. Yet this privilege only works *a contrario*, by what contests it: the type of spatiality that the State produces, at the same time as it finds in it the condition and the field in which to exercise its power is never produced *only* by its power of capture but always due to a complex and conflictual articulation with other powers that produce heterogeneous spaces. It is therefore a new, political-geographical formulation of the impossible closing of the structure of self-presupposition of the State-form. It implies that the typology of historico-machinic processes, and the topology of their relationships of extrinsic and intrinsic coexistence are transversally intersected by a typology and a topology of *spatial logics* or *types of territorialization*: which the 12th Plateau carries out (Propositions V and VII).

c) The assembly of the hypothesis ends in a historico-machinic disassembly of the *modern* State and its specific monopolistic structure. While the State form is defined by Deleuze and Guattari through its structure of self-presupposition, the modern State is defined by this "surprising monopoly, the monopoly of political decision," according to Carl Schmitt, who developed its two-fold historical implication: on the one hand, the repression of internal antagonisms (feudal rivalries and wars of faith), or at least their *relativization*, neutralizing their signification as "war" and reducing them to *private* disagreements; on the other, the monopolistic appropriation of external relationships, circumscribing war to a modality of strictly inter-State relationships. A dual structure of monopolization, therefore, or rather a bipolarized one, combining the monopolization of political authority on the "inside" (producing a de-politicization of internal space as "police" space), and a monopolization of political will on the "outside" (making possible a codification of international relationships as relationships between sovereign political wills recognizing each other mutually as such). Sovereignty as monopolistic subject of decisions and of political relationships only found its particularly modern figure from a certain articulation between sovereignty, politics, *and war*. Faced with this situation, the hypothesis of the war machine, starting with the affirmation that the power of war is not intrinsic to the State-form, and war not an intrinsic modality of politics, finds itself caught up in the perspective of a historical genealogy of State war power, which is formulated in historico-machinic concepts: a genealogy of ways of *appropriation of the power of the war machine by the State power of capture*, transforming a relationship of *extrinsic coexistence* to one of *intrinsic coexistence*. It is thus a heterogenesis of State power through its conflictual interactions with the historical forces that escape it or turn against it.

From there, the critical scope of the hypothesis takes on effective meaning touching on the history of the modern State and the historicity of the concept of politics that it determined. The hypothesis aims to follow closely the historical processes that first conditioned the synthesis of the modern State (the synthesis of territorial sovereignty connecting the monopoly on internal civil authority and the monopoly on external war decisions, and through which Statified sovereignty, as Carl Schmitt noted after Clausewitz, *effectively became* the "presupposition" of war), but also the processes that led to the dislocation of this synthesis with historico-machinic conceptuality, making it therefore possible to think retrospectively about its contingency and formation, and prospectively about its historical finitude which combines 1/the internal politicization of conflicts turned against the sovereign State as a "superior and neutral third party" (be it in the name of another sovereignty, or against the very principle of sovereign authority) and 2/the external subordination of inter-State wars to interests and power relationships for which State sovereignty and capture tend to become simple means. Which explains how the hypothesis of the war machine can be read in turns as an anti-Hegelian and yet Schmittian hypothesis, as post-Clausewitzian and even "neo-Leninist." It should be noted that while a tenacious denial wants Deleuze and Guattari to have kept themselves purely and simply outside of the range of questions related to Marxism-Leninism, our authors themselves seem to have had a much sharper awareness of the difficulties of escaping so miraculously from the ideological-political forces of their time, and from the systems of positions, displacements, and critical "depositions" that they made possible. In this very context, the term, or at least the concept, of "war machine" was introduced as early as 1973 to express the "direct political problem" of the day: the invention of modes of organization of revolutionary forces that would not model their "party" on the form of a State organ, which would not imitate the "self-supposing" organization of an apparatus of capture.[3] At the other extreme end of the curve of development of the war machine hypothesis, in 1980, in the 13th Plateau, Deleuze and Guattari restate: the problem is still "that of smashing capitalism, of redefining socialism, of constituting a war machine capable of countering the world war machine by other means. [...] constituting a war machine whose aim is neither the war of extermination nor the peace of generalized terror, but revolutionary movement."[4] Instead of a liquidation without inventory, it is necessary to examine the fact that this direct political problem is developed in a program of considerable scope, one that aims to recast the theoretical problem of war and the relationship between politics and the State that, in the modern era, defined its codes, manners, rules, and meanings, through an unprecedented reworking of Clausewitz's "Formula," and culminating in a new theory of the "*nomos* of the earth" placing all of the categories of historico-machinic materialism at the service of an analysis of the conflictual modes of territorialization of power.

Nomadism and its "Machine": *Nomos* of the Earth and State Territorialization

"1227: Treatise on Nomadology—The War Machine." Giving the year of Genghis Khan's death as a date for the war machine does not mean assigning it a historical beginning. According to the Sinologist René Grousset, no one knows when nomadism began. In his comprehensive work, *The Empire of the Steppes*, he describes remains that date back to the Neolithic, which leads us to believe that nomadic ways of life were present alongside the entire history of Asian civilization.[5] Undoubtedly, one of the motives that Deleuze and Guattari had in elaborating it as a philosophical concept is precisely the fact that cultural sciences had so often attributed an ambivalent universality to nomadism, which could even be called a *negative universality*. There are few countries or times that have not known it, in very diverse ethnological and historical forms, and nomadism was often seen not only as a set of sociocultural forms genetically distinct from sedentary societies but as a state that preceded sedentarity. More than its prehistory, it would be the name of its *anti*-historical origin: an origin that had to be repressed, domesticated, or dominated so that something like "civilization" could emerge, and that humanity could be born to itself as a process of self-civilization. Sedentarity, or what Gordon Childe calls the "Neolithic revolution," is the condition of conditions for this process: condition of the mastery of food production by the increase in agricultural and craft techniques and by the domestication of animals; correlative condition of a demographic development of space; condition of the appearance of writing, forms of thought, and symbolic structures dependent on writing; condition of urban formations and the first forms of political government.... Against the evolutionist approach, Deleuze and Guattari turned their interest to the hypothesis of Mikhail Gryaznov, who considered nomadism not as a condition "of the origin" but on the contrary as a becoming affecting populations constrained to abandon their sedentarity.[6] Yet instead of contesting this representation of nomadism as myth of the origin, the expansion of the nomadism motif to all kinds of scientific or pseudo-scientific discourse adds a new variant. At the price of a vague metaphorization intended to echo the complex transformations of contemporary forms of encouraged, deliberate, or forced displacements of vast masses of people within and across the borders of States, the success of this motif tends to invert the myth of the origin in a myth of the end of history, where humanity, unshackled from the sedentism established over the course of centuries, to detach cultural, social, and political territories to rework planetary space into a space for generalized nomadism, for better or worse.[7] It is better to recall that the negative universalism of nomadism was not thought of as this origin that would have had to have been repressed to make way for a civilizing sedentariness without seeing it constantly return at the same time, from an "outside" where major historical fables and apocalyptic visions are combined: from waves of barbarian invasions unfurling onto sedentary land and overthrowing dynasties to the proletarian hordes that returned to haunt bourgeois fantasies of the 19th century. Periodically ravaging carefully cultivated fields, raiding cities of the empire, bringing entire civilizations to a brutal end, nomadism has also continued to be a delirium of the sedentary. Kafka gave a hallucinatory tale of it in *The Great Wall of China*—"they are obviously nomads from the North. In some way that is incomprehensible to me they have pushed right into the capital, although it is a long way from the frontier. At any rate, here they are; it seems that every morning there are more of them." To come at it from the opposite angle, sedentism is also a sedentism of thought that attempts to think nomadism and can only think of it in privative terms, in terms of the civilization it lacks, or paranoid ones, in terms of the civilization that it threatens to destroy. More profoundly than the accumulation of culture, knowledge and techniques, signs and goods, sedentism, the condition of conditions, would be their common condition of possibility: the pure form of time much more than space, or historicity as the formal condition of any possible accumulation. It may be a paradox: sedentism, total conquest of space opening the history of its mastery, its domestication, the discipline of its arrangements, and the exploitation of its resources, is in many ways also its repression or its foreclosure—its "external enclosure"—such that its exteriority can only return from an excess exteriority, taken to its absolute since it is no longer relative to an interiority. Not an exteriority in space (as a form of distinction and division of relative interiors and exteriors), but an exteriority of space to itself. What Blanchot, in *The Infinite Conversation*, called desert space, nomad space, or even the "outside" is the result of this sort of reversed reflexivity of spatial exteriority with itself, therefore "outside" itself, a flexion as a power of unbinding, a fluxion undoing identities, a flux.[8] It is significant that Western thought was keenly aware of this paradox of the external meaning of space and could only reduce it by multiplying the privative characterizations of space, as was done with the nomads. In the litany of "societies without," the nomads were not forgotten: without writing (or borrowing it from others), without cities and without State (or incapable of administering those conquered), without history, or without religion (or content with a rudimentary one).

Deleuze and Guattari's construction of a philosophical concept of nomadism, and the cartography of the field of problematics in which it takes on meaning (a "nomadology" of the war machine), engage in a complex—if not warped—way with these worn schemas of the thought of civilization, which confers original values on the anthropological and historical singularities mobilized, of which the meaning varies in function of the conceptual and argumentative context. This nomadology does not claim to provide a more "objective" understanding of nomad cultures and societies[9] (others are obviously better situated to do it); it does not aim for an understanding finally liberated from the two perceptions of nomadism mentioned above, excessive as they are: its hallucinatory projection by sedentary thought, its speculative exhaustion in Blanchot's "outside thought." What the concept of nomadism carries out in *A Thousand Plateaus* is a way of having these two perceptions play within each other, instead of against each other. Far from dismissing purely and simply the fantastic or imaginary values of nomadism, Deleuze and Guattari work on the contrary, at least in art, within them.[10] From this point of view, nomadology is a schizo-analytic process: by the inversions of perspective that it imposes, it is an analyzer of the imaginary and fantastic structures of sedentary thought and, in the final analysis, of the functioning of the State-form that overdetermines the sedentism implicit in our intellectual pragmatics. Yet in this way, nomadology is taken to a speculative level, by shifting the standard anthropological opposition between nomadism and sedentism. Deleuze and Guattari do not oppose the nomad with the sedentary but *with the State*, which is not defined by its sedentariness but first by a form of interiority, or in the Hegelian sense, by its concept, in other words its structure of self-presupposition *from which* specific treatments of space-time come: methods of capture of territoriality within which the State appears to itself necessarily as the sole "subject."[11]

> History is always written from the sedentary point of view and in the name of a unitary State apparatus, at least a possible one, even when the topic is nomads. What is lacking is a Nomadology, the opposite of a history.[12]
>
> The warrior is in the position of betraying everything, including the function of the military, or of understanding nothing. It happens that historians, both bourgeois and Soviet, will follow this negative tradition and explain how Genghis Khan understood nothing: he "didn't understand" the phenomenon of the city. An easy thing to say. The problem is that the exteriority of the war machine in relation to the State apparatus is everywhere apparent but remains difficult to conceptualize. It is not enough to affirm that the war machine is external to the apparatus. It is necessary to reach the point of conceiving the war machine as itself a pure form of exteriority, whereas the State apparatus constitutes the form of interiority we habitually take as a model, or according to which we are in the habit of thinking.[13]

Deleuze and Guattari qualify nomadism as a "war machine" on this second level, as "pure Idea" or "pure form of exteriority," which contests the form of State interiority, contravenes its modes of historicity and territoriality, and can at that point only be embodied *from the point of view of the State* in an inchoative phenomenon of destruction, thus failing to both cross the threshold of political history and to integrate an order of territorial coexistence of political powers (a "*nomos* of the earth" as Carl Schmitt would put it). The Genghis Khan sequence takes on an emblematic role for Deleuze and Guattari precisely because of this double relationship, of *formal exteriority* and *material destruction*, of a nomad war machine with the grand imperial formation that understands it in its own civilizational era. While it remains to be seen what form of power they see as corresponding to the war machine as "process," for the moment, it is essential to highlight the primacy that they confer on the relationship of formal exteriority that defines the war machine in relation to the process of material abolition or State destruction that only issues from it, and even must issue from it necessarily. This point is enough to illuminate the reversal of perspective that nomadology imposes in relationship to the State-centric point of view, and in return, what makes it so difficult for the major thinkers of the rational State to recognize an effective political signification in nomad peoples, both from the point of view of the history of development of State rationality and from the point of view of the legal-territorial coding of relationships between State powers. For Hegel and for Carl Schmitt, nomadism fails to make history, make a State, and to make "*nomos*." However, it can only fail, first of all, because *the point of view of the form of State interiority* imposes a certain order of primacy of the material process of destruction on the formal relationship of exteriority, leading to a reduction of the form of exteriority to unformed, contingent violence without any effectiveness and destined to self-destruction in the dust of history. As for the State, it will thus never know an effective exteriority except through the other States with which it has relations. Its exteriority will always be *relative* to its form of interiority; it will be its form of interiority even when finally developed in its full universality. This is why Hegel can say, in the *Elements of the Philosophy of Right*, that one cannot wage war on nomads, precisely for the reason underlying the political rationality of war, its internal signification in the rational concept of the State. Schmitt, in a sense, does not say anything else, but he elaborates the properly *spatial* meaning of the point of view of the "*nomos* of the Earth." Mentioning nomadic formations of power in passing, Schmitt only sees three possibilities: nomadism is only the temporary appearance taken by a migration that will become the source of a new territorial order between imperial or State powers; it will find its historical destiny in becoming part of one of these formations; or, refusing these first two possibilities, it only gives rise to "mere acts of violence that quickly destroy themselves."[14] What cannot be called into question, however, is the *homogeneity of the space of coexistence* of powers judged to be politically, historically, and legally significant, that this homogeneity is based on the development of the State concept, or that it is based on the legal-political concept of land acquisition (*Landnahme*). For Hegel, the plurality of States does not contradict the universality of the State concept; on the contrary, it is the way in which this concept realizes its rationality: inter-State relations, including the contingency, arbitrariness, and violence they contain, refer to relationships of negativity internal to the concept of the State. Its universality defines an interiority, but this interiority saturates the field of exteriority of sovereignty as a space of "mutual recognition," of which war is also one modality. There is no formal exteriority: the form of State interiority is without an outside.

Schmitt returns to the concept of "land acquisition" to perform this homogenizing universalization, as an act of power constituting an order of coexistence structured by territorial division corresponding to the land taken and, as such, capable of legal formalization. And this order of coexistence of powers "having acquired land" implies an area of exteriority, the one that the *jus gentium* would define as "free lands" and "free seas." Yet this exteriority is only free relative to the powers of capture capable of territorializing their sovereignty there: free lands and seas are only free to be "an open and 'unoccupied' space 'free' for conquest."[15]

Only a change in point of view can offer an exit from this circle of self-presupposition of Stateness. What fails to be thought in the concept of the rational State—or rather what must be foreclosed from it to maintain the fiction of unity and universality, and the (political, juridical, diplomatic, and military) staging of the debate between sovereign wills—is precisely the heterogeneity of relationships of power in a given historical or territorial field.[16] Precisely because it builds on a pluralism of forms of power, as we have seen, historico-machinic materialism possesses a specific concept of irreducible heterogeneity of fields of historico-political coexistence. It can therefore thematize a *formal* exteriority, a form of power that asserts an exteriority in relation to the State-form due to this power that constitutes its positive essence, and therefore in relation to the inter-State relations immersed in the same homogenous interiority. It is therefore finally able to assume the primacy of the relationship of formal exteriority over the relationship of material destruction, and by the same token, to account for the positivity of the indetermination of the war machine, *starting with its polyvocal relationship with war itself.* "The first theoretical element of importance is the fact that the war machine has many varied meanings, and this is *precisely because the war machine has an extremely variable relation to war itself*," in that it does not in itself express a State power or a relationship between States in a conflict situation. "The war machine is not uniformly defined, and comprises something other than increasing quantities of force."[17] The indetermination that the State-centered point of view, placing all the historico-political determination in the movement of differentiation and negativity internal to the concept, perceives as a loss of form, takes in the form of exteriority the positivity of an essentially plastic and transformable process. The positive power of the inform is not the absence of form but metamorphosis, like the mythological figures of the warrior analyzed by Dumézil;[18] such that, in the end, almost anything could potentialize a war machine, "an industrial innovation," a "technological invention," a "trade route," a "religious creation," as soon as they are removed from the stability conferred on them by their signification in the ethical totality of a State or an inter-State relationship and that they actualize this milieu as formally external to State capture, in other words, it is not part of the mosaic of States as the universal context of interiority.[19]

Needless to say, isolating a "war machine" power as an autonomous process does not mean defining this power *through* war. War, as an anthropological, sociological, or political phenomenon, remains a phenomenon always defined by fields of coexistence between heterogenic machinic processes, and does not belong specifically or "in itself" to anyone (like the "savage war" analyzed by Clastres, in a process of anticipation-warding off of State capture). Deleuze and Guattari identify the proper object of this power as "composition of a *nomos*,"[20] a nomadic *nomos* or a certain type of production or investment of space. Naturally, the war machine cannot be defined as a process, and its positive content defined as "nomadic" without changing the meaning of nomadism. It involves building a non-anthropological and non-ethnic but properly territorial concept of nomadism, defining it as "nothing to do with war but to do with a particular way of occupying, taking up, space-time, or inventing new space-times."[21] It is important to distinguish the status of nomadism for Deleuze and Guattari. From the perspective of global history, the nomads of the steppes invent a war machine as a form of exteriority of imperial or State formations.[22] From the perspective of conceptual constructivism, ethnological and historical studies of different nomadic peoples allow the elaboration by comparison and contrast of content adequate to the process of such a machine (a distinctive assemblage of productions of space). The ecological, economic, technical, and artistic practices forming the anthropological-historical content of the *Treatise on Nomadology* weave together these empirical singularities from which a nomadic "territorial principal" can be defined ("smooth space"). Finally, from the point of view of historical-machinic materialism itself, nomadism carries out this machinic process, or in other words affirms its specific power: to produce a form of exteriority to the State, occupy or "hold" a type of space that counters State territorial capture in collective arrangements that escape it or turn against it. At the same time as this territorial determination explains the form of power by which nomadism is defined positively (rather than by the politicalness or Stateness that it supposedly lacks), the de-ethicized concept of the nomad that results from it can be used in a non-metaphorical way to think other phenomena than those defined as such in the framework of historical and ethnological study: "However, in conformity with the essence, the nomads do not hold the secret: an 'ideological,' scientific, or artistic movement can be a potential war machine, to the precise extent to which it draws, in relation to a *phylum*, a plane of consistency, a creative line of flight, a smooth space of displacement. It is not the nomad who defines this constellation of characteristics; it is this constellation that defines the nomad, and at the same time the essence of the war machine."[23]

The hypothesis of the nomad war machine calls into question the type of territorialization or production of space implied by the accumulation of power of the State-form. In line with the analyses of the first part, it therefore involves both the theory of material apparatuses of capture and the theory of the relationship of sovereignty between *power* and *law*. On the one hand, among the three apparatuses of State capture, territorial capture takes the privilege of acting as an *empirical-transcendental doublet*, which makes State territorialization both, in circular fashion, the empirical positivity of the State and what could be called its metapolitical condition of possibility. This is what the hypothesis of the nomad war machine brings to light, albeit *a contrario* by the very fact that it contests this doubling. As for the second aspect of the State-form (sovereignty itself), the hypothesis of the war machine highlights, while destabilizing it again, the *internal* function realized by State territorialization within the structural relationship of sovereignty between Power and Law. It shows that State territorialization constitutes not only an external field of application of sovereignty, intervention of its power, or regulation of its law, as an unformed matter on which sovereign power would be applied, but first and fundamentally the instance that *gives it reason*, in other words that regulates, makes commensurate, and proportions together the symbolic-religious power of the *nexxum* and the obligation of the rule of law—which can be read precisely as a rewriting of the (speculative) crux of the (non-speculative but historico-political and legal) theory of Carl Schmitt's "*nomos* of the earth." In this perspective, Deleuze and Guattari's theory of the "nomadic nomos" becomes intelligible as a critical rethinking of Schmitt's analysis in *Nomos der Erde*, the *contrastive proximity* of their respective problematizations of the concept of *nomos* producing on each other an illumination that is as captivating as the silence shown by our authors towards the thinker of the nomos of the earth.

Nomadic *Nomos*: Anti-Hegelian or Neo-Schmittian Thesis?

Starting in the 1960s, Deleuze had taken up the concept of *nomos* to turn it against its classically "nomological" definition, to separate *nomos* and *law*, and by so doing to oppose *nomos* and *logos* as a "system of judgment," or the judicative structure under which reality would be submitted to the laws of discursive thought. It meant questioning, following to a Nietzschean inspiration that remained present in the elaboration of the nomad *nomos* in 1980, the theological-moral presuppositions of the concept of law. It meant especially relating these presuppositions to a certain *territorial structure of judgment*. The form of judgment itself, short of the divisions between theoretical and practical judgment, between fact and law, or between natural legality and human or divine legislation, originates in a procedure of distributive justice that fundamentally has land as its object, good property as its ideal, and the hierarchy of "proprietors" as the rule or reason for just, or in other words justly unequal, appropriation. Deleuze did not elaborate on the anthropological, historical, and political references for this distributive and appropriative treatment of land presupposed by the form of judgment and its model of justice. He mainly wanted to show how acts of objectivization of land as property that could be divided into parts, of differential attribution of the property to people, and of measurement proportioning these parts to the hierarchy of qualities, social titles, or ontological merits recognized of the beneficiaries later internally informed the philosophical doctrines of judgment of

Aristotle and Thomas of Aquinas to Kant and Husserl and inscribed within them onto-theological presuppositions inherent in the idea of a categorial division of meanings of being, presuppositions that take their own basis in a politics of occupation and administration of land, of exploitation of income, and infinitisation of debt: the "agrarian question" as *arche terra* suppressed by the idealism of doctrines of judgment or of "*attribution*."[24] Against them, Deleuze was already elaborating the irreducibility of a nomadology of thought, opposing the categorial divisions of being with "all the extensity of a univocal and undistributed Being"; the procedures of unequal attribution of property to beings with "a completely other distribution which must be called nomadic, a nomad *nomos*, without property, enclosure, or measure"; and the hierarchy of beings proportioning the part that each one "deserves" in function of his or her internal *logos* with "crowned anarchy": "Here, there is no longer a division of that which is distributed but rather a division among those who distribute *themselves* in an open space—a space which is unlimited, or at least without precise limits. [...] It is an errant and even 'delirious' distribution [...]. It is not a matter of being which is distributed according to the requirements of representation, but of all things being divided up within being in the univocity of simple presence."[25]

Relying notably on Emmanuel Laroche's study *Histoire de la racine NEM en Grec ancient*, which gave philological support to Deleuze's thinking in 1968,[26] Carl Schmitt had argued fifteen years earlier for a reevaluation of the "original meaning" of the word *nomos*: an originally concrete and concretely spatial meaning still perceptible in the degradation inflicted on it by the dissolution of the *polis* and the rise of sophistry,[27] and for which modern legal positivism completed the de-semantization by reducing the notion of *nomos* to that of law or *Gesetz*, that "fateful word" that hides the concrete meaning under the representation of rules and abstract norms. Against this, the first meaning of *nomos* must recall this fact—which Schmitt made the cornerstone of his historical study of the *Jus publicum Europaeum* and his analysis of the structures of international law in the 20th century, although its effects more fundamentally reach legal conceptuality as such and the general structures of law—that legal notions are always spatialized. Even more, they are localized and localizing: they only gain meaning, systemic cohesion, and effectively normative value *under territorializing acts*, which Schmitt identifies in the proven concept from the history of the rights of people who "take land" (*landnahme*) and for which the constitutive effectiveness cannot be misunderstood without reducing the norms of law to prescriptive statements empty of meaning, and without blinding oneself to the powers that use these abstractions that can be mercilessly manipulated to benefit their own territorial ambitions. Legal norms do not stop at setting limits: they anchor themselves in indissociably conceptual and socio-spatial systems that inscribe the play of norms in manifest spatial delimitations in virtue of which human activities and social, economic and political practices are differentiated and polarized. While categories of law are always statements of *limit*, and while legal rationality presupposes the possibility of establishing univocal disjunctions, it is spatial delimitation, under the paradigmatic figure of the *frontier*, that fundamentally materializes each limit and gives its effectiveness with disjunctive categories of law (interior/exterior, public/private…). The concept of "land taking," a regional legal concept of human law, thus takes on a deeper, non-regional meaning for Schmitt. It is the legal expression of the very condition of a legal order: a "*nomos* of the earth," or a system of spatial order, of localizations and spatial delimitations, expressing events of land taking by powers that objectivized and made manifest their limits there, thus both their relationships of coexistence and the determined, defined, and "circumscribed" field of their competitions, alliances, and confrontations within this order of coexistence.

From this point of proximity between their respective problematizations we can measure what disjoints, separates, and finally gives a diametrically opposed meaning to the Schmittian and Deleuzian concepts of *nomos*. For Schmitt and for Deleuze, territoriality, spatial configurations of occupying land, the production of space, of differentiation of lands by frontier delimitations, allow a dual renewal: from abstract prescriptions to spatial configurations of division and differentiated separation that concretely support the position, predetermine its meaning, and condition its normative effectiveness; but also from these separations themselves to an act of first investment of the land, an act of power that must be said to be "constituent" because it is first "self-objective," it produces the spatial objectivity in which this power is constituted and manifested. Yet for Schmitt, this act (*nomos* as *nomen actionis*, *nemein* as "act and process") is determined as *taking*, capture or original appropriation that is the foundation of the subsequent partitions and repartitions. Whereas for Deleuze, the *nomos* is a process that undoes the divisions and distributions of the existing spatial order and which, so to speak, *defounds* them. It does not counter them with a new order of territorial takings or captures and a new system of delimitation, it produces and invests a type of space that makes it unlimited, and makes its capture impossible.

"The primary determination of nomads is to occupy and hold a smooth space: it is this aspect that determines them as nomad (essence)."[28] *Holding a space* is not *taking* it, it is even the exact opposite. One can only hold a space that cannot be taken, or that resists being taken (partisan war), precisely by becoming unlimited, in other words impossible to circumscribe in fixed limits, delimitations of contour and interior sharing, dimensions, and unvarying directions. An unlimited space in this sense is called *smooth*. We would then say that a space is "smoothed" by what happens in it (modes of distribution of people and things, movements, and events), not when it is homogenized but on the contrary when the constant markers that allow modes of occupation of space to be related to constants of objectivation are placed in variation. Space "is striated, by walls, enclosures, and roads between enclosures, while nomad space is smooth, marked only by "traits" that are effaced and displaced with the trajectory," like vectors that vary in function of events that affect the movement through this space "throughout which things-flows are distributed, rather than plotting out a closed space for linear and solid things."[29] Thus in the ecological conditions of steppes or deserts, "orientations are not constant but change according to temporary vegetation, occupations, and precipitation." For example again in the habitat and iconographic practices of the Sarmatians, the Mongols, or the Larbaa, spaces appear with "neither horizon nor background nor perspective nor limit nor outline or form nor center."[30] A phenomenon is defined as nomad as soon as it produces, "occupies and holds a smooth space," space "open and unlimited in all directions," without any other mode of scouting and orientation than the material and semiotic values expressed by the trajectory that encounters or elicits them. These values determine a field of event-related singularities, vectors or mobile "traits" that vary both the directions and the spatial markers that allow them to be identified, to the point that the trajectories are altered at each step, and that the space itself tends to become confused with the movements that occur there. Nomadic territorialization, by smoothing, is a mobilization of space rather than a movement *in* a supposedly immobile space. This is a variation of a subjectively unappropriable and objectively unappropriated space, and not the occupation of a space objectivated as a property ("taking land" or territorial capture). The State, on the contrary, needs these invariable markers (striations) to *immobilize space*, a fundamental condition enabling not only to take the land but within the taken territory to identify and control the people and the things according to their positions and their movements in this space, to delimit it, segment it, and make it appropriable, directly when the State itself determines the rules of residentiality of people and the division of goods, or indirectly when it sets the legal rules of their appropriation and their private exchanges. Operations that are not only foreign to the modes of nomadic territorialization but incompatible with them.

It is clear that from the point of view of Deleuze and Guattari's "nomadology," Schmitt's determination of the *nomos* of the earth as a system of order and localizations resulting from a historic series of "takings of land," is only supported by a tautological circle. It sheds all the more light on the contrastive proximity of the two perspectives. From Schmitt's point of view, the fact that the *nomos* of the earth expresses a circle, and in definitive the pure tautology of an "ontonomous judgment"—source of law because of conformance to what is, in other words to the taking of land and to the order of coexistence of powers that set their relationships there-is apparently not a disqualifying objection. It is on the contrary the sign of its originarity and the means by which the *nomos* makes a *foundation*. The metaphors of foundation, rooting, and frontier that are threaded throughout the corollaries of the *Nomos der Erde*, and to which Schmitt gives a literal and telluric meaning (counter to the abstract metaphor of the *Grundnorm* of legal positivism), bear witness to this tautological closure in the Schmittian text itself. As a system of order and localizations expressing the land taking by powers that objectify and make manifest their limits and their coexistence there, a *nomos* of the earth only works as a foundation because it already encloses *in itself* what it is supposed to make possible after it. For this reason, Schmittian analysis oscillates between the political-legal language of the constitution (taking land is the act originally constituting the law) and the idealist language of expression or of manifestation (the norms of law, internal and external legal relationships, and also the economic systems of production, circulation, and exchange, are only the expression of the order of coexistence of powers having taken land, and having therefore imposed the fundamental division and repartition of land for a given era). For this reason again, in 1953, when he makes use of the etymological resources of the substantive of *nemein*, at the same time *taking*, *sharing*, and the act of *grazing* or *making graze*, Schmitt can either turn it into a "topic" articulating the three dimensions of politics (taking and the power that does it), law (division and its distributive justice), and economics (growing what is shared, its productive use, and the commutative justice of its exchange), or consider that taking and dividing, sharing and distributing, using and producing, are only aspects of the *nomos*, with commutative and distributive justice finding their roots in a telluric justice, immanent to the land, a justice of which the earth itself is not only the object but the subject.[31] Land taking makes possible a division, a partition, and a repartition of land in attributable and exploitable parts, as an object of law and economy, because taking is already in itself "*original sharing*," original judgment, *Ur-teil*, as expressed in the Old Testament: "So Joshua took [seized] the whole land, according to all that the Lord said unto Moses; and Joshua gave it for an inheritance unto Israel according to their divisions by their tribes. And the land rested from war."[32] As an act of meta-legal power, taking is at the same time an already legal act, and takes value within the order that it establishes as *radical title* or "original legal title." It therefore has the exact same structure as the State violence that I analyzed in the first part, as the sovereign pole of "magical capture": the structure of the *nexum*, of which the Schmittian *nomos* is the territorial transposition. At the limits of the law, taking land *makes law* in that it inaugurates, conditions, and pre-configures an order of spatial divisions, in other words a system of limits and exclusive disjunctions of which the structures of the law only formalize the major articulations (between interior and exterior, between *imperium and dominum*, between public law and private law, etc.). In this way, State territorialization, as I suggested before, enjoys a relative privilege that makes it more than one of the three apparatuses of capture. It is already in itself *the principle of articulation of the two heads of sovereignty*, power and law: it balances them with each other, constituting their common reason, preventing the ideological abstraction of a law shorn of any relationship of power, but also the illimitation of conflicts of powers freed of all law, and finally the instrumentalization of one by the other. In this way, we can understand why the *nomos* takes on all the attributes of sovereignty for Schmitt starting in the 1950s, and land taking restates the "decision of the situation of exception" or of the constitutive act that reestablishes the normative orders constituted. The reason is that the earth constitutes in itself *the unity of power and law*. It names the original moment of their indistinction (the "meaning of the earth"), from which power and law are disjoined, articulated, and unarticulated, in other words enter into history which is only a series of major articulations between powers of taking and the legal orders that formalize the relationships of coexistence. The mythological moment internal to law, as Deleuze and Guattari's interpretation of the *nexum* suggests, is confirmed: when Schmitt opens the *Nomos der Erde* by positing the original telluric unity in the language of myths, it is not a liminal concession to a mythical-speculative meditation destined to disappear after the positive analysis of the history of law of European peoples, but on the contrary the cornerstone on which his conception of the driving powers of history rests.[33] The earth is already justice, immanent justice, original unity of power and law, in other words source of the rule or the *limit*, because it is *the fundamental limiting instance*. Thus any structural problematization of the law, or the limit, and singularly of international law and the "circumscription" of war, is a questioning of the territorial structures in which, in a given historical sequence, powers can coexist.

Nomos in the Deleuzian, and therefore nomadic sense, works on the contrary like an instance of illimitation. It makes the earth the great Deterritorialized but also the highest deterritorializing power:[34] not the foundation of divided, jurisdictioned, economically invested territories, but on the contrary that which opens territories onto their outside, their disinvestment, or their transformation. In fact, this type of smooth, uncapturable, illimiting space is not at all unknown to Schmitt. The paradigmatic figure of it in *The Nomos of the Earth* is maritime space; another is the tactical space of the partisan, given the importance Schmitt gives partisans in decolonization struggles and revolutionary wars. "The *sea* knows no such apparent unity of space and law, of order and orientation. [...]On the sea, fields cannot be planted and firm lines cannot be engraved. Ships that sail across the sea leave no trace. 'On the waves, there is nothing but waves.' The sea has no character, in the original sense of the word, which comes from the Greek *charassein*, meaning to engrave, to scratch, to imprint."[35] As for partisans, it is true that Schmitt insists they are a "particularly terrestrial type of combatant" as distinct from pirates and corsairs, and bearing witness to the way that "land and sea are distinguished as (two different) elemental spaces [Elementarräume] of human activity and martial engagement between peoples. Land and sea have developed not only different vehicles of warfare, and not only distinctive theaters of war [Kriegsschauplätze], but they have also developed separate concepts of war, peace, and spoils." Yet he notes with no less insistence how much the land/sea opposition is constantly relativized by the partisan's tactics, to the extent that "[t]o the space of the regular traditional theater of war he, thus, adds another, darker dimension, a dimension of depth," and "he provides an unexpected (but no less effective for that) terrestrial analogy to the sub-marine."[36]

Significantly, Deleuze and Guattari see maritime space as a typically nomadic smooth space. "The sea as a smooth space is a specific problem of the war machine. As Virilio shows, it is at sea that the problem of the fleet in being is posed, in other words, the task of occupying an open space with a vortical movement that can rise up at any point."[37] Nevertheless, the essential point here is not found in a repertory of elements or a classification of general "dimensions" of space, but in modes of investment and production of regimes of spatialization and territorialization. Where Schmitt underlines how much the sea, outside the "thalassocracies" or at least until the geopolitical upheaval caused by what he considered the exemplary thalassocracy, the British Empire,[38] had long represented an element of illimitation and excess, draining the telluric principles of a circumscribed play of political powers, escaping capture and its spatial dimension, and thereby stymieing the determinations of univocal and legally formalizeable coexistence, Deleuze and Guattari emphasize how the sea has constantly (and perhaps first) been subject to striating forces, while land has constantly been invested "maritimely," which does not mean in a "vague" manner as good-old terrestrial sense would have it.[39] If the nomadic *nomos* has an objective affinity with deserts, it is in the sense that deserts are a terrestrial sea, or at least lend themselves to the type of investment that makes them a "non-metric ensemble."

More generally, the earth constitutes a maritime phylum each time that it is to be "held" instead of "taken," occupied and not captured, mobilized without being measured (like fish in the water...). It is therefore not a question of "elementary elements" or substantial dimensions of space (according to a series to which Schmitt sometimes gives an evolutionary meaning, leading from feudal land law to European-centric, interstate individual laws, to the great British industrial and maritime power, to the aerial powers of the age of total war in the first part of the 20th century to the cosmic dimension of conquering space during the Cold War).[40] And it is not merely a question of techniques of spatial production, although numerous examples from the 12th Plateau show how Deleuze and Guattari give as much importance as Schmitt to the history of technologies, and particularly military technology, in the modes of production of space.[41] Deleuze-Guattari and Schmitt agree more on this point: while spaces of sea and guerilla are very significant (highly anomic spaces for Schmitt, while for Deleuze and Guattari, they bear witness to a *nomos* or a territorialization in smooth space typical of a nomad war machine), it is not for purely technical reasons which, as determinant as they may be, never constitute an independent variable. The way in which technical-military methods intervene in the production and destruction of spaces is always *determined to be determinant* by other factors, tactical-strategic factors, and in the final instance political factors (in other words, for Deleuze and Guattari, coming from relationships of intrinsic and extrinsic coexistence of processes of power mapping the historical-political field in question).

The question of guerilla and minority wars in contemporary history is a prime illustration for the three authors. "And each time there is an operation against the State—insubordination, rioting, guerrilla warfare, or revolution as act—it can be said that a war machine has revived, that a new nomadic potential has appeared, accompanied by the reconstitution of a smooth space or a manner of being in space as though it were smooth."[42] From the point of view of nomadology, it allows us to think a "confrontation of spaces,"[43] heteronomic forms of production of smooth spaces that combine with the methods of striation necessitated by regular armies, but also partial appropriations of smooth spaces by State military power (which prevents conferring on them a univocal political and ideological meaning).[44] First, the characteristics of smooth space can be found in the space of irregular conflicts, without which, the *asymmetrical* nature of the conflict remains undetermined. Conflicts are said to be dissymmetrical when they bring together homogenous tactical forces, means, and procedures, with quantitative differences. They find their "center of gravity" in the *battle*, their condition of possibility in State policies and relationships between States, and their formal tendency for development in the quantitative one-upmanship of regular forces (the form that allowed Clausewitz to describe the movement of realization of the pure concept of war towards absolute war as an asymptotic movement or ascension to extremes).[45] *Asymmetrical* conflicts differ from dissymmetrical ones not by the disproportion of forces and means engaged but by the qualitative heterogeneity of tactical procedures. Their paradigm is found in guerrilla operations and not in battle; their condition of possibility in an at least relative autonomy of groups and modes of decision-making and of action in relation to the organizations for strategic planning; their form of action and deployment, not in the dissymmetrical development of the forces in presence, but in the invention of means to displace the forces in the heterogeneous (becoming).[46] In all of the real combinations, the passages and borrowings from one logic to the other (problems of counter-insurrection, but also terrorism and policing), their heterogeneity is confirmed.

It can be seen immediately in the tactical investments of space, under a principle of non-battle that reverses the inferiority of forces in principle positive of asymmetricalization of the conditions and modalities of attacks: harassment and "hit-and-run" more than "engagement" in the strict sense; turbulent movement instead of encircling; a moving, continually mobile and fractalized front instead of a "front line" or "line of conflict" between warring forces. There results a special temporality—relationships of speed and slowness allowing the combination of a strategy of long attrition and surprise tactics[47]—and correspondingly a *logic of movement* that cannot be reduced to the classic conception of maneuvering or to the too broad opposition between "war of movement" and "war of position" where the strategic alternative remains subordinate to the battle as center of gravity of the antagonism. The imperative of permanent mobility imposes the reduction of attachments to the ground in favor of moving camps that minimize the role of external sanctuary and bases, and an easily transportable, minimal logistics in conformance with the requirement to *hold space*, in other words to have a strict correlation between current movement and the possibility of appearing anywhere at any time instead of occupying it as an object to appropriate and defend.[48] The principle of movements with variable vectors in an unstable and non-dimensional directional space comes from this as well, as motivation of the tactical primacy of turning movements: "No fixed line of demarcation, as the front is everywhere where the adversary is found…" (Vo N. Giap), the space of conflict is not that of the confrontation between two armies according to an arithmetic of the forces involved, but the open space in which non-relationships are distributed, where weak points or *ordinary critical points*[49] move about. Thus the privileged targets of guerilla forces (breaking lines of communication, human movement, or transportation of supplies) aim primarily at "de-striating" the space, increasing the capacity and speed of movement, de-linearizing directions, and fractalizing the dimensions of an unappropriable space:[50] in short, reestablishing a smooth space of which T.E. Lawrence gives the purest description, according to Deleuze: "the Algebraical element [...] dealt with known variables, fixed conditions, space and time, inorganic things like hills and climates and railways, with mankind in type-masses too great for individual variety [...]. It was essentially formulable. [...] but suppose we were(as we might be) an influence, and idea, a thing intangible, invulnerable, without front or back, drifting about like a gas? Armies were like plants, immobile, firm-rooted, nourished through long stems to the head. We might be a vapour, blowing where we listed."[51]

Yet the main point in all this remains that these methods for producing smooth space do not respond to tactical problems alone but directly touch a question of *politics*—as Carl Schmitt emphasized in his *Theory of the Partisan*. Not only because of the over-investment of ideology and politics in the confrontation between combatants, but because of the forms of spatiality that come along with it. Ideas change with spaces, and according to Deleuze and Guattari, smooth space contains a subversion of the very Stateness of politics. To come at it from the other direction, the fact of reducing smooth spaces to purely tactical options is already a political act that aims to neutralize *another* politics implied by this type of space. Thus the importance of State armies appropriating some guerilla tactics, which transfers techniques and knowledge of asymmetrical war or war by the minority[52] to the repressive apparatus. The doctrine of the "ordinary enemy" forged by the theorist of national defense in the mid-1970s was of particular interest to Deleuze and Guattari, precisely because it introduced a concept typical of smooth space ("ordinary critical point") into a control technology for the internal social sphere.[53] Yet there is also the importance of the hesitations or disagreements between State strategists concerning these appropriations and the "theories of the same element,"[54] and symmetrically and no less significantly, of the conflicts that can come *from popular resistance itself* when irregular forces are integrated into the regular army.[55] Once again, Deleuze and Guattari find in Lawrence the most admirable and limpid expression of the politics implied by smooth space:

> the tribes were convinced that they had made a free and Arab Government, and that each of them was It. They were independent and would enjoy themselves—a conviction and resolution which might have led to anarchy, if they had not made more stringent the family tie, and the bonds of kin-responsibility. But this entailed a negation of central power. The Sherif might have legal sovereignty abroad, if he hiked the high-sounding toy; but home affairs were to be customary. The problem of the foreign theorists—Is Damascus to rule the Hejaz, or can Hejaz rule Damascus?' did not trouble them at all, for they would not have it set. The Semites' idea of nationality was the independence of clans and villages, and their ideal of national union was episodic combined resistance to an intruder. Constructive policies, an organized state, an extended empire, were not so much beyond their sight as hateful in it. They were fighting to get rid of Empire, not to win it. The feeling of the Syrians and Mesopotamians in these Arab armies was indirect. They believed that by fighting in the local ranks, even here in Hejaz, they were vindicating the general rights of all Arabs to national existence; and without envisaging one State, or even a confederation of States, they were definitely looking northward, wishing to add an autonomous Damascus and Bagdad to the Arab family.[56]

I will conclude the confrontation with Carl Schmitt with a final remark. Guerilla warfare offers a particularly captivating case to show that these spaces do not provide a simple foundation or empty framework for antagonism but determine dynamics that partially decide positions, confrontations, and displacements because the concepts of politics—starting with those of the State, law, war, hostility, and enemies, but more generally the concepts in which politics are thought and practiced through its divisions and con-flicts—are only worthwhile, at whatever level we approach them (legally, philosophically, ideologically, strategically, or politically), *in determined spaces*, in function of specific territorializations that they contribute to schematizing (to dramatizing, as Deleuze would say) at the same time as they find their meaning and effectiveness (as illustrated by the perfectly ambivalent concepts of "ordinary point" and "ordinary enemy"). Modes of territorialization and deterrito-rialization of practices, techniques, and institutional codes are always at the same time territorializations and deterritorializations of concepts that find in them their conditions of formation and transformation before finding their "object" and their "subject." This is the properly *"geophilosophical"* thesis that underlies historico-machinic materialism: *the problem of thought is not posited first in the relationships between subject and object but in the relationships between land and territories.*[57] The incompatibility of the diagnoses proposed by Schmitt on the one hand and Deleuze and Guattari on the other for the crisis of modern State territoriality is nonetheless insur-mountable. Yet the political and ideological motivations, as massively evident as they may be, are only instructive in considering the conceptualities in which they are put in play.

When opposed to Deleuze and Guattari, critical thinkers of the State-form, Schmitt remains a State thinker of the crisis of State. The assumptions on which the *very thinkability* of politics relies for

Schmitt remain determined by the State-form. The *presupposition of the State* underlies Schmitt's continual expansion of his diagnosis of the dismemberment of this presupposition: it is, as we know, the point of departure of his approach to the "concept of politics." Yet it is also, we should add, its immanent end, calling for a new authority to take its place.[58] Modern Stateness, of which the rationality is carried by the State, analytically connected for Schmitt to a territorial striation that is supposed to be unequivocal, absolutely unequivocal, and therefore ideally unequivocal (the entire question—as we saw in the first part—is to know how far one can think the State "in a Stately manner" without idealizing it). This territorialization of the State-form expressed by its legal-political codification and in the first place, the three major conceptual frontiers that the European *Jus Publicum* was able to (self-)impose unequivocally between war and peace, between civilians and combatants, and between enemies and criminals, the *Nomos of the Earth* shows that it relied on a *nomos* held together by (a) State monopolization of sovereign borders (or the *sovereignization of the borders* of European nation-States), and (b) a no less intangible separation between the continental space of their coexistence (as space of mutual recognition of the inalienable sovereignty of each State) and the extra-European "free lands" (as free field of competition for their territorial ambitions). From there, neither of the two spatial determinations could be called into question without weakening the other, as illustrated in the disturbing play of mirrors that Schmitt constantly sees between civil war and "anti-colonial" war, and the inexorable vicious circle where communist "revolutionary war" draws them as a trend towards "global civil war," at least bearing witness to the spectral schema of *Kat-echeon* in Schmitt's thought and the apocalyptic figure that underlies it, of Evil or the Antichrist. From the historico-machinic point of view at present, the historic sequence of the "modern State" and its legal, philosophical, and geopolitical rationalization was only, on the contrary, the precarious and provisional effect of a dominant process of capture. This dominance condenses the complex ways in which the State is able to appropriate, or subordinate the other machinic processes to itself *relatively*: urban polarization (problem of the conflict between State sovereignties and free cities), the war machine (problem of the constitution and monopoly of State armies), ecumenical envelopment (problem of State control of long distance trade, access to raw materials, and more). In the next section, we will see how the synthesis of the modern State (the State as the exclusive subject of politics, and war as means of exclusively inter-State relationships) as it is expressed exemplarily by Clausewitz, fundamentally relies on such a highly contradictory and unstable historical process of subordination of other machinic processes to State capture and singularly on a movement of "appropriation" of the war machine power to the State-form.

This conceptual arrangement, while it goes against Schmitt's requirement to reserve the concept of State to the modern State (superior, autonomous, and neutral sovereign power, inseparable from its legal-political codification, from its philosophical elaboration, and in the end from the *nomos* of the earth of which one and the other are supported and that is expressed by the Eurocentric Human Rights), allows a much greater conceptual and analytical flexibility than the fetishistic antithesis of reactionary thought of Order and Disorder. By making the State-form a variable of coexistence currently or virtually present in any historical field (a machinic process in a relationship of extrinsic and intrinsic coexistence with others), it does not eliminate the concept of State in the abstract generalities feared by Schmitt. On the contrary, by breaking the back-and-forth between idealization of a Golden Age of the modern State and a melancholy for its great legal and philosophical edifices of which the long decline is constantly bemoaned, it allows first an analysis of the internal contradictions that have constantly beset this State, its apparatus of capture, and its sovereignty, then the *transformations* of the State-form and even the new functions and the new powers that the State could gain when their machinic process, by ceasing to be dominant, becomes subordinate to new processes (of polarization, of envelopment, of the war machine) which are in turn relatively re-autonomized in relationship to State capture and sovereignty. It is up to the systematic presentation of the "hypothesis as a whole" to show it: in the end, rather than the advent of "global civil war," Deleuze and Guattari predict the advent of a global police-legal order of "absolute Peace," and instead of the arrival of the Antichrist against which the State was supposed to be the final rampart, the promise of a New Jerusalem where States will not have the final share: "Whenever a radiant city is programmed, we can be assured that it is a way to destroy the world, to render it 'uninhabitable,' and to begin the hunt for the unspecified enemy. […] The Apocalypse is not a concentration camp (Antichrist); it is the great military, police, and civil security of the new State (the Heavenly Jerusalem).[59] Yet how much is this reversal capable of shedding light on the troubling affinities between these thinkers that everything opposes?

Machinic Processes and Spatial Logics

Let us conclude this trip through the manufacture of the war machine hypothesis by taking some conceptual clarifications for historico-machinic materialism·

a) The binary opposition between State/War Machine has a heuristic function. In the privileged conditions of the Genghis Khan sequence, it finds the way to illustrate above all an autonomous machinic process, in other words an affirmation of a form of power qualitatively distinct from the State power of capture. (b) This "simplification of antagonism" remains purely theoretical: every geohistorical field articulates relationships of coexistence of *all* of the machinic processes (polarization, anticipation-warding-off, envelopment, among others) at degrees of intensity and in relationships of subordination that are all the more varied. (c) The reciprocal is even more important: while the War Machine/State antagonism is always overdetermined by a field of coexistence of all the machinic processes, it cannot be enough to oppose a nomadic territoriality and a State territoriality, or the smooth space of a nomadic *nomos* and the striated space of land capture. As the machinic processes are not homogenous from the point of view of the form of power that constitutes its essence as each time positive, they cannot be any more homogenous from the point of view of their productions of space. The study of the modes of territorialization must therefore pluralize its categories of analysis, adopting the typology of machinic processes as its guiding thread, and overlapping it transversally. We should not be too hasty to identify in Deleuze and Guattari, in a similar series of equivalencies, always the same opposition between the nomad and sedentary, between the war machine and the State apparatus, between smooth space and striated space. For not only do these oppositions express a different point of view locally on the critique of the State-form, but they all form a system of highly overdetermined *multiplicities* in which the oppositional or binary antagonisms come from the play of dominance and subordination articulating multiplicities that are not of the same epistemic level: the multiplicity of forms of power (machinic processes) but also the multiplicity of productions of space (modes of territorialization). We will recognize this in identifying the new threshold of categorization that the Nomadology of the 12th Plateau has historico-machinic materialism cross.

The analysis of territorialities leads in fact to an articulation, which is still typological and topological here, of spatial logics, or of forms of spatialization produced by heterogeneous logics of move-ment and displacement.[60] I have already underlined that the research enlisted from cultural and historical anthropology, placed in the service of identification of a nomadic "territorial principle," produced the paradoxical effect of breaking with an ethnicized representation of nomadism, and with the standard opposition that comes from it between nomadic and sedentary peoples. To repeat: nomadism is not defined in opposition to sedentariness but to the State, not because the State is missing but because it affirms its own essence, in other words the form of power that defines it as nomadism: the composition of a *nomos*, a smooth space incom-patible with State territorial capture (the striation of space as circular condition, effect and cause of State power). These two types of spatiality, smooth and striated, are themselves complex forma-tions that involve modalities of heterogeneous movement, displacement, and circulation which are themselves caught up in variable relationships of dominance and subordination (according to relationships of coexistence of the machinic processes present). The incompatibility between smooth and striated space therefore refers more deeply to a pluralist typology of circulatory logics, of which the types are composed diversely and can all be identified in social formations that are only globally or statistically called nomadic or sedentary. I will start with a synthetic expression of them that highlights the implicitly structural inspiration of the pro-cedure. Take the four types distinguished first by a dual opposition two by two thus allowing the suggestion of an affinity of crossed couples: a *nomadic displacement* and a *migratory displacement* as opposed according to the relationship of inverse subordination between the two values of *points/trajectories*; an *ambulatory or itinerant displacement* and a *transhumatory displacement* are opposed according to the relationship of inverse subordination between the two values of *flux/rotation*; a *transhumatory circuit* submits a flux to points (affinity with migration), an *ambulatory flux* submits points of passage to the trajectory traced materially by the flux itself (affinity with nomadism).[61]

	Trajectories/Points		Flux/Rotation	
Nomadism	+	-		
Migration	-	+		
Itinerancy	+	-	+	-
Transhumance	-	+	-	+

This formula allows us to highlight the play of overdetermination necessarily at work in every territorial multiplicity:

1) The specificity of *Nomadic* displacement would be to subordinate the "points" of stops, starts, passage, or destination to *trajectories* that start to have value for themselves—eliciting practices, modes of being and thinking, specific scientific or artistic technological inventions—and that only connect the points, stages, or coordinates of movement by means of consequence or as a subordinate condition. "A path is always between two points, but the in-between has taken on all the consistency and enjoys both an autonomy and a direction of its own."[62] This is emblematically the case when these points tend to be affected themselves by their own variability or mobility, for example under the influence of some ecological conditions (steppes, oceans, deserts, or ice).

2) *Migratory* displacement would then be distinct, marked by the inverse subversion of trajectories to points that refer them to a

system of coordinates, guarantee them a source and an end, and fix their meaning and their arrangement of mediations to realize it. "The nomad is not at all the same as the migrant; for the migrant goes principally from one point to another, even if the second point is uncertain, unforeseen, or not well localized. But the nomad goes from point to point only as a consequence and as a factual necessity; in principle, points for him are relays along a trajectory."[63]

3) Displacement becomes specifically *ambulatory* or *itinerant* when movement occurs not by subordination of trajectories to points (migratory movement), nor by subordination of points to trajectories (nomadic movement), but by their common subordination to a *material flux* possessing its own variables (*phylum*). Ambulation is an itinerancy of flows, "to follow the flow of matter is to itinerate, to ambulate. [...]Of course, there are second-order itinerancies where it is no longer a flow of matter that one prospects and follows, but, for example, a market. Nevertheless, it is always a flow that is followed, even if the flow is not always that of matter" but in this case a flow of monetary signs, goods, and buyers, that the ambulant seller or producer follows.[64]

4) Yet flows themselves can be integrated into a system of coordinates or "points" of a migratory type, defining a *circuit* which is in turn subordinate to ambulation. The itinerancy of a circuit, in contrast with the itinerancy of flows, defines a transhumance, in other words, a *rotation*: "a transhumant, whether a farmer or an animal raiser, changes land after it is worn out, or else seasonally; but transhumants only secondarily follow a land flow, because they undertake a rotation meant from the start to return them to the point from which they left, after the forest has regenerated, the land has rested, the weather has changed. Transhumants do not follow a flow, they draw a circuit; they only follow the part of the flow that enters into the circuit, even an ever-widening one. Transhumants

are therefore itinerant only consequentially, or become itinerant only when their circuit of land or pasture has been exhausted, or when the rotation has become so wide that the flows escape the circuit. Even the merchant is a transhumant, to the extent that mercantile flows are subordinated to the rotation between a point of departure and a point of arrival (go get-bring back, import-export, buy-sell)."[65]

The distinction between these four logics of movement is inseparable from the analysis of their variable articulations depending on the case. They do not define ethnic or cultural traits, sociological groups, or "ways of life" but heterogeneous logics of circulation that can become entangled, complementary, or contradictory within the same group, society, or even individual. The question then becomes what determines the dominant and subordinate types of displacement within one multiplicity or another, and the division of "primary" and "secondary" in each type.

Thus there is a second level of formalization where this typology not only does not restore an opposition between nomadism and sedentarism, but confers no privilege on the two territorial principles of *smooth* and *striated*, the opposition of which does not exhaust all of the possibilities of the conceptual map. A territorial principle does not define a simple space or an unequivocal spatial investment, but *a principle of articulation of the four types of itinerancy and of determination of their unequal relationships*. Relationships of dominance and subordination between machinic processes are what govern the relationships of dominance and subordination between types of movements, and therefore the divisions between primary and secondary (between trajectories and points, between flows and circuits). While a war machine process imposes the dominance of a nomadic movement, a process of the *urban polarization* type would impose instead the dominance of a movement of circuit or *rotation*, and mechanisms of *anticipation-warding off* would privilege movements of the *itinerant* type.[66] As for the opposition between smooth and striated space, it is not a binary opposition or bi-univocal (like that between nomadic and sedentary, or between two ways of life), but between two territorial principles or two articulations of the four types of displacement. In this sense, it is a structural opposition: it does not oppose one type of territoriality to another two by two, but on the contrary, two forms of *overdetermination of displacement* in that these four logics of movement are *always* and always *unequally* combined there. Deleuze and Guattari can say in this sense that these territorial principles allow an accounting of their "mix—on when it is produced, on the form in which it is produced, and on the order in which it is produced,"[67] or that what is primary in the "mix" (for example, the affinity of *nomadic* movement, subordinating stops to trajectories, with the *ambulant* movement, subordinating the trajectory to a flow of matter to explore or follow; or for example the connection between migration from one point to another, and *transhumance* in a circuit of rotation which is itself "punctuated").

In this sense, a smooth space of displacement can be qualified as nomadic: it corresponds to an investment or a production of space that accounts both for the primary value taken by trajectories (relegating "points" to the rank of secondary or derivative conditions, but no less necessary), and the objective reason for which the nomadic displacement is subordinated to migratory displacement, no less than the itinerant and transhumant types of displacement. "The primary determination of nomads is to occupy and hold a smooth space: it is this aspect that determines them as nomad (essence). On their own account, they will be transhumants, or itinerants, only by virtue of the imperatives imposed by the smooth spaces"[68] (nomadism is destroyed just as well by taking away its "transhumant" segments as its "itinerant" ones). We have seen how these spaces should be called smooth by what happens on them: modes of distribution of people and things, movements and events, vary in function of the events that affect the very crossing of this space that has become "open and unlimited in every direction." It is precisely when trajectories are subordinate to points that the latter then take on the value of vectorial lines "that are erased and displaced with the trajectory," to the point that the space itself becomes mobile.[69] That which is opposed to the nomadic territorial principle is therefore not sedentariness as such (which can tolerate vast expanses of smooth space) but a territorial principle that counters smooth space and which subordinates nomadic movements to migratory displacements (going from one point to another), no less than the itinerancies of flows to circuits of rotation (only following "from a flow what passes in the circuit"). What Deleuze and Guattari call a *striation of space* is just such an objective of a surface of immobilized inscription that turns the space into a homogenous expanse made divisible, separable into identifiable segments, controllable according to constant references that allow an appreciation in each point of the variation of the relative positions and movements of things, people and signs, and that allow a distribution of the space itself by "assigning each person a share and regulating the communication between shares."[70] Why is the nomadic territorial principle opposed to a specifically State territoriality instead of a generic sedentariness? One can certainly conceive of countless techniques for striating space, and semiotic, social and even mental arrangements of striated territories. However the question, for Deleuze and Guattari, lies elsewhere: what makes this striation of space a *principle*, in other words a treatment of space that should apply universally, *by right for every case*, for all movements, or all assignments of space? The State, "if it can help it, [...] does not dissociate itself from a process of capture of flows of all kinds, populations, commodities or commerce, money or capital, etc. There is still a need for fixed paths in well-defined directions, which restrict speed, regulate circulation, relativize movement, and measure in detail the relative movements of subjects and objects."[71] From there, we can add three or four corollaries:

a) First, just as the nomadic territorial principle does not establish a bi-univocal correlation between smooth space and nomadic movement, but a structural correlation between smooth and complex space of heterogeneous movements (nomadic, migratory, itinerant, or "ambulant," rotational or "transhumant") *under the dominance* of a nomadic movement, the State territorial principle establishes a structural correlation between striated and complex spaces of heterogeneous displacements *under the subordination* of nomadic displacements, the elimination of which can only ever be underlying: "One of the fundamental tasks of the State is to striate the space over which it reigns, or to utilize smooth spaces as a means of communication in the service of striated space. It is a vital concern of every State not only to vanquish nomadism but to control migrations and, more generally, to establish a zone of rights over an entire "exterior," over all of the flows traversing the ecumenon. [...]Conversely, when a State does not succeed in striating its interior or neighboring space, the flows traversing that State necessarily adopt the stance of a war machine directed against it, deployed in a hostile or rebellious smooth space."[72]

b) If we then ask what displacements striated space makes dominant, the response can certainly not be univocal. Nevertheless, State sedentarism, based *in principle* on the striation of space, necessarily privileges *migratory* movement (directly) and the movement of rotation (indirectly). "It is not at all that the State knows nothing of speed; but it requires that movement, even the fastest, cease to be the absolute state of a moving body occupying a smooth space, to become the relative characteristic of a "moved body" going from one point to another in a striated space. In this sense the State never ceases to decompose, recompose, and transform movement, or to regulate speed. The State as town surveyor, converter, or highway interchange."[73] If migration is defined as an itinerancy that subordinates trajectories to invariable coordinates or to predetermined points, it is clear that residential territorialization as a principle of subjects belonging to a State has as its correlate countless migrations that are local, daily, social, and professional. The problem of State territorialization is therefore the *selective differentiation* of migrations and circulations, therefore the rules, means, and goals of their discrimination in function of points of departure, transit, and arrival (city/county, intra-/inter-regional, and intra-/trans-frontier migrations, among others).

c) Third, the State territorial principle, while channeling or repressing nomadic itinerancy in the strict sense, leaves open an entire field of possible tensions and contradictions between the other itinerancies that it can privilege: migratory, ambulant (of flows), and transhumant (of circuit-rotation). Think, for example, of the modes of territorialization of signs of economic power during the 15th to the 18th centuries: in historic articulations between Venetian and Genovese cities, then Holland, followed by England on the one hand and the major monarchal States on the other, striation by domination of transhumant circuits was in particular in the cities, which expanded the rotation of banking and merchant capital, while striation by migratory trajectories was ensured by States, including by fixing on both sides of the Atlantic points of passage of capital, raw materials, and slave labor. As States replaced free cities and appropriated all of the functions of capitalist accumulation on a global scale, they also internalized the possible contradictions and conflicts between these different types of territorialization (and between the different types of associated itinerancy). Under these new generalized conditions, it seems that the circuits of rotation essentially concern banking capital, merchant capital, and debt, while migrations mainly concern investment capital as much as variable capital (displacing the labor force of one production site to another, from one branch of production to another, from one pool of labor to another) as constant capital (determining the productive "points" materialized in machines and equipment, between which the labor force must migrate). As for the ambulation that consists of following a flow, it can be said that in the first place it concerns an autonomized financial capital, an abstract flow indifferent both to the rotations of merchant capital that only capture what happens in its circuit and to the migrations and relocalizations of variable and constant capital. In the following chapter, we will see how, in the framework of this logic of territorializations as overdetermined spatial multiplicities, the problematic of distinction and articulation between "territorial logic" and "capitalist logic" of power (according to the categories of Harvey and Arrighi) is taken up, and why Deleuze and Guattari are led to displace economic-political disjunctions of constant/variable capital and fixed/circulating capital towards a distinction articulating political-economic processes with the modes of territorialization of capital, between "*striated capital*" and "*smooth capital*."[74]

4

The Formula and the Hypothesis:

State Appropriation and Genealogy of War Power

The hypothesis of the nomad war machine finds its full presentation at the end of the 12th Plateau in the context of a discussion of Carl von Clausewitz. Yet in relation to Clausewitz, it functions on two levels simultaneously, which I will examine in succession, although they play off of one another. First, it proposes a new interpretation, which is itself already paradoxical. On the one hand, it deconstructs the grand synthesis of the modern State for which Clausewitz's concept of war as "instrument of politics" was the magisterial expression, by presenting its historico-machinic conditions of effectiveness (first of which, the *appropriation* of the power of the war machine by the apparatus of State capture), and therefore the limits of validity. At the same time, however, Deleuze and Guattari show that the principle of this deconstruction is found to be already formulated by Clausewitz himself. The hypothesis can thus be exposed as a post-Clausewitzian hypothesis, but because Clausewitz is the first post-Clausewitzian: the history of its posterity is made intelligible in his own language. On a second level, the hypothesis of the war machine can then function as an analyzer of this very posterity and, more precisely, of some of the figures of the *excessive Clausewitzianism* that was built up around a gesture of "inversion" of Clausewitz's Formula, and rapidly (in fact, as soon as it is formulated explicitly by Erich Ludendorff in the 1930s), around the contradictory interpretations of this gesture. For this reason, I will attempt to show that, if the hypothesis of the war machine explicitly leads to a discussion of the theses of Ludendorff on the inversion that the age of total wars imposes on the relationship between war and politics as theorized by Clausewitz, this inversion does not allow any conclusion on the caducity of this Formula, as Ludendorff saw it. On the contrary, it imposes the need to re-problematize it, to re-question the intrinsically litigious relationship between politics and the State (as Schmitt perceived in his *Concept of the Political*), and leads for this reason to interpretive and ideological-political options that are radically antinomic. By pushing Deleuze and Guattari's analysis to the limit, while remaining faithful to the hermeneutical lines that it clearly traces (further testimony to its "between-the-wars tropism"), we will see that, when it is applied to the age of total wars and to the contradictions that they inscribe in relationships between the State, war, politics, and beyond, up to the new sequence of capitalist globalization of the post-war decades, the Hypothesis opens "symptomatically" onto several readings of the Clauzewitzian significations of the period, meeting the interpretation sketched out by Foucault in 1976–1977, as well as Schmitt's problematic of the "total State" and finally reconnecting unexpectedly with the revolutionary appropriation of Clausewitz by Lenin, continued by other means.

Clausewitz, or the Formula: History and Presuppositions of the Instrumental Rationality of War

The textual location of the theoretical reference to Clausewitz immediately suggests its importance: sketched in the first Proposition of the *Treatise on Nomadology*, it is picked up again and developed in the ninth and last Proposition, where it organizes another approach to the body of problems implicated by the theory of the war machine in a systematic exposition which "recapitulates the hypothesis in its entirety." This reference envelops a paradox upon first reading in regards to what constitutes the core of Clausewitz's polemical thought (at least that to which his controversial posthumous reputation was attached): the thesis of a *political* determination of wars. Expressed in the well-known formula, "War is not merely a political act, but also a real political instrument, a continuation of political commerce, a carrying out of the same by other means,"[1] this argument affirms an instrumental conception of war, and more profoundly, it bases war upon the premise of a strictly statist determination of the political itself. Yet Deleuze and Guattari's hypothesis of the war machine is based on anthropological and historical considerations that prove to differ with such a simplified Clausewitzian thesis. Against the supposition which would have war be "in essence" an affair of the State, a mode of interaction between States, and thus an (albeit extreme) modality of the political, the hypothesis postulates a relationship of exteriority between the State and the power of war, process or *continuum* of power that can be actualized in infinitely varied sociotechnical environments, but without necessarily taking war as its object, nor as goal the submission or destruction of an enemy.[2]

This same hypothesis, however, far from distancing us from the Prussian theoretician, seems to bring us closer to him, by inviting us to reexamine the presuppositions and political determination of wars. As Deleuze and Guattari recall, his Formula does not exist alone. It is found within a "theoretical and practical, historic and transhistorical aggregate whose parts are interconnected," and which is not unrelated to the ideal determination of the war machine as pure continuum or process of power:

(1) There is a pure concept of war as absolute, unconditioned war, an Idea not given in experience (bring down or 'upset' the enemy, who is assumed to have no other determination, with no political, economic, or social considerations entering in). (2) What is given are real wars as submitted to State aims; States are better or worse 'conductors' in relation to absolute war, and in any case condition its realization in experience. (3) Real wars swing between two poles, both subject to State politics: the war of annihilation, which can escalate to total war (depending on the objectives of the annihilation) and tends to approach the unconditioned concept via an ascent to extremes; and limited war, which is no 'less' a war, but one that effects a descent toward limiting conditions, and can de-escalate to mere 'armed observation.'[3]

In inscribing into such a theoretical mechanism his theory of the political determination of war, Clausewitz draws out its conditions of validity, and thus its limits, which are simultaneously of a historical, theoretical, and even speculative order. First, it is known that the Clausewitzian concept of "absolute war" is constructed from the historical singularity of the Napoleonic Wars and from the twofold upheaval that followed, in the political equilibrium of the European balance of power, and even in the art of making war (radical offensive war, systematic utilization of the maneuver, mobilization of the entire nation, or at least of an enlarged fraction of "the people" in the war effort). But if this historical singularity must orient the construction of the pure concept of war, of which it reveals, in asymptotically approaching it in a new way, the essential content, this is because it appears at the end of a historical series that passes from the "Tartar hordes," through the Roman Republic and then Empire, through the vassal systems of the feudal monarchy, through "the great merchant cities and small republics" of the Renaissance, to the great State monarchies of the Classical European Age.[4] It is not that wars took a more and more absolute form: Clausewitz emphasizes on the contrary the strictly limited character, until the French Revolution, of the political goals of war, and thus of its objectives and its military means. The essential part of this historical series is rather the transformative curve *of the political itself,* and in particular, of the development of the "state cohesion," through consolidation of territorial sovereignties, through the development of public fiscal concerns permitting the transformation of personal allegiances into material taxation and the insertion of the State's military power into the institution of a permanent army, and finally through state monopolization, not only of "legitimate physical violence," but of the political relationships between groupings of power in European space:

> Inside [this space], almost all the States had become absolute royalties, and the rights of states [*Stände*] and their privileges had gradually disappeared; political power was thereafter a unified institution, capable of representing the State for foreign powers. The evolution of things had created an efficient instrument and an independent power capable of impressing upon war a direction conforming to its nature.[5]

Thus if wars are always politically determined, or in other words are *not "ever an independent reality* but in all cases conceivable as a political instrument," as the Clausewitzian formula announces, this proposition does not become *historically and in practice true* until the moment where the political determination is itself monopolized by the State. Yet far from deducing that State politics is an intrinsic determination of war itself, that is to say an internal given to absolute war as adequate content to the pure concept of war,

Clausewitz draws the inverse conclusion. The historical limit of validity of the Formula is thus reinforced by a properly speculative limit dealing with the relation between the "essential" and the "real," between the "pure concept" and historical effectiveness. In fact, if real wars are always politically determined, this is not because war is intrinsically or essentially political, but on the contrary *because it is not*. If it belongs to political power to provide the *reason* for wars— in the double sense of the term, in that it is at the same time their final cause, and the principle that *proportions* to this end their sequence of events, their objectives, and their tactical and strategic means[6]—it is precisely because war in its pure concept has no other object than its pure autonomous movement, and no other proportion than a disproportioned race toward the extreme where, *at the limit*, the political would dissolve itself (the end of history?). In other words, effective war is the continuation of politics, and one of the forms of realization of political relations, precisely because its effectiveness does not coincide with its concept or essence. "If wars between civilized nations are far less cruel and destructive than wars between savages, the reason lies in the social conditions of the states themselves and in their relationships to one another. These are the forces that give rise to war; the same forces circumscribe and moderate it. They themselves however are not part of war; they already exist before fighting starts."[7] Closer to Kant than to Hegel, politics finds its proper place in this irreducible distance between the concept and history, which is for Clausewitz a distance between the absolute form of war and the various ways in which States determine, and simultaneously condition and limit, the empirical realizations of this form. This is condensed in the striking expression: "War is sometimes more, sometimes less than Itself."[8]

For Deleuze and Guattari, this Clausewitzian mechanism provides a valid point of departure on the condition of being adjusted according to the hypothesis of the heteronomy between the power of the war machine and State power. This adjustment takes on the appearance of a radicalization of the distance enveloped in the Formula. In relation to this theoretical mechanism, what exactly does this displacement have to do with? They find a hint in Clausewitz himself:

> Whenever the irruption of war power is confused with the line of State domination, everything gets muddled; the war machine can then be understood only through the categories of the negative, since nothing is left that remains outside the State. But, returned to its milieu of exteriority, the war machine is seen to be of another species, of another nature, of another origin [than State]. [...] *The State has no war machine of its own*; it can only appropriate one in the form of a military institution, one that will continually cause it problems. This explains the mistrust States have toward their military institutions, in that the military institution inherits an extrinsic war machine. Karl von Clausewitz has a general sense [*un pressentiment*] of this situation when he treats the flow of absolute war as an Idea that States partially appropriate according to their political needs, and in relation to which they are more or less good 'conductors.'[9]

Already in Book I of *On War*, and then again in Book VIII, Clausewitz senses the tension that is introduced into the theoretical conception of war by his distinction between real empirical wars and the pure concept of war as the "inherent tendency of the war machine," the "natural tendency for which States are only more or less conductors or offer more or less resistance or friction."[10] Without ceasing to be a State affair, absolute war compels one to think, as adequate content to the pure concept as limit-concept, an ideational flux of power that States only seem to be able to partially appropriate according to their political determinations, and that must be conceived as *exterior in theory* to this political sphere of the State and of relations between States. What is symptomatic is that this ideational determination is not sensed by Clausewitz any more than as a "presentiment," that is to say that it is, for a theoretician of war as political instrument, inevitably maintained in the implicit, and that it can only reveal the flaws or the hesitations of his text which makes of absolute war at times the *political* exacerbation of the process of war, and at other times the "inherent tendency" of a war machine which abstracts itself from every political relation.[11] These vacillations mark *in the theory* what this very theory cannot manage to think. What is it then that prevents it from bringing to explicit thematization this exteriority of the war machine to the State-form, which the Formula covers up and disguises rather than expresses? "The problem is that the exteriority of the war machine in relation to the State apparatus is everywhere apparent but remains difficult to conceptualize," while "the State apparatus constitutes the form of interiority we habitually take as a model, or according to which we are in the habit of thinking."[12] What remains unsatisfying is not the distance that Clausewitz places between a pure concept of the power of war (as an absolute or an unconditioned Idea) and real conditioned wars through their insertion in historical and institutional, as well as social and moral milieus where they find *ipso facto* a political signification. The problem is on the contrary that this distance is not envisaged in its full radicalness, because it remains a distance interior to the State-form. In *Difference and Repetition*, Deleuze defined his program of "transcendental empiricism" by reproaching Kant for having conserved too many empirical presuppositions in his criticism, and at the same time, for having just as much compromised the exploration of the "true structures of the transcendental" which distorted the critical thrust of the empiricism itself.[13] In a similar sense, Clausewitz finds himself reproached in *A Thousand Plateaus* for having put *too much* of the political in the pure concept, or inversely, for having not put enough heteronomy of the power of war in the State—heteronomy of which the recurrent conflicts, in the history of modern States, between civil and military authorities and the constant mistrust of the former vis-à-vis the latter, are the institutional symptoms, just as Clausewitz's hesitation had previously formed the theoretical symptom. In sum, Clausewitz presupposes already "too much State" in the pure concept of the power of war itself. Thus, when he determines the fundamental objective of the military action as the "destruction of the enemy" (i.e., in the "overcoming of his ability to resist")[14] and considers this objective as the intrinsic property of the pure concept,[15] and when, correlatively, he inserts in the pure concept a dynamic of ascent to the extremes of antagonistic forces, it is clear that the supposedly "intrinsic" goal *presupposes* already a political determination of the enemy, and that the ascent to extremes presupposes a *qualitative* homogeneity of the forces in presence of which the tactical paradigm remains the battle between regular armies, as a function of powers in conflict.

This difficulty in thinking the formal heterogeneity of the war machine exposes us to the risk of a theoretical double blockage: First, a disfiguration of the content of the pure concept—a power of war incarnated in a "machine" as an Idea unconditioned by State political coordinates—but also, on the other hand, an illusion in the theory of the State-form itself which compromises the historical analysis of its transformations. The speculative problem and the analytic-concrete problem are here intimately related (as usual in the work of Deleuze and Guattari). In missing the pure concept or the war machine as process and form of power *sui generis*, the risk is as much to mistakenly obscure the effective operations by which the States succeed in incorporating this war machine (and in transforming it while incorporating it), as it is, simultaneously, to misread the limits of this incorporation, the mutations that it imposes on the State-form itself, the contradictions and the antagonisms that the heteronomy of the war machine introduces into the apparatuses and structures of the State power. In sum, we risk missing the fundamental problem of a genealogy of military power in the material history of societies. We must then see at present how the critical recapture of the Clausewitzian mechanism leads to developing systematically "the entirety of the hypothesis," in order to remove these two blockages and to specify the groundwork of the corresponding genealogical program.

Systematic Exposition of the Hypothesis

The critical return to the Clausewitzian mechanism allows a systematic exposition of the hypothesis of the war machine by directly identifying its problematic core: "The distinction between absolute war as Idea and real wars seems to us to be of great importance, but only if a different criterion than that of Clausewitz is applied. The pure Idea is not that of the abstract elimination of the adversary but that of a war machine *that does not have war as its object*."[16] The problem consists in uncoupling two things that remained indistinct for Clausewitz: the absolute concept of the power of war (this power as form or unconditioned Idea), and the concept *of* absolute war. Such a decoupling implies, more fundamentally, a reconsideration of the conceptual form conditioning the instrumental representation of war: the form of a *practical syllogism* where "the political intention is the desired end, war is the means, and the means cannot be conceived without the end."[17] The overall exposition of the hypothesis of the war machine follows from it, and is deployed in a twofold problematic series. The first series explains in what sense the war machine does not satisfy *a priori* this syllogistic form, cannot be determined as the State instrument of war, cannot then either be determined by the goal "to overthrow or defeat the enemy," and in short it does not enter "by its nature" in the practical syllogism of ends and means expressing the political signification of inter-State war. It is thus an analytic and critical series: it aims at separating the war machine from war itself. Thus its main problem becomes: How to re-determine the positive object of the war machine, in other words, the intrinsic content of the Idea, if this object is paradoxically not war itself? Yet this first problematic series leads to a second, this time synthetic and historic, where the problem is to know how the war machine becomes an instrument of State power, by which means States appropriate it and integrate it into the political syllo- gism of (military) means, of the object (of war), and of the ends (political wills or goals) accorded to the inter-State relations, and at the price of what tensions or what contradictions in the historical developments of the State-form.

PROBLEMATIC SERIES I

Analytic-critical Series (conceptual division war machine / State apparatus).

PROBLEM 1: Is battle the necessary "object" (objective form) of war?

THESIS 1: The principle of non-battle, such as is illustrated notably in irregular conflicts, and such as it can also enter into State strategies, suggests otherwise. Clausewitz already emphasized how the modern exploitation of the war of movement, as well as new strategic uses of defense in wars of resistance, had come to compli- cate the forms and strategic issues of battle. However, he maintained its privileged position. "The center of gravity of the whole conflict or of the campaign," the battle is the only means of war that one can immediately deduce from its concept: "The primordial objective of military action [being] to overcome the enemy and thus to destroy his armed forces [...], the battle is the only means disposed of by military activity to achieve it."[18] The first problem thus places the analysis on the concrete, polemological ground of tactics, strategy, and of their relationship; in response, there is a re-evaluation of forms of confrontation that are not subordinated to this model of military engagement. Let us note in any case that this first thesis— "the battle and the non-battle are the double object of war," without exclusivity of the one nor of the other[19]—does not resolve the corresponding problem. It emphasizes rather that this problem remains irresolvable as long as not only the tactical situation but also the political implications of the modes of territorialization are not taken into account.

PROBLEM 2: Is war the object (objective) of the war machine?

THESIS 2: The war machine does not have as its suitable or direct objective war itself, but the composition of a "smooth space," as a mode of collective organization of life. The formal heterogeneity of the war machine in relation to the State-form has for intrinsic content, not military confrontation, but the heterogeneity of modes of inscription or investment of space and time by the two formations of power. For if there are States without armies, and even confrontations without the objective of forcing an opposing political will to submit (of the pillage or "razzia" type, for example), it is difficult to conceive, on the other hand, a State, however "transcendent" or inadequately socialized it may be, that does not implicate a minimum of development of territory, assembling material infrastructures and symbolic-imaginary investments of the inhabited space. What is usually called the "territorial principle" of State domination is as much the result as it is the presupposition of this inscription (as variable as it might be, depending on the historical formations) by which the State compensates for the specific deterritorialization of its apparatuses in relation to immanent social practices. The "exteriority" of the war machine is not then an exteriority *in* space (geographical distance), but an exteriority *of* space to itself (to be "from the outside," wherever one is), which prevents its complete interiorization into the State-form, in conformance with the determination of the nomadic nomos: smooth space, that cannot be "taken" but only "held," and that makes the territorial correlates (socioeconomic, institutional, symbolic correlates) of a State apparatus actively impossible.

Why then do we still speak of a *war* machine, with all of the ambiguity that this expression contains, since its object is not war but a mode of production of space? It is because if the production and investment of smooth spaces is truly its intrinsic process, it cannot present itself as such without encountering that which escapes it, without running into that which it excludes from itself outside it. The ambiguity is not in the expression but in the thing itself:[20] "If war necessarily results, it is because the war machine collides with States and cities, as forces (of striation) opposing its positive object: from then on, the war machine has as its enemy the State, the city, the state and urban phenomenon, and adopts as its objective their annihilation."[21] War does not ensue *analytically* from the war machine and its arrangements of smooth space; but these very arrangements make it so that war must necessarily ensue from the nomad machine, according to a *synthetic* connection. (The problem therefore becomes: what controls and operates this synthesis, and imposes this necessity?)

PROBLEM 3: Is the war machine the object (means) of the State apparatus?

THESIS 3: If the war machine is not in itself the object of the State apparatus, it *becomes* it when the State *appropriates it* as a subordinated instrument to its own ends, and this historical process of appropriation is reflected in the two preceding problems: it is when the State appropriates the war machine as a means, that the war machine itself takes war as a direct objective, and that war in turn takes battle as its privileged objective form. It is thus the privileged form of the *polémos*, and the nature of the "synthesis" which change. As long as the war machine is not appropriated by the State, its relation to war is synthetically necessary, but the synthesis itself returns to an *exterior encounter* between the State-form and a war machine: this meeting "over-determines" the synthesis, establishes the *contingency of its necessity*, and ensures that the war machine maintains autonomy in its own process (as we saw in terms of the Arab resistance in T.E. Lawrence). Yet as soon as the war machine is appropriated by the State: subordinated to the politics of States and to their ends, it "changes in nature and function, since it is afterward directed against the nomad and all State destroyers, or else expresses relations between States, to the extent that a State undertakes exclusively to destroy another State or impose its aims upon it."[22] If it then enters into a synthetically necessary relation to war, it is not because of an exterior encounter, but because henceforth the State masters the power of synthesis, transforms the objective form of war into battles between regular armies, and even becomes capable of locally integrating, not without mistrust or resistance, irregular elements of asymmetrical conflict.

What is the power of synthesis here? The conditions and means of this State appropriation of the war machine, thus in final analysis the machinic process proper to State power. This is the major displacement of the Clausewitzian mechanism imposed by the hypothesis: the main problem is not that of the *"realization"* of the pure concept of war, of the realization of absolute war in more or less limiting conditions of States according to their political, social, economic and technical, moral and juridical parameters. The problem is at first that of *material appropriation* of the war machine by the State. It is the conditions, the forms and the historically variable means of this appropriation that can account for the modes of realization of war, which depend on it. This leads to the second problematic series, which deals directly with the genealogical process of appropriation, and of which the exposition reactivates the theory of the State-form and the redefinition of its apparatuses as "apparatuses of capture."

PROBLEMATIC SERIES II

(Synthetic-dynamic series: the process of appropriation of war machines by States).

PROBLEM 4: What are the conditions of possibility of such an appropriation?

THESIS 4: The principle condition of this state appropriation is found in the *ambiguity internal* to the war machine itself, as an objective "hesitation" of the Idea, according to Thesis 2. "It is precisely because war is only the supplementary or synthetic object of the nomad war machine that it experiences the hesitation that proves fatal to it, and that the State apparatus for its part is able to lay hold of war and thus turn the war machine back against the nomads. [...] The integration of the nomads into the conquered empires was one of the most powerful factors of appropriation of the war machine by the State apparatus: the inevitable danger to which the nomads succumbed."[23] If the State first meets war not in waging it, but in suffering it, we must also say that "the State learns fast!"[24] The dating of the *Treatise on Nomadology* not only refers to the exteriority of Genghis Khan's power which for several decades succeeded in subordinating the Chinese imperial centers, but also the ambiguity which traverses it (and which traverses it, "from the very beginning, from the first act of war against the State"), since the great nomad warriors who followed, such as Kublai, and especially Timur, would appear in turn as new founders of Empires, turning the war machine against the nomads of the Steppes themselves.[25] The year 1227 resonates as the date of this historic turning point, which returns back to this "hesitation" in the Idea, this *fluctuatio animi* of the Idea, of which the State takes advantage, without hesitating.

PROBLEM 5: What are the concrete forms of this appropriation?

THESIS 5: Deleuze and Guattari distinguish two principle methods according to two poles of sovereignty ("with all possible mixtures between them"): On the one hand, there can be an "encastment" of social groups which remain exogenous to the political sovereignty, and which thus conserve a heterogeneity and a relative autonomy (historical problem of mercenaries, militias, *condottiere*, special corps, etc.);[26] on the other hand, they describe an "appropriation proper" which constitutes the power of war as a public function incorporated into the institutional structure of the State apparatus according to the rules of the sovereignty itself, which thus tends to withdraw from it as much autonomy as possible.

PROBLEM 6: What are the effective means of this appropriation?

THESIS 6: These means cannot be directly military or juridical, because the military institution and the correlated transformations of the law in its relationship to repressive force, are the result of appropriation. The genealogy of the State power of war is not itself warlike, the juridicization of State violence does not come from a juridical evolution: both depend on three organic apparatuses of State capture: the management of territory and the control of norms of residency and of the circulation of people and of things; the organization of work and the control of norms of exploitation of surplus labor; the tax system and control of the issuing of money.[27] Throughout history, the permanent co-functioning of this triple monopoly is illustrated it in the enterprise of territorialization of warriors and the incorporation of their forces into the State-form, combining territorial attachment with duties of military service and economic ground rent which in turn stimulate the fiscal apparatus and the monetarization of the economy (inifinitization of debt). Institutions such as the *hatru* in Achaemenid Babylonia, the Cleruchy in Lagid Egypt, and the *kleros* in fifth-century Greece are aimed at binding down the mercenary warriors by ceding land in compensation for military benefits, but according to conditions such as that this territorialization profits especially from the development of the public tax system and from the state capture of the monetary economy. At the same time as it represents a powerful way to absorb the imperial surplus, the territorialization of warriors participates closely in the rise of public fiscality and the monetarization of the economy.[28] Under very different historical conditions, when emerging modern States were confronted with the dismemberment of feudality and the dynamism of free cities to establish the territorial unification of their dominion, the solution invented by the French monarchy permitted the territorialization of the ancient warrior aristocracy by directly utilizing a series of economic and financial factors: the ruin of the feudal nobility crippled with debts at the end of the wars of Religion and deprived of their lands by creditors, the state promotion of a bourgeoisie on the rise, the correlative development of the monetary economy and of public financing, which make possible a financial subjection of the armed nobility by the sovereign, and the substitutive putting in place of a soon enlarged conscription of all the social strata of the population.[29] The link between development of the public tax system and the constitution of military institutions attests to the iteration, in the creative evolution of States, of the convergent action of capture of territories, of activities, and of capital.

What is at stake in the theory of the apparatuses of capture, as we have seen, is the construction of a non-juridical concept of State monopoly.[30] More precisely, it targets an original operation of monopolization by which is realized an auto-constitution of State power in the interior of social and economic structures on which this power simultaneously exercises its domination. This reopens a materialist decryption of the transformations of State through the conflicts and adversarial forces which it incorporates within itself throughout its history. As I also noted, the retranscription of this concept of State capture in the Marxian analysis of primitive accumulation, calling for an identification of the transformations of the economy of repressive State violence, and of its relationship to the mutations of the juridical apparatus, through the historical process of decomposition of pre-capitalist modes of production, and the progressive establishment of the relation of production of capital. This analysis takes on new relief in light of the hypothesis of the war machine. Under a first aspect, this hypothesis is inserted into this historical process: it adds to the primitive accumulation of capital a *primitive accumulation of the State power of repression*, in a way that is more than a simple analogy with Marx's analysis. The two processes should, however, be distinguished, since they are not inscribed in the same level in the same State economy of violence. The transformation of the relationship between repressive power and juridical apparatus in the establishment of the structure of capitalist production concerns above all internal repression as State policing or "legal violence," while the process of appropriation of the war machine seems to concern essentially an external violence, defensive or offensive, turned against other territories or other States. From this point of view, the two processes even seem to be in an inverse relationship: on the one hand, internalization of an increasingly less manifest violence as it is materially incorporated into the social structure. On the other, reinforcement and monopolistic concentration in the State of a material war power destined to manifest itself "sovereignly" on the international stage in ever more considerable proportions. Yet a remark mentioned above from Clausewitz opens up another route for us: the development of a "state cohesion," which will determine the tendency of nineteenth-century wars to return to attaining an absolute form, itself took place in an epoch when wars did not at all display such a tendency; it is not in the age of the *politics* of total war that a *power* of total war developed, but previously, when the politics gave war (and proportionally the military means to war) strictly *limited* objectives.[31]

From the perspective of Deleuze and Guattari, this acknowledgment must be explained by a new problematic engaged by the Hypothesis: the question of modes of *realization* of wars between States is second in relation to modes of *appropriation* of the war machine by the State. This process of appropriation must then be conceived as that of a "primitive accumulation" of a political power of total war, that is to say an accumulation which *cannot be explained by the political determination* of war, but by the transformations of the war machine in the Classical Age according to new relations in which the State and the socioeconomic field are determined to enter. According to this last point of view, the determining historical sequence is that where the genealogy of the military power of the State enters into a relation of reciprocal determination with the genealogy of the social power of capital. Two movements reveal themselves from this moment as more and more indissociable: the integration of the war machine into the State-form, but also the integration of State apparatuses into the immanence of social production. In *Anti-Oedipus*, Deleuze and Guattari designated as a "tendency to concretization" this historical movement of incorporation of the power and of the apparatuses of State into socioeconomic structures and in the corresponding social antagonisms. And they deduce from it not an abstractly considered loss of State power, but on the contrary its intensive socialization bestowing it with an unheard-of social power and more and more differentiated functions, in its new task of regulating decoded flows of capital, of merchandise and human labor force.[32] In *A Thousand Plateaus*, the new hypothesis takes this correlative tendency as a consequence: the more the war machine is interiorized by the State, the more the institutionalization of war, its administration and not only its political but industrial, financial, and populational organization become factors of intense creativity for this State which is itself more and more immanent to the social field. In other terms, the appropriated war machine becomes itself a direct instrument not only of the policies of war, but of the growing implication of the State throughout the social relations of production, at once as a stimulant and economic regulator and as an instrument of domination at the core of class conflicts. The recurrent use of the war machine as an organ of repression in the multiple insurrectional junctures which rocked Europe and the colonized world, has as its reverse the functions that it takes on in the invention of new forms of socialization of labor. Marx remarked in a letter to Engels on September 25, 1857, that the military institution had constituted a formidable laboratory of experimentation of the relations of production that would then be "developed at the heart of bourgeois society" (for example the systematization of wages, the division of work to the interior of a branch, "machinism"). In this perspective, Deleuze and Guattari recall the determining role that military engineers, from the Middle Ages on, assumed in the state management of territory, "not only in the case of fortresses and fortified cities, but also in strategic communication, the logistical structure, the industrial infra-structure, etc."[33] In a similar manner, from the point of view of the transformations in modes of division and connection of the process of labor in the seventeenth- and eighteenth-centuries, they comple-ment the analyses of Michel Foucault of military models of the "*dispositifs disciplinaires*" mobilized to territorialize productive bodies onto the apparatuses of burgeoning industrial production. It is in the barracks, the arsenals and the weapons factories where take place experimentations and systemizations of the techniques which permit the "settling, sedentarizing labor force, regulating the movement of the flow of labor, assigning it channels and conduits," by means of a striation of a "closed space, detached, surveyed in all its points, where individuals are inserted into a fixed place, where the smallest movements are controlled, where all events are recorded."[34]

In short, the genealogical program opened up by "the entirety of the hypothesis" is not only to study the role of the public tax system, of the state management of territories and of connections of productive work, in the appropriation of the war machine. It is also, in return, to analyze how this machine, appropriated in the form of institutions and of military functions, becomes an intense vector of creation of knowledge and techniques of power for the State stria-tion of the social field, without which the capitalist relation of production would not have been able to establish itself nor to extend its social domination. This program thus articulates the primitive accumulation of the military power to the accumulation of capital, as the two processes that the State-form incorporates, and in which the modern State transforms itself. The major effect of this incorporation pointed out by Deleuze and Guattari will be the inex-tricable link of determination and of reciprocal stimulation, between the rise of industrial capitalism and the development of economies of war. It is at the core of the same complex tendency that the modern State is militarized, that it assumes its new regulatory functions in a decoded capitalist field, and that the material organization of the power of war becomes an intrinsic condition of the accumulation and of the enlarged reproduction of capital. The Clausewitzian Formula must therefore be re-envisaged in light of this trend to unity along with the evaluation of its limits in the *Treatise on Nomadology*: it is precisely at the level of these limits that the genealogical program engages with a political diagnostic of the situation at the time: 1980.

Current Situation and Illimitation of Violence: Inversion of the Formula or Reversion of the Hypothesis

The limits of the Formula were often enunciated by the necessity, for historical analysis and/or for the strategic calculation of new twentieth-century conflicts, to operate an "inversion." Politics became a continuation of war by other means, and States, the instrument of a perpetual war (whether overt or concealed), in any case in which the political States would no longer be the ultimate subjects. Nevertheless, from Erich von Ludendorff to Paul Virilio, from Carl Schmitt to Foucault, this took on such diverse meanings that Deleuze and Guattari did not adopt it without the precaution of immediately reinscribing it into the system of their hypothesis. "It is not enough to invert the order of the words as if they could be spoken in either direction; it is necessary to follow the real movement at the conclusion of which the States, having appropriated a war machine, and having adapted it to their aims, re-impart a war machine that takes charge of the aim, appropriates the States, and assumes increasingly wider political functions."[35] A first point: the inversion must include an historical process which implicates not only the parameters of the political State in the oscillation of real wars between simple armed observation and tremendous surges of military hostility, but more profoundly, the evolution of the material factor of appropriation uncovered by the hypothesis. In light of this criterion, we can evaluate the interpretation of the inversion of the Formula first posited by Ludendorff.[36]

I should note first that the proposition is bolstered by counting Deleuze and Guattari, with the Schmitt of *The Concept of the Political* and the Lenin of the years 1914–1917 and of the *Tetradska*, among those that I previously called *excessive Clausewitzians*, those who "go beyond" Clausewitz less than they push to their ultimate consequences the intuitions through which Clausewitz's conception of the relationships between war and politics already exceeded his historical and conceptual premises. At the heart of the debate over Clausewitz's posterity, the problem of the transformations of modern imperialist war as "total war" is naturally posed, and, singularly, even before its Ludendorffian formulation,[37] the crisis of a strictly instrumental concept of war as "means of politics." Its decomposition was the object of anxious thought for a generation of thinkers such as Walter Benjamin, Ernst Jünger, and Schmitt, and even a heightened sense of the tragedy of history—even if it favored a new mysticism of war for some, as Benjamin reproached the Jünger brothers in his review of *War and Warriors* in 1930.[38] Benjamin showed how this warrior mystique, which idealized a combative ethos in profound contradiction with military technology that had become impersonal and massive, exalted a representation of war as "universal effectivity" that expressed while misunderstanding it the material process of modern total wars, within which the goals and political conditions tended to become contingent if not indifferent.[39] Jünger himself, in *Total Mobilization*, offered a striking portrait of it as "forges of Vulcan built by industrial States at war," materializing war in a generalized machinism of which the constraints and inter-connections made the former "decision-making" figure of the sovereign and the "monarchic instinct" of Prussian politics at the turn of the century seem anachronistic.[40] In this sense as well, Benjamin welcomed some articles of *War and Warriors* for presenting the problem brutally exposed by the Great War—and which remains one of the main motives of the war machine hypothesis, confirming once again that this "between-the-wars tropism" which I have already noted on several occasions, anchoring here and there the macro-political thought of Deleuze and Guattari in the constitutive crisis of contemporary Europe, imperialist war, the failure of the revolutionary labor movement in Western Europe and the rise of fascism on a global scale:

> It is understandable that the question of "governmental checks on war" arises in the best, most well-reasoned essay in this volume. For in this mystical theory of war, the State naturally plays more than a minor role. These checks should not for a moment be understood in a pacifist sense. Rather, what is demanded of the State is that its structure and its disposition adapt themselves to, and appear worthy of, the magical forces that the State itself must mobilize in the event of war. Otherwise it will not succeed in bending war to its purpose. It was this failure of the powers of State in the face of war that instigated the first independent thinking of the authors gathered here.[41]

In his analysis of the total character of the First World War, Ludendorff gives Clausewitz credit for having recognized, after the Napoleonic wars and the new forms of resistance that they caused to emerge in Spain and Russia, the new and inevitably decisive importance of the "popular" dimension of modern conflicts.[42] He nonetheless reproaches him for having failed to draw out all the implications of this realization, due to a three-fold presupposition: Clausewitz abusively subordinated the military instrument to diplomatic action, since he limited his notion of the political to exterior politics while at the same time continuing to think of armies as the only subjects and objects of confrontations. Ludendorff objects to this by pointing out that, after the passage from the Napoleonic Wars to contemporary total wars, the hostility henceforth opposed entire nations, the entirety of their civil population, economy, and their ideological forces (which he refers to as the "spiritual cohesion" of the people in question). The strategic objectives were no longer only armies and their reserve bases; they included their industrial infrastructure, their financial resources, the human and moral "reserves," all enlisted and involved in the war effort.[43] In other words, the strategic "center of gravity" is no longer a *center*, but the *totality* of the opposing society and of its State. This leads Ludendorff to the theoretical necessity of extending the notion of the political in order to take into account the increasingly determining role of domestic politics in the enterprise of war, and the strategic necessity of entrusting to a military High Command the decision-making power over the entirety of the military *and* political (diplomatic, economic, psychological, etc.) means in view of the sole final objective which is henceforth adequate: no longer to confer through armaments an advantageous relation to the political State in order to negotiate the conditions of peace, but to impose militarily on the vanquished an unconditional capitulation. That such a situation results directly from the underlying unity previously identified, is easily conceived: the entanglement of the militarization of the State and the tendency to its concretization in the immanence of the capitalist social relations means that the war machine cannot be appropriated by the State-form without simultaneously being materialized in the increasingly intense network of interconnections of socioeconomic, political and ideological relations (which also means that at no historical moment is the appropriated war machine to be confused with the military institution alone). It is in this sense that Deleuze and Guattari write that "the factors that make State war total war are closely connected to capitalism." It is in the same movement that capital "totalizes" the social field (which Marx called the "real subsumption" of social relations and the process of production by capital) and that the State military power is incarnated in the total war machine, in other words, in a war machine of which the *means* and the *object* tend to become *unlimited*: the means are no longer limited to the military institutions but extend themselves to the totality of "the investment of constant capital in equipment, industry, and war economy, and the investment of variable capital in the population in its physical and mental aspects (both as warmaker and as victim of war)";[44] the objective is no longer limited to striking the enemy army in order to bring about the submission of the political authority upon which that army depends, but tends to annihilate the entirety of the forces of the opposing nation.

Nevertheless, as Raymond Aron has rightly demonstrated, the Ludendorffian inversion of the Formula is not without ambiguity. First, because Clausewitz does at times recognize the importance of domestic politics in the war effort, and especially because the unconditional capitulation of the enemy remains extremely vague outside of a political will, even should we only be dealing with a will capable of proportioning this ultimate objective to the conservation of its own State.[45] Now this ambiguity is not simply theoretical. It is an effective ambiguity of the *politics of total war*, which is revealed historically in the contradiction into which may enter the political goal and the processes of a now unlimited war machine, and which, at the *limit of this contradiction*, does not lead so much to the inversion of the hierarchical relation war/politics announced by the Clausewitzian instrumental conception as to an *abolition of the political* as such, the absorption of the political goal by a material process of war which has become autonomous. The concept of total war has sometimes been reproached for its vagueness, beyond Ludendorff's formulation.[46] For Deleuze and Guattari, this concept is by no means vague; it is theoretically (starting with those who use it as State thinkers and strategists) and *politically* untenable, which is very different. This concept only has meaning as a function of an assumed State, which is totalized itself while the war becomes total (which leads to the trend of indiscernibility between the State and a war machine incorporated in all the workings of industrial society, like the "forges of Vulcan" described by Jünger in the inextricably historical and fantastical register of the "Age of the Worker"), but which only finds its full effectiveness at the limit of a process that can only be autonomous in the horizon of a subordination of the State to the process of the war machine, and a collapse of politics (not an inversion). The historical effectiveness of this limit, which brings both the Clausewitzian thesis and its Ludendorffian critique to their common "*unthinkable*," is identified by Deleuze and Guattari in the global war machine of the Nazi State. In its process of total war, this machine tends to free itself from every political goal, to become an unconditioned process of war, i.e., removed from any political conditioning whatsoever. It is not only that the political goal tends to mix with the objective of war (in the conditions described by Ludendorff), but this objective itself tends to become a process without end, autonomous, and whose political goals are now only subordinated means. The total war machine is no longer only simply appropriated to the State and to its political ends; it becomes capable on the contrary of subordinating or even engendering "a State apparatus which is no longer useful for anything save destruction," eventually reaching a state of contradiction with every limiting condition of a political end, even with the fundamental requirement of the political: the conservation of the State. Thus the difference between the National-Socialist State and a totalitarian State:

> Totalitarianism is a State affair: it essentially concerns the relation between the State as a localized assemblage and the abstract machine of overcoding it effectuates. Even in the case of a military dictatorship, it is a State army, not a war machine, that takes power and elevates the State to the totalitarian stage. Totalitarianism is quintessentially conservative. Fascism, on the other hand, involves a war machine. When fascism builds itself a totalitarian State, it is not in the sense of a State army taking power, but of a war machine taking over the State.[47]

The specificity of the National-Socialist total State cannot be fully determined without recognizing the dynamics of virtually unlimited war in which *and through which it realizes its totalization*—by the militarization of civil society, by the total mobilization of the population in the war effort, the ideological mobilization towards imperialist expansionism exploiting all of the resources of the "historical-global delirium,"[48] by the conversion of the entire economy into a war economy by the movement of investments to means of production and consumption toward the production of means of destruction. Yet at the center of this dynamic, the State tends to become a simple means of acceleration of a process of annihilation into which it plunges. In this sense, the full realization of the National-Socialist total State is less totalitarianism as such (total domination would be rather its "synthetically" necessary object, according to the requirements of total mobilization, which is, after all, the work of the Party rather than the State) than its realization in a "suicidal State."[49] Even though she did not distinguish between fascism and totalitarianism, Hannah Arendt wrote in a similar vein that the National Socialist idea of domination "could be realized neither by a State nor by a simple apparatus of violence, but only by a movement which is constantly moving [...]; as for the political objective which the end of this movement would constitute, it simply does not exist."[50] At this point, Deleuze and Guattari add, the war, and even the risk of losing the war, and finally the inevitability of defeat, come into play as accelerators of this now unlimited movement. March 19, 1945—Hitler—telegram 71: "If the war is lost, may the nation perish."[51]

In what historical situation would the Formula be "inverted," properly speaking, and not simply brought to the limit where it loses all sense? We have reached the end of the Hypothesis, that is, the point where the historical movement of the factor of *appropriation* meets up with the time of Deuelze and Guattari's utterance of the Hypothesis itself. More than ever, we must reaffirm its fundamental theoretical sense: the over-determination of the relation politics/war by the relation war machine/State, without which the supposed "inversion" of the Formula remains a pointless verbal artifice. What the first phase of the inversion which culminates in the Second World War has shown us is that a global war machine which tends toward autonomy from States, at the outcome of a trend where the rise of industrial capitalism and the development of war economics progressively merged, and where the intensive militarization of European States made of the material organization of the power of war an intrinsic condition of capitalist accumulation. But in this first phase, this inversion of the relation of appropriation of the war machine and State *does not bring about* an inversion of the relation of politics and war. This is because the war machine only appropriates the political

State in and by *enacted* war, in the form of total war; it is in continuing to take war as its direct objective that the war machine materializes in the ensemble of the socio-economic field (economy of war and total mobilization). In this way, the relation of appropriation is inverted, but under conditions where the political goal (to subjugate or destroy the enemy) remains the determining motive, and where war remains that of the Clausewitzian Formula, "the continuation of politics by other means," even though these other means become incompatible with all political and diplomatic solutions, and despite the fact that the political ends enter into contradiction with a process of war leading the political State inevitably toward self-destruction. If a new threshold is crossed during the post-war decades, it is precisely insofar as the inversion of the relation of appropriation between war machine and State is embodied in a global configuration where the militarization of States, the rise of the war economy in the structures of capitalism, the subsumption under the material power of unlimited war of the ensemble of the planetary social environment, come to be realized *without enacted total war*.

> This worldwide war machine, which in a way 'reissues' from the States, displays two successive figures: first, that of fascism, which makes war an unlimited movement with no other aim than itself; but fascism is only a rough sketch, and the second, postfascist, figure is that of a war machine that takes peace as its object directly, as the peace of Terror or Survival. The war machine reforms a smooth space that now claims to control, to surround the entire earth. Total war itself is surpassed, toward a form of peace more terrifying still. The war machine has taken charge of the aim, worldwide order, and the States are now no more than objects or means adapted to that machine. This is the point at which Clausewitz's formula is effectively reversed.[52]

We are in the presence of a configuration where the political effec-tively becomes the continuation of war by other means, but precisely because the global war machine *ceases to have war as its object*, while war *ceases to be subordinated to political ends*. The first important factor of the reconstitution of such an autonomous war machine is of course geopolitical and strategic, according to new axes of international politics, the displacement of imperialist rivalries of European States toward the axes of the Cold War and the new North-South relations. This is first the meaning of the remark according to which "*it is peace that technologically frees the unlimited material process of total war.*"[53] The ominous peace in the new strategy of nuclear deterrence, the "peace of Terror or Survival," makes of the global war machine the object and means of a techno-logical, scientific and economic capitalization without precedent, which no longer even needs the triggering of total war itself in order to develop. But there is a second, more profound factor, which explains that the reformation of a worldwide war machine in the post-second world war decades is not for Deleuze and Guattari simply a prolongation, a broadening to new technological and geopolitical dimensions, or a continuation of imperialist strategies of the Nation-States of the first half of the twentieth century, but a new situation. Geopolitics itself in fact depends on a "meta-economy" which determines the relations between the system of the world-economy and the political States which effectuate its conditions.[55] This point is at the heart of the thematization of the accumulation of capital on a global scale in terms of "axiomatics" that I will discuss in the last section. Yet we can already say, in a general way, that the autonomy of the global war machine in relation to State structures remains determined, as much in the first phase as in the second phase of the inversion, by the *degree of relative autonomy* (not of "indepen-dence") of the process of accumulation and reproduction of capital in relation to these same structures. Certainly, the process of accumulation of capital passes increasingly through an international division of labor, a transnational circulation of capital and a worldwide market, but it is still obviously up to States to manage the corresponding relations of production, to overcome the systematic disequilibria and the crises of under-investment and overproduction, and to regulate for better or for worse their social repercussions inside national structures. The novelty of the post-war decades is that the new worldwide war machine which the States "unleash" appears henceforth endowed with a degree of autonomy far superior to anything heard of before the Second World War. This provides evidence of the extreme integration of this machine in the capitalist structure which itself has crossed a new threshold of autonomization vis-à-vis State institutions. At the same time that a trans-State monopolistic capitalism is developing, which grafts itself onto State monopoly capitalism, which complicates it rather than supplants it, and which is embodied in multinational firms and a worldwide financial oligarchy, the global war machine itself is embodied "in financial, industrial, and military technological complexes that are in continuity with one another," traversing the administrative, juridical and economic frontiers of national States.[55]

I can now clarify what I was suggesting earlier: when States tend to reconstitute a global autonomous war machine "of which they are no longer anything more than the opposable or apposed parts," it has less to do with a binary "inversion" of the Clausewitzian Formula (is it war that is the continuation of politics, or politics that continues war...) than with a profound redistribution of all the terms of its syllogism, in other words a systematic transformation of the relationships between *goal, objective,* and *means,* and, consequently, a mutation of the meaning of the objective form of both war and politics itself:

a) First, if the war machine now ceases to be subordinated to a political *end*, it is first of all because the end itself ceases to be political and becomes *immediately economic*: the accumulation of capital and its enlarged reproduction to global scale, in systemic contradictions that remain for Deleuze and Guattari those that Marx uncovered in his analysis of the tendency of the general rate of profit to fall and of crises of overaccumulation. As alpha and omega of Deleuze and Guattari's appropriation of Marx, these analyses polarize their entire reading of *Capital* and, without an ideological work, would have been enough to consume the reception of *Capitalism and Schizophrenia* for a long time outside the stakes of the critique of political economy. In Book III of *Capital*, he emphasized the radical originality of capitalism with respect to all other known modes of production: having no other goal but the production of surplus value, to make of growth of social productivity an "end in itself," having thus no exterior limit to its own process of accumulation, but only interior or "immanent" limits, such as the delimited conditions of the valorization of existent capital: limits of productive forces in the creation of surplus value according to the relations between population and rate of exploitation of labor, but also limits in the absorption or "realization" of surplus value according to "the proportionality of the different branches of production and of the power of consumption of the society." As embodied in excess capital, unemployment and crises of overproduction, such bounds generated by the process of accumulation in itself may only be surmounted by the periodic depreciation of existing capital, by the augmentation of investment in constant capital and the "continual upheaval of the methods of production," by the creation of new markets and the expansion of the scale of production, which does not destroy the immanent limits but displaces them only to find them again farther away, or which only destroys them in reproducing them on an increasingly large scale.[56]

b) Inside of this dynamic of the process of capitalist accumulation on a worldwide scale, the new aim of the war machine must then be doubly determined. First, this aim becomes *effectively unlimited*. Total war still needed a political end fixing an extrinsic limit to the war machine (annihilate the enemy); but as soon as it crosses its new threshold of integration into the structures of global capitalism, the war machine becomes effectively unlimited, i.e., rejoins the base determination of the process of accumulation: not to meet any exterior limit to this process itself as an end in itself. Second, this end is only limited because it is *intrinsically critical*; the process breaks any exterior limit only insomuch as it generates its own immanent bounds (crises). From this point of view, the capitalist motivation of the war machine and its specific illimitation (smooth space) depends not only on the geopolitical relations of capitalist powers, but more immediately on the compositions of production and reproduction of capital on a global scale: "It is as though, at the outcome of the striation that capitalism was able to carry to an unequaled point of perfection, circulating capital necessarily recreated, reconstituted, a sort of smooth space in which the destiny of human beings is recast. Striation, of course, survives in the most perfect and severest of forms [...]; however, it relates primarily to the state pole of capitalism, in other words, to the role of the modern State apparatuses in the organization of capital. On the other hand, at the complementary and dominant level of *integrated* (or rather integrating) *world capitalism*, a new smooth space is produced [...]. The multinationals fabricate a kind of deterritorialized smooth space in which points of occupation as well as poles of exchange become quite independent of the classical paths to striation."[57] Taking up the concept of smooth space again in the context of contemporary capitalism is underpinned by the determination of trends in capitalist illimitation, touching both the relationship of constant capital/variable capital—and the becoming-indiscernible of this relationship in the development of the organic composition of capital or the socio-technical composition of exploitation—and the relationship of fixed capital/circulating capital—and the becoming-indiscernible of this relationship through the acceleration of rhythms of rotation in the reproduction of capital on the global level. This dual trend leads Deleuze and Guattari, who are contemporaries of the rise of new transnational industrial and financial bodies, to bring out a new differential that extends the two previous distinctions while relativizing them, and in particular by relating their critical forms to the geographies of capital, the modes of territorialisation and deterritorialization implied by its hold on the labor force, on territories and their facilities, on States and their populations. The distinction between "smooth capital" and "striated capital," combining both factors of organic composition and rhythms of reproduction of capital marks the point of critical junction between the two series of factors in the scale of impact of the depreciation of capital necessitated by crises of over-accumulation. As this capital is materialized not only in facilities, but in cities, regions or even countries, its destruction could from one day to the next make the entire land *uninhabitable* for entire populations—the "deterritorialization" of capital has no other correlate than the "depopulation of people."[58] This is precisely the point where capitalist illimitation, its "endo-violence" or the *destructivism* that sustains the cast-iron law of its productivism, cannot be deployed without directly mobilizing the "global war machine" and its own power of illimitation: the production of a smooth space: "The growing importance of constant capital in the [capitalist] axiomatic means that the depreciation of existing capital and the formation of new capital assume a rhythm and scale that necessarily take the route of a war machine now incarnated in the [militaroindustrial and financial] complexes [...]. There is a continuous 'threshold' of power that accompanies in every instance the shifting of the axiomatic's limits; it is as though the power of war always supersaturated the system's saturation, and was its necessary condition."[59]

c) At this point of incorporation into the process of globalized accumulation, the war machine no longer has as its *objective* war as such, nor even war carried to the absolute. The objective is rather, Deleuze and Guattari write, the worldwide order as "absolute peace of survival." This is obviously not to say that wars diminish in frequency—indeed, this is far from the case! Rather, at the same time as the war machine is regaining an autonomy from the State form, war becomes once again its only *synthetic* object. Its analytic object, on the other hand, is to assure the displacement of bounds of the valorization of existing capital, through the extension of the scale of production within the integrated worldwide market, through the correlative intensification of exploitation of energy and planetary resources and of "peripheral" labor, through the consequential reconfiguring of the international division of labor and of the relations of unequal dependence between the regions of the world-economy. Without a doubt, none of these operations take place without tensions between States, or without confrontations between political wills. But these are integrated henceforth as wheels of a planetary security order which is planned throughout all civil disorders which the reproduction of the capitalist mode of production does not cease to generate. It is in this sense that "war ceases to be the materialization of the war machine; *the war machine itself becomes materialized war;*"[60] incorporated into "the order" and the "security" of the global capitalist axiomatic, which no longer even needs to pass through military operations, and which passes more systematically through the decoding of alimentary flows which generate famine, the recoding of population flows through

destructions of settlement, forced migrations and remote urbanizations, the decodings of flows of energy-matter which generate
political and monetary instabilities: ravages of war which have
become perfectly immanent to the systematically destabilized and
"unsecure" social and existential territories, of which even the military outburst of enacted total war was only a premonition from
above, like the "moral bombing" of Arthur T. Harris.

d) It is to wars themselves that we must return. The "peace" of
the worldwide security order does not imply any political pacification, or any quantitative reduction of wars, which may even contain
certain of their functions from the imperialist age, according to new
geopolitical polarities and new relations of unequal exchange
between North and South.[61] Nevertheless these partial continuities
are capable of masking the crux of the matter. Once again, the
realization of war depends upon variable relations of *appropriation*
between State and war machine. Now, as soon as the war machine
ceases to be a means of State wars and becomes itself materialized
war or organized insecurity, a power of destruction of concrete social
territories in the "normal" order of a world-economy which, as Paul
Virilio has written, tends to disqualify "the ensemble of the planetary settlement while stripping peoples of their quality of
inhabitants,"[62] wars tend to take new objective forms. The convergence with Schmitt becomes prevalent again here. In the first place,
Deleuze and Guattari observe, they enter into alliances with *police
interventions*, police operations interior to the "society" of the global
market, which (relatively) subordinates the political and diplomatic
leverage of States. An indication can be found in the growing
transfer of public functions of States to the war machine itself—or
to say this inversely, in the fact that military technologies are more
and more frequently transferred to the domain of civil government,
of repression and population control. Take the example, analyzed by

Virilio, of "the famous McNamara Line which was constructed, through an electronic system, to prevent Vietcong infiltration, and which was reinstalled, in the course of the summer of 1973, in the south of the United States, on the frontier of Mexico, in order this time to prevent the clandestine migration of workers. In France also, after the arson of certain factories and fuel depots, the same electronic processes of detection were put in place as those of American forces in the Far East, but this time around industrial zones. Spy-cameras no longer only watched a declared enemy, but also the misbehaving spectator at a stadium, the bad driver, etc."[63] The new objective forms of wars, as internal parts of the security global order, thus combine a "policification" of international space and a militarization of civil interior spaces. In the second place, such a correlation causes the wavering of the double partition war/peace and interior/exterior, upon which is based the coding of military conflicts in the State-form (political, juridical and diplomatic coding). Here again, Virilio made the following case: "At the moment where, throughout the "operational defense of territory," the military institution attends increasingly to interior security, while the police tends to identify itself to public welfare. For the army, there is no longer even a clear distinction between the "interior" enemy and the "exterior" enemy, there is only a general *threat* to all domains (demography, economy, delinquency, etc.), and thus *only one enemy* without location, since it can be discovered here or there, at the whim of propaganda."[64] At the same time as the diplomatic and strategic distinction between peacetime and wartime tends to fade away, the qualification of the enemy tends to be decreasingly political and becomes juridical, economic, moral, religious… It is no less a "total enemy," but this total characteristic must not only be overcoded by an exclusive hostility that has it correspond to a univocal figure; it must also, contradictorily, be molecularized in an innumerable multiplicity of possible equivocal figures.[65] Thus the interest already noted for the strategic concept of the "unspecified enemy" formed by French theoreticians of the National Defense beginning in the 1970s, a perfectly adequate concept to the security continuum in smooth space constituted by a new global war machine.[66] When General Guy Brossollet presents himself as the fervent partisan of an integration of anti-insurrectional techniques in strategies of Defense, he explains that this is to deal not only with potential exterior aggressions, but especially with all sorts of much less localizable threats, "of moral, political, subversive or economic order, etc.": "The adversary is multiform, maneuvering and omnipresent. The threats which France must deal with are found everywhere and affect very diverse sectors of national potential. This is an alarming realization and implies a defense conceived according to the diversity and ubiquity of the threats."[67] In short, at the same time that war takes a police-juridical objective form, the enemy becomes abstract, virtually omnipresent, similar to a non-individualized and unqualified threat capable of springing up at any locus of social space and in unpredictable forms (smooth space), independently of political criteria of association with a State or relations between States.

We could call this state of affairs a paranoiac reign of *"insecuritizing security"*: "The global entente between States, the organization of a global police and jurisdiction such as those in preparation, necessarily clear the way for an extension where more and more people will be considered 'virtual' terrorists."[68] From there, the task is to understand how new combinations of the military and the police implicate new procedures of discursive construction of the figure of the enemy, procedures necessary in relation to the symbolic and imaginary repertories in which the contradictions and resistances of capitalist domination are subjectivized. We have seen in what sense the new global war machine was closely linked to the process of accumulation of capital on the worldwide scale, which only traverses its internal crises in precipitating cycles of depreciation of existing capital and of the formation of new capital, with an unheard-of scope and speed of rotation. Precisely, such an expansion of the capitalist axiomatic necessarily passes through a generalized virtualization of the enemy becoming unspecified or unqualified, and correlatively, through an acceleration of procedures of qualification of the enemy, and of continuous requalification of the enemy, at the price of an enlarged criminalization of social practices not in conformance with the institutions of capital. Such is the last correlate of the transformation of objective forms of war diagnosed by Deleuze and Guattari: the rise of an "informative" power, in the shape of assemblages of utterances capable of constantly revising the figure of the "threat," assuring this discursive reproduction of an enemy which may be recorded, at the limit, in any fragment of discursive code: variables of age, confession, profession, residence, political ideology, social, sexual, or economic conduct...[69]

Clausewitz, Lenin, Schmitt, Foucault, Deleuze-Guattari: Dialogical Fictions

The theory of the war machine, first presented by its authors as a working hypothesis in 1980, can be read as the basis of a genealogical program articulating the long-term history of the concept as well as its contemporary relevance. A conjectural analysis of the latest analyses referring the global war machine to the formation of a security, police-military, and police space, allowing a situation of Deleuze and Guattari's hypothesis further forward, in the turn of the 1970s–1980s, thus at the point where its theoretical development became contemporaneous with its utterance: there are combined, a/ displacements of the geopolitical relationships of force between the two "blocks" but also and increasingly the relationships between the "center" of global capitalism and the "Peripheries," finally their effects on the intra-European relationships of force (in the context of the early Reagan administration, the renewal of military investments and the intensification of pressure to reinforce the United States' sphere of influence in Western Europe); b/ at the same time, the cycle of violence which, in Western Europe, in the ebb of the protest forces of the 1950s–1960s, culminated in the 1976–1978 years with a succession of terrorism and State terrorism (emergency laws in Germany, the Klaus Croissant Affair, the real or imaginary circulation between Palestinian resistance and the conflicts of the extreme left in Western cities, the massive mobilization of new media in State propaganda, etc.).[70] At the intersection of these different events, the program of work is defined on which this hypothesis ultimately opens; one of its aspects is the analysis of control technologies in smooth space, in particular transfers of technology from the military to the civil domain, and that would also include a semiological analysis of media, discursive, and audiovisual constructions of the unspecified enemy.

It is clear that this *theoretical* program seems difficult to dissociate from *practices* of collective resistance capable of rebuilding habitable territories, and thus recreating new political practices capable of responding as much to military coding as to the juridical-moral, security, and police diversions of "politics." Starting in 1975–1976, the intensification of Deleuze and Guattari's thinking on the "becoming-minor of everyone," which is also the reversal of an undetermined extension of minoritization as a technique of power capable of subjecting, in favor of circumstances and political opportunities, ever larger portions of the population, here finds one of its most immediate, if not the most urgent motives. Yet even then, the category of war machine, precisely in what is excessive in relation to the State coordinates of politics, and because it includes an antagonistic power that itself has a "variable relationship with war," will continue to name, for Deleuze and Guattari, an instance capable of *separating the State from its war power*: to *divide war*. From there, it allows place to be made (in one sense, against Schmitt) for a use of conflict that *transforms* (which does not necessarily mean: neutralize) the meaning of war itself. That this transformation, referring to the war machine as power of/in metamorphosis, did not in turn have any univocal "meaning" that would predestine its revolutionary or reactionary, emancipatory or destructive, or even pacifist or militarist results—that more profoundly nothing can decide in advance whether the war machine, even when losing war as a direct object, takes on an even more considerable destructive power than those that imperialist States developed with their total wars, or if the war machine can constitute itself as an antagonistic power reintroducing politics into war where "civil" or "interstate" war tends to destroy the possibility of politics—this is a certainty of which this chapter has shown the effective or objective, and not simply theoretical, character.

To conclude, I would suggest three more possible readings of the hypothesis that came together during this overview. While only the third is developed by Deleuze and Guattari, the two others have no less coherence in relation to presenting the entire hypothesis; moreover, the three are articulated, as much by their common distance from Schmitt's "concept of politics," as in relation to the Ludendorffian *perversion* of the Formula:

a) Let us call *perversion* of the Formula the Foucaldian operation that identifies in Clausewitz's axiom the results of an "inversion" of a previous movement that, in the process of construction of the modern State, interiorized both an internal military technology and a discourse of "social war."[71] It has the effect of immediately lodging a contradiction at the heart of what Schmitt saw as the emergence of a superior and neutral Power supposed to impose itself through a relativization of internal conflicts reduced to de-politicized and "private" dissensions (as objects of simple policing)—as if this sovereign power was only effectively able to *make itself State* by incorporating contradictorily, and in part by contributing to invent, these figures of internal war and the "domestic enemy" that it should have repressed.

b) *Subversion* of the Formula would be the Leninist operation, carried by the command to "transform imperialist war into revolutionary civil war," and that makes civil war, not a means to "realize" a class politics by raising the antagonism to armed conflict until the instauration of a new proletarian State (following Schmitt's reading of Lenin in *The Concept of the Political*),[72] but the form that class struggle can and must take to repoliticize violence in a context of war that tends on the contrary to destroy any political content (or any content to emancipate class) to the sole benefit of inter-State and inter-imperialist rivalries.[73] We have seen that Deleuze and Guattari's concept of the war machine (remarkably dialectical from this point of view) targets precisely in one of these moments an instance of transformation of war[74]—short of the opposition of bellicism and pacifism, or rather deciding the political consistency of their alternative.[75] To put it another way, this concept aims to reproblematize the contradictory movement through which politics, which tends to "fuse" with and disappear into the process of war materialized by capitalist States, can impose on itself the task of "revolutionizing war" to re-impose political antagonism. This leads reciprocally to thinking the war machine as the instance of a transformation of politics itself, on the condition that this instance divides war or separates the power of war from the capitalist class interests focused on State monopolization.

c) I reserve the term of inversion of the Formula, this time in the limited and unprecedented sense developed in the 12th and 13th Plateaus, to characterize a new configuration of the war machine appropriated to the power of "englobing" of capitalist accumulation on a worldwide scale, making States themselves the instruments of an "order of Peace" as police-judicial order. This reformulates, under new conditions, the question of the forces and strategic possibilities of alternative war machines capable of repoliticizing a historical-political field otherwise saturated with combinations of neo-imperialist economic wars or that criminalize any force of contestation of the order and disorder of the world— capable of transforming the global war machine into a revolutionary war machine, or in the terms of Deleuze and Guattari themselves (for which, for better or for worse, the Leninist background is very clear): "smashing capitalism, of redefining socialism, of constituting a war machine capable of countering the world war machine by other means [...]a war machine whose aim is neither the war of extermination nor the peace of generalized terror, *but revolutionary movement*."[76] Why do they see in the fight of minorities rather than class struggle (which means in part in their place, calling both returns and displacements, and "continuing them by other means," rather than an abstract permutation from one term to the other), the resources of these alternative war machines? What are the relationships with the articulation of machinic processes of anticipation-warding off, polarization, englobing, capture, and war machine, and according to what contextual analysis? These are the problems to be dealt with In the last part of this study, starting with a reexamination of the form of power of global capitalism, in other words, its specific machinic process.

PART THREE

ENDO-VIOLENCE:
THE CAPITALIST AXIOMATIC

5

The Axiomatic of Capital:

States and Accumulation on a Global Scale

The macropolitics of Deleuze and Guattari finds its final reasons in an analysis of contemporary capitalism, and in a critical examination of the conceptual apparatuses available to account for its singularity. In *A Thousand Plateaus*, they have it correspond to a machinic process or a specific form of power called "ecumenical englobing," reopening a dialog with historians of the world economy and theorists of the dependency on relationships of inequality and power internal to the accumulation of capital of a global scale. Starting in 1972, however, the dynamic of capitalist accumulation is informed by a rereading of the Marxist critique of political economy, the analysis of modes of production and circulation of capital, and fundamentally the capitalist social relationships, the radical singularity of which Deleuze and Guattari reformulate in the concept of *axiomatic*, or *social relations "axiomatized by capital."* I will begin here with a reminder of how this concept is set up in *Anti-Oedipus* before turning to a more specific analysis of its reformulation in the framework of historico-machinic materialism in 1980.

Capitalist Illimitation: Code, Decoding, Axiomatics

The concept of axiomatics is introduced in 1972, first to conceive, not only the specificity of the capitalist social relationship, but the singular form that capital confers on "social relations." Thus it is determined differentially in relation to the other concepts of social relations (coding, over-coding), which places its thematization in two areas: that of economic anthropology and that of an analytics of the mode of capitalist production, the latter of which involves a three part analysis: genealogical, structural and dynamic-trending.[1] It is most important, however, to take the *difference* of these two points of view into account, the distance that separates them and prevents them from being placed in continuity: the operations that Deleuze and Guattari perform on Marxist analyses of capital and on the critique of political economy depend on it.

In fact, the economic anthropology forged in Chapter 3 is not aimed at identifying, in terms of sociological or anthropological invariants, the universal foundations on which different modes could be distinguished for human groups to produce their material conditions of existence, but the *quasi-universal* conditions under which *almost all* of these modes of social production are articulated ("extra-economic coding" of social relations). Almost all: *with the exception, precisely, of the capitalist mode of production*, which only imposes itself by relativization and in a tendential way by the destruction of these very conditions (decoding). This calls for two possible formulae, between which there is no way to choose, but the oscillation between them allows us to account for the theoretical challenge that capitalism, in its already long history, continues to pose to an understanding of it: capitalism is an economy that destroys the anthropological possibilities of collectivities; capitalism is an aneconomy, or it is not defined as an economy except by redefining the economy itself *a contrario* and by negation of all non-capitalist social economies. In sum, capital does not dominate "social relations" without changing the meaning of these relations and the way that they make a society, starting in particular by destroying its "social" character. Which places the mode of capitalist production in a *limit-relationship* with the very possibility of an economic anthropology, of which it also represents the "most profound negative," "*the negative* of all social formations" within which it occupies a literally impossible place.[2]

It follows that there is no system of simple *transformation* that allows passage, genetically or structurally, from "pre-capitalist" modes of production to the capitalist mode: the latter is on the contrary inseparable from a radical *cut*—a "diachronic schizze." Yet the structural perspective of the transformation is not disqualified, but it must be coupled and placed in tension with the perspective of *destruction*, for which the key concept is *decoding*, which is nothing other than a reinterpretation of the Marxist concept of *primitive accumulation*.[3] Precisely this tension between these two ways to analyze the "capitalist cut," in terms of *transformation* and *destruction*, allows an accounting of the internal role, not subsidiary but essential to their argument, that Deleuze and Guattari attribute in *Anti-Oedipus* to the work of the Althusserians.[4] The obstinacy often shown to deny this fact renders the contrastive determination of notions of code and axiomatic well and truly unintelligible, making them into vague metaphors and, by obliterating the mediations through which Deleuze and Guattari reread Marx in 1972, turning their reproblematization of the stakes of the critique of political economy into a mere incantation.

The first trait that Deleuze and Guattari note relates to an understanding that simultaneously rejects a combinatory conception of structural transformations and a teleological conception of the genesis of the capitalist relationship of production.[5] The capitalist schizze is radical first in the sense that a multiplicity of heterogeneous historical processes come together in it, independent of each other, of which the genealogical lines no less than their historical conjunction are highly contingent. When Deleuze and Guattari transcribe the "dissolutions" analyzed by Marx in the chapter of *Capital* on primitive accumulation (dissolution of the corporative organization of jobs, the feudal structure of the countryside, forms of communal property, "personal ties" of subjection in exploitation by slavery and servitude, among others) in the language of "decoding flows of exchanges and production," it is to underline immediately its great diversity which makes its conjugation almost improbable: diverse processes of decoding by *privatization of productive factors*, bearing on the means of production and communes, and first on these two "instruments of every instrument" which are land and the body itself;[6] diverse processes of decoding by *abstraction of value*, by different historical paths leading to the rise of monetary signs, by different ways of market expansion, generalization of the commodity-form, and objectification of an "abstract work" or quantity of social work"; diverse processes of *deterritorialization*, bearing on producers (expropriation, rural exodus…), but also on property and trade capital as simple forms or "metamorphoses" of a power of investment independent of the particular object-states of "wealth"; processes of decoding State power itself, its control of territorialities, commercial exchanges and monetary flows, and fiscal and debt mechanisms.[7] It is often written that Deleuze and Guattari define capitalism as the decoding of social fluxes: this is all the more imprecise in that decoding is the generic name of this wide variety of heterogeneous historical processes that pass through *all* social formations. When Deleuze and Guattari quote historians, such as Pierre Chaunu or Étienne Balazs,

Braudel or Marx himself, to show "in China, in Rome, in Byzantium, in the Middle Ages…" vast sequences of decoding of the fluxes of proletarized populations, monetary fluxes, fluxes of private property and goods, they do so to show that decoding fluxes *is not enough* to crystallize a capitalist mode of production or even relationship of production.[8] At most, it makes it so that "The capitalists appear in succession in a series that institutes a kind of creativity of history, a strange menagerie: the schizoid time of the new creative break." However, "the encounter of all these flows will be necessary, their conjunction, and their reaction on one another—and the contingent nature of this encounter, this conjunction, and this reaction, which occur one time—in order for capitalism to be born, and for the old system to die."[9]

The scope of this "schizoid" temporality within historical capitalism still needs to be determined. What makes it singular, in fact, is not only this "general axiomatization of decoded flows," but additionally the intrinsically contradictory character of this axiomatization, which can only connect social relations by bringing back a decoding of flows on a wider scale, such that its procedures of privatization, abstraction, and deterritorialization become tasks that must be constantly re-performed, both in virtue of its own internal limits as in reason of the resistances and conflicts that these procedures elicit.[10] For this reason, there is a dual focalization in the reading of *Capital* in Chapter III of *Anti-Oedipus*: on the one hand, the Marxian analysis of these internal limits themselves, of which they follow the most developed formulations in the section of Book III on the tendency to a falling rate of profit and on crises of overproduction; on the other, the analysis of methods of primitive accumulation In Book I, considered however not only from the point of view of a genealogy of the relationship of capitalist production or its "factors," but from the point of view of historical accumulation of capital of which these methods remain a constant. The socio-anthropological and conceptual discontinuity produced by the capitalist break, at the same time as it invalidates the claim to overcome it through its invariants, is also combined with the essentially "diachronic" appearance of this break under this double relationship: because it "takes time" to come about, and because once it has come about it continuously has to come about again. As for the decoding of flows, it does not *define* the capitalist mode of production (CMP) in either of the two cases. It first generically designates a set of *historical conditions* that the CMP does not explain because it presupposes them; it then includes processes that the CMP elicits over the course of its process of expanded accumulation: in other words, the two aspects of a "primitive" accumulation which accounts for capital never being contemporary to its own conditions, never synchronous with itself or with its own break, and that its break is unending, a schizoid time making capital into an interminable "neo-archaism."[11]

If we consider the *permanent effect* of this break, then we have to face a new mode of subsumption of social flows, or a new way to make "social relations." Between *coded* socioeconomic (non-capitalist) relations and *axiomized* social relations (by capital), the difference can only be understood by adopting a structural and tendential, as Deleuze and Guattari explain when they recap its distinctive traits based once again on the work of *Reading Capital*.[12]

a) A code is an operation to *qualify* social flows, and it is only *indirectly* a social relationship, in function of the respective qualities of heterogeneous flows. According to a prototypical example, the economy of the Tiv in Nigeria codes three types of flows, consumer goods, prestige goods, and women and children: "When money supervenes, it can only be coded as an object of prestige, yet merchants use it to lay hold of sectors of consumer goods traditionally held by the women: all the codes vacillate. [...] seeing the trucks that leave loaded with export goods, "the Tiv elders deplore this situation, and know what is happening, but do not know where to place their blame."[13] What the coding of social relations averts under this first aspect is the generalization of a developed form of value, and *a fortiori* of a general equivalent that would be capable of expressing any type of good indifferently, notwithstanding their respective qualifications making them socially incommensurable. *b/* More profoundly, however, "coded relations" already avert the emergence of a *simple* form of value, to the extent that social services and counter-services include non-circulating, non-exchangeable, and non-consumable elements that are nonetheless the object of a deduction from the transaction but without a principle of commensurability or equivalency that would open onto an *illimited* series of exchanges (M-A-M'...). These elements (that Deleuze and Guattari call "surplus value of code"), such as a relationship of prestige or obligation, status or responsibility, marker of allegiance or authority, are extra-economic "values" expressed in relationships of *debt* rather than exchange, and bearing witness to how the economic relationship is rigorously determined and circumscribed by non-economic factors but sociopolitical, genealogical, religious, or even cosmological ones. *c/* Yet if we ask what determines that these non-economic factors themselves come to dominate the social relationships in circulation by averting the autonomization of an economic determination of value, Deleuze and Guattari invoke the relationship of production, the type of organization of surplus labor and the correlating conditions of appropriation of its surplus production, which it expresses or not in terms of surplus value:

All these code characteristics—indirect, qualitative, and limited— are sufficient to show that a code is not, and can never be, economic: on the contrary, it expresses the apparent objective movement according to which the economic forces or productive connections are attributed to an extraeconomic instance as though they emanated from it, an instance that serves as a support and an agent of inscription. That is what Althusser and Balibar show so well: how juridical and political relations are determined as dominant—in the case of feudalism, for example—because surplus labor as a form of surplus value constitutes a flux that is qualitatively and temporally distinct from that of labor, and consequently must enter into a composite that is itself qualitative and implies noneconomic factors. Or the way the autochthonous relations of alliance and filiation are determined as dominant in the so-called primitive societies, where the economic forces and flows are inscribed on the full body of the earth and are attributed to it. […]That is why the sign of desire, as an economic sign that consists in producing and breaking flows, is accompanied by a sign of necessarily extraeconomic power, although its causes and effects lie within the economy.[14]

The operation of axiomatization of a social relationship is defined by contrast, its concept synthesizing a plurality of determinations that concern both the mode of production and the mode of circulation of capital, and that are articulated together but not deducible from one another by means of a linear theoretical beginning. The concept of axiomatic first denotes the structural singularity of the CMP, which is based on posing its own relationship of production as its own presupposition, and the only rightful presupposition of the social system as a whole. This gives it a sense of "immanence": it destroys extra-economic codes or relegates them to the subordinate rank of conditions for reproducing social relations and the agents decided on to occupy the places in them. Deleuze and

Guattari have this basic characterization correspond, not directly to the illimitation of the commodity form or the circulation of exchange value, nor to the illimitation of capital-money as such, but to the singularity of the relationship of exploitation in which capital-money is realized as a relationship of power, appropriation, or ordering of labor, under conditions where an *immediately economic* appropriation occurs, internal to the process of production, of surplus labor, without the intermediary of extra-economic factors. According to their reading of Marx, the singularity of the relationship of capitalist exploitation appears in final analysis in the unprecedented aspect of surplus value, the very aspect that the interpretations of economists and quantitavists constantly tend to gloss over. We have already seen how, under the "Asian" paradigm, the surplus labor organized in the major hydraulic and monumental works was not added to a presupposed labor but represented on the contrary the basic objective layer from which more or less broad sectors of productive activity took on a "labor-form," as if so-called necessary labor was obtained by subtracting surplus labor, and presupposed it (either the precapitalist interpretation of the materialist axiom: the relationship of force of exploitation is first in relation to production and its economic measures). The capitalist mode of production—the "real" subsumption of the labor process, the forms of division and cooperation of collective workers, the socio-anthropological and socio-technological connections in mechanization and major industry—carries the labor/surplus labor differential to a superior degree of *real non-distinction*. And this non-distinction materialized in social relationships has the effect of making surplus value *non-localizable in the objectivity of capitalist society*. It confirms what economism tends to hide: surplus value is not an *economic fact*, like a "phenomenon" that would be a "given" in the objective representation of this social formation, but the mode of presence-absence of relationships of power of exploitation in a socioeconomic field that these relations form, but in which they disappear in the very movement where they condition its objective presentation (save in favor of a relationship of force capable of *imposing* its recognition).[15] This is one of the main motifs for which Deleuze and Guattari formalize the relationship of capitalist exploitation as a *differential relationship*.[16]

We can determine a final distinctive trait of the concept of axiomatic towards which all of the others converge: if capital axiomatizes social relations, and if its nuclear relationship of power—the relationship of exploitation and surplus-exploitation of the labor force—must be conceived of as a differential relationship, it is in the sense that neither of them encounter any outside limit to their development (such as extra-economic constraints predetermining productive forms of connections, the conditions and extension of market circulation, the rules and forms of dividing and consuming social products), but only the internal contradictions that imprint their own tendencies, as Marx identifies them in his theory of crises.[17] The CMP only promotes the development of social productivity as "end in itself" under the limited conditions of the process of valorizing existing capital. In other words, the development and productivity of labor and surplus value production, as the only determinant goal immanent to production itself, does not avoid creating its own limits which are immanent to the relationship of production: limits of productive forces in function of the capacities of "productive consumption" of labor force, and relationships between the rates of exploitation and rates of profit, limits in the "realization" of surplus value in function of the "proportionality of different branches of production and society's consumer power." Embodied in over-accumulated capital, mass unemployment, and crises of overproduction, these limits generated by the process of accumulation and valorization can only be overcome by methods of chronic destruction of existing capital and of displacement of investments towards new branches, by the creation of new prospects and new markets, and, in final analysis, by an expansion of the scale of production that also reproduces these limits at this constantly increasing scale—"at risk of falling into ruin...."[18] Capitalism functions as an axiomatics "because capitalism for its part has no exterior limit, but only an interior limit that is capital itself and that it does not encounter, but reproduces by always displacing it," in other words by always deferring its own *saturation*.[19]

Here we touch on one of the most constantly reaffirmed points from *Anti-Oedipus* to *A Thousand Plateaus*, and which allows us to better discern its displacements in Deleuze and Guattari's analysis of capitalism and the reading of Marx that underlies it. From 1972 to 1980, the reproblematization of capital as an axiomatics is validated and even strengthened, yet at the cost of a displacement of its center of gravity. In the first work, the opposition between axiomatic and code, focusing on the radical singularity of the social relationship of production and the capitalist mode of production, and in final analysis, on the radical singularity of the relationship implied by this mode of production, between its process of accumulation and its *limit* as "immanent limit," led, on the basis of an analysis combining historical references and partial logical beginnings, to advancing two major questions on the historical accumulation of capital. On the one hand, the new functions occupied within this axiomatics by the capitalist State, its apparatuses, and the political power that they concentrate: the State is indeed *exterior* to the mechanisms of extortion and appropriation of surplus value which are now determined within relationships of production that have become private; but it is at the same time *immanent* in that it intervenes in the becoming-concrete of a real abstraction, in other words finds itself in the service of reproducing social relations within which the valorization of value occurs, and even the reproduction of value of these "special commodities" which are labor force and money.[20] This "becoming-immanent" or this *socialization of the State* makes it simultaneously the regulating principle of the contradictions of accumulation, first agent of the displacement of immanent limits, by opposing the tendency to decline of the rate of profit, by absorbing capital through its apparatuses of anti-production,[21] by destroying excess capital and depreciating the labor force by facilitating or ensuring on its own the expansion of the base of accumulation by capturing new resources, opening new markets, and proletarizing new labor reserves. In this context, Deleuze and Guattari also underline, in 1972, the determinant function of the "deterritorialization" of capital, embodied in an international division of labor and a global structure of the process of accumulation, unfair exchange, the asymmetrical circulation of capital, and the unequal distribution of methods of exploitation and over-exploitation.

It can be said that in 1980, these two final aspects are moved into the heart of the analysis, while *the* mode of capitalist production, considered in its internal physiognomy alone, is relegated to the background as an overly abstract point of departure. In my view, this displacement is a sign of the new perspective of historico-machinic materialism.[22] It imposes an approach to capitalism not through its characteristic or dominant mode of production but through the specific form of power that it accomplishes (and on which this dominant—but not exclusive—mode of production depends). This form of power is defined in *A Thousand Plateaus* as an "ecumenical power of englobing," and it turns capital into an *immediately global* process, and more precisely, into a process that is inseparable from the relationships it establishes between heterogeneous social formations *which are not necessarily regulated by capitalist relationships and modes of production*. This new focus of the analysis is highlighted by the at first formal description of the machinic process of "ecumenical englobing."

Before a reminder of its main traits, and before seeing how the definition of capital as an axiomatics and the question of the relationship between globalized capitalism and States is reinvigorated by it, we should note that the above displacement correlates to another one related to the point of view adopted by global history. As I already indicated in Chapter 1, from the "universal history" of 1972 to the analysis of the "world-economy" in 1980, Deleuze and Guattari's political thought is even more intensively inscribed in the already dense fabric of debates between theories of unfair exchange and the dependency coming out of the decolonization battles and the emergence of the "Third World" on the international stage, as well as the renewal, in Braudel's inventive posterity, of economic historiography related to the question of "world-systems." Here again, misunderstanding of these debates poses the risk of obscuring the fields of problems in which Deleuze and Guattari are operating— debates that have not lost their importance today, as shown by the reception of work by David Harvey or the controversies rekindled from Kenneth Pomeranz's *The Great Divergence* to Giovanni Arrighi's *Adam Smith in Beijing* on the question of the "Chinese way," although some of the terms have apparently changed. At their center is first a *theoretical* problem touching the concepts of "mode of production" and "social formation," a theoretical problem that would not have been so massively and polemically invested if it had not been translated into a *political* problem that the splitting up of ways to "construct socialism," in the Soviet Union, China, and certain countries recently freed from colonial domination brought back to the forefront of Marxist controversies: the problem of "transition to socialism," and what was its immediate opposite (to the extent that it was to shed light on this first problem, or at least give academic support to the conviction that this transition would no less necessarily have taken place than another that preceded it), the problem of "transition" to the capitalist mode of production itself from another ("feudal") predecessor. This problem touched the limits that affected the Euro-centric and even "Britanno-centric" analysis produced by Marx of the period of "primitive accumulation," and the very difficulty of sequencing a periodization—to say nothing of a "break"—of the emergence of capitalism.[23] It came more profoundly to test the tacit identification of historical capitalism with its nuclear mode of production. It imposed a complexity on the instruments of intelligibility of *capitalist social formation*, in that its dynamics revealed themselves to be irreducible to the sole tendencies of the mode of production of capital, or even in that they required a return to what Marx first had presented as tendencies, and not as teleological lines of a progressive development or realization. Deleuze and Guattari's interest in the questions raised by historians concerning the "birth" of capitalism ("Why not Rome? [...] why not in China in the 13th century?"), and which led them to affirm in 1972 the *continued* characteristic of the capitalist *schizze*—a break that both recurs in its genealogical anterior (as if capitalism constantly announced itself through factors that oppose its advent)[24] and constantly has to be reperformed throughout its history (leading to the insistence by our authors on the permanence of techniques of primitive accumulation throughout historical capitalism, on their unequal geographical distribution, and on the combinations that they can form with institutions of broader accumulation)—bears witness to how their reflection is anchored in these debates, which become all the more enlightening in the second volume of *Capitalism and Schizophrenia*.

Global Capitalist Subsumption: Ecumenical Globalization and the Typology of Modern States

Let us start back at the formal description of the machinic process called "ecumenical" and its specific power ("power of englobing"). First remark: globalized capitalism is not what allows a definition of a machinic process of englobing but the opposite: "international aggregates [...] obviously did not wait for capitalism before forming: as early as Neolithic times, even Paleolithic, we find traces of ecumenical organizations that testify to the existence of long-distance trade, and simultaneously cut across the most varied of social formations."[25] Second, these international aggregates actualize a process of power *sui generis*, one that is qualitatively distinct from the power of capture of the State type or even the power of polarization of the urban type in virtue of the power that they demonstrate to diffuse themselves, to penetrate or impose themselves on heterogeneous formations, precisely by using their unequal existence and taking advantage of this heterogeneity:

An international ecumenical organization does not proceed from an imperial center that imposes itself upon and homogenizes an exterior milieu; neither is it reducible to relations between formations of the same order, between States, for example (the League of Nations, the United Nations). On the contrary, it constitutes an intermediate milieu between the different coexistent orders. Therefore it is not exclusively commercial or economic, but is also religious, artistic, etc. From this standpoint, we shall call an international organization anything that has the capacity to move through diverse social formations simultaneously: States, towns, deserts, war machines, primitive societies. The great commercial formations in history do not simply have city-poles, but also primitive, imperial, and nomadic segments through which they pass, perhaps issuing out again in another form. [...] The point of departure for ecumenical organization is not a State, even an imperial one; the imperial State is only one part of it, and it constitutes a part of it in its own mode, according to its own order, which consists in capturing everything it can. It does not proceed by progressive homogenization, or by totalization, but by the taking on of consistency or the consolidation of the diverse as such. For example, monotheistic religion is distinguished from territorial worship by its pretension to universality. But this pretension is not homogenizing, it makes itself felt only by spreading everywhere; this was the case with Christianity, which became imperial and urban, but not without giving rise to bands, deserts, war machines of its own. Similarly, there is no artistic movement that does not have its towns and empires, but also its nomads, bands, and primitives.[26]

The problem then becomes understanding how capitalism, as an "international organization," inserts itself in a process of this type while giving it an entirely unprecedented allure. As it was for Samir Amin, the importance attributed to commercial organizations that develop their activities between the major imperial, State, and urban civilizations is helpful in this regard. It allows a return to the Marxian distinction between "formal subsumption" and "real subsumption," while considering the passage from one to the other not as an historical sequence that occurs once and for all but as a *permanent tendency* of capital's hold on social relations, and especially by having this tendency carry, not directly on a mode of production, but on the relationships between *social formations* which themselves combine difference relationships and modes of production. A geo-economy and even geopolitics are thus inscribed in the heart of capitalist social relations that cannot be dissociated from them. Capitalism is an ecumenical organization, not only because of the planetary dimension of its process and its hold, but because this global dimension—or its unequally and "equivocally" global organization—is always already included in its elements, even those that are the most analytically discernable. The new homology between an historico-machinic distinction and a Marxian distinction can be stated as follows: there is a *formal subsumption* of diverse social formations by an ecumenical organization, when the latter finds as a *given condition* the heterogeneity of formations between which it develops its power (for example a commercial organization taking a commercial profit from transactions that it ensures between formations of which it does not modify the modes of production and consumption), in other words its power of englobing presupposes and benefits from the *extrinsic coexistence* between these formations. There is *real subsumption* when this power of englobement enters into a relationship of *intrinsic coexistence*, relatively subordinates or appropriates the powers that until then dominated these formations (of capture, polarization, war machine, and others), and rearticulates through their means the relationships between them no less than their internal relationships. In this sense, "capitalism marks a mutation in worldwide or ecumenical organizations, which now take on a consistency of their own: the worldwide axiomatic, instead of resulting from heterogeneous social formations and their relations, for the most part distributes these formations, determines their relations, while organizing an international division of labor."[27] Let me add two remarks:

a) Precisely because this "passage" from a formal englobement to a real one ("axiomatic") is a *tendency*—a movement that constantly remakes itself in what undoes it, or to make itself into something else through that which opposes it—the conceptual distinction between the two forms of englobement leaves room for irreducibly ambivalent situations. A search for profits takes advantage, for example, of differentials in productivity, financing and indirect wages, socio-institutional constraints and legal frameworks regulating the conditions of productive "consumption" of the labor force, social norms or production and consumption, and the class relations that these norms concentrate, among others. In this exploitation of social and fiscal "dumping," however, the two dimensions of subsumption by an englobement taking advantage of the existing differences but also, *at the same time*, accentuating, displacing, or provoking these heterogeneities themselves as differences in potential favoring new sources of exploitation or increases in the rate of profit. From there, the objective difficulty of passing an impermeable border between politicist interpretations and economist interpretations of imperialism, as seen for example in David Harvey, where the "political or territorial logic of power" (the *State* logic of power following specific modes of State territorialization) either comes to "maintain" or reproduce the spatial asymmetries that are characteristic of unequal exchange (which are presupposed as given, without intervention of the "political dimension"), or contributes to producing these asymmetries.[28]

b) Second, the refusal to define the capitalist system as a *global social formation*—not only globalized but globalizing—by its dominant mode of production alone, does not lead (as Gunder Frank goes so far as to claim) to dissipating the question of the *specificity of this social formation itself*. The problem is precisely to think of capitalism as a systemic or "ecumenical" formation by taking into account the fact that it has historically transformed the form of the *very systematicity of the world*. From this point of view, the aporia between the discontinuist thesis (and the difficulties of assigning a "1500 break" to the capitalist world-system) and the continuist thesis (and the weak analytical impact of representing only one "global system" over a single five-thousand year cycle) is, if not lifted, then at least displaced. It is not so much a question of knowing if we are dealing with the same cycle of a single global system or with a transition from one world-system to another, than to understand, to divert one of Gunder Frank's expressions, how the transition is always a transition between two or *n* transitions, through which the "terms" themselves while the world-systems form a system *in another way*, such that the systematicity of the system is changed. It also requires breaking with the simple identification between capitalist social formation and mode of production, but not to eliminate purely and simply the questions related to modes of production and their "articulations" (through which we understand, for example, how Samir Amin remains a central interlocutor in the presentation of the global capitalist axiomatic in the 13th Plateau).

On this basis, the conception of the social relationship of capital as an axiomatic relationship is renewed. In one sense, the stakes remain the same as in 1972: grasping the articulation between the two main series of problems that organized Deleuze and Guattari's reading of Marx: the implications of the idea of *real abstraction* (and finally the problem of thinking the way in which this abstraction *is realized* or *concretized* as a relationship of production and exploitation), the implications of the idea of *immanent limit* (and the two related questions of the tendency to a decline in rates of profit and crises of overproduction). Yet when the formula of real abstraction is brought back in 1980, it is less to highlight the structural correlation (the immediate economic capture of surplus labor, without the intermediate of "extra-economic factors inscribed in a code") than to emphasize the way in which State capture is included in the becoming-concrete of real abstraction, placed at the service of the very constitution of relationships of production and circulation of capital. Already heavily emphasized in *Anti-Oedipus* as we have seen, this becoming immanent of the State is even more accentuated, as its territorial, employment, and monetary axioms (its three "powers" or apparatuses of capture) being immediately involved in the formation, reproduction, and limits of variation of value:

> we must review what distinguishes an axiomatic from all manner of codes, overcodings, and recodings: the axiomatic deals directly with purely functional elements and relations whose nature is not specified, and which are immediately realized in highly varied domains simultaneously; codes, on the other hand, are relative to those domains and express specific relations between qualified elements that cannot be subsumed by a higher formal unity (overcoding) except by transcendence and in an indirect fashion. The immanent axiomatic finds in the domains it moves through so many models, termed models of realization. It could similarly be said that capital as right, as a "qualitatively homogeneous and quantitatively commensurable element," is realized in sectors and means of production (or that "unified capital" is realized in "differentiated capital"). However, the different sectors are not alone in serving as models of realization—the States do too. Each of them groups together and combines several sectors, according to its resources, population, wealth, industrial capacity, etc. Thus the States, in capitalism, are not canceled out but change form and take on a new meaning: models of realization for a worldwide axiomatic that exceeds them. But to exceed is not at all the same thing as doing without.[29]

As for the second motive for conceiving of capitalist globalization as an axiomatic (the problem of its "saturation" or of the limits that it elicits in itself, and that it only destroys or overcomes by displacing them and by reproducing them on a wider scale), when it is taken up again in 1980, it is not only to recognize the intervention of a "capitalist State" considered generally, but on the contrary to index a distinctive identification of States, their forms of heterogeneity, and their inequalities as they are required, used, and in large part produced by capitalist globalization in virtue of its special unity. Before returning in more detail to the two aspects developed in the last proposition of the 13th Plateau ("*Proposition XIV: Axiomatics and the presentday situation*"), let us examine the way in which they lead to deepening the concept of capitalist axiomatic by the detour of an analogy with logical axiomatics, which could be exposed to several misunderstandings if we do not follow both the multiple theoretico-political aspects and the overall signification together.

Indeed, the concept of "axiomatic of capital" is not based on a comparison of the two terms, which would represent globalized capitalism in resemblance to a logical-deductive axiomatic, but on an analogy, a relation of relations: between the problems encountered attempts to axiomatize and the related practices on the one hand, and the problems created by capitalist accumulation on a global scale and the political practices that confront them and are assigned responsibility for them on the other.[30] The analogy is therefore based on this point of view, not in the imaginary resemblance of an economic system to a system of logic but in a confrontation between a *politics internal to scientific fields* that include relationships of force and power that bear on their own operations and their own factors (physical and semiotic flows), and a politics *internal* to the capitalist economy, which is not applied there *afterwards* but which constitutively determines its own factors (physical flows of territories, populations, and goods; monetary, commercial, debt and financial semiotic flows), and which makes it so that "capitalism has always required there to be a new force and a new law of States, on the level of the flow of labor as on the level of the flow of independent capital."[31] If the hypothesis of the capitalist axiomatic leads to a concept of *capitalist politics*, the latter takes no prestige from this analogy of logical univocity and deductive rigor, but on the contrary the factors of equivocalness, contingency and indecision, decision and uncertainty that work the procedures of logical axiomatization themselves. "Politics is by no means an apodictic science" (it "proceeds by experimentation, groping in the dark, injection, withdrawal, advances, retreats. The factors of decision and prediction are limited"); precisely, neither is the axiomatic method:

> In science an axiomatic is not at all a transcendent, autonomous, and decision-making power opposed to experimentation and intuition. On the one hand, it has its own gropings in the dark, experimentations, modes of intuition. Axioms being independent of each other, can they be added, and up to what point (a saturated system)? Can they be withdrawn (a "weakened" system)? On the other hand, it is of the nature of axiomatics to come up against *so-called undecidable propositions*, to confront *necessarily higher powers* that it cannot master. Finally, axiomatics does not constitute the cutting edge of science; it is much more a stopping point, a reordering that prevents decoded semiotic flows in physics and mathematics from escaping in all directions. The great axiomaticians are the men of State of science, who seal off the lines of flight that are so frequent in mathematics, who would impose a new *nexum*, if only a temporary one, and who lay down the official policies of science.[32]

Second, the series of political-economic problems that this analogy helps expose and articulate together is inseparable from the representations over which capitalist powers endeavored to strengthen their hold over the course of the 1970s. First, there was the combination of two symmetrical and reversible representations to which American economic and political-military hegemony, the weakening of the Soviet bloc, and the forced integration of former colonies and Third-World countries in the process of capitalist accumulation give renewed vigor: on the one hand, a capitalist System that overhangs frontiers and States, indifferent to their institutions, their sociopolitical contexts, and their internal relationships of forces (from where Deleuze and Guattari take the contrastive thematization of the States of globalized capitalism as "immanent models of realization for [its] axiomatic"); on the other hand, a world-economy that would be orderable by a political authority capable of harmonizing their evolutions, a State of supra-State authority as represented in international organizations of the IBRD, the GATT, and the IMF through which industrial and financial oligarchies have extended their sphere of influence since the end of the war and taken on the post-decolonization struggles and the collapse of the Bretton Wood system in Third World countries, and such as it was displayed in the 1975 creation of the G6 by the bloc of advanced capitalist States. Against which Deleuze and Guattari castigate the "absurdity to postulate a world supergovernment that makes the final decisions" ("No one is even capable of predicting the growth in the money supply…"), whereas the concept of capitalist axiomatics comes to oppose, while taking it at its word to dismantle it from the inside, the technocratic and scientific self-representation that the liberal governmentality produces itself through its institutions, but also through its scientific productions, placing the economic sciences under the authority of its characteristic mixes of deregulationist ideology, technocratic management, and logical-mathematical modelling.

The hypothesis of global capitalism as an axiomatic finally aims to keep open the problem that these dominant representations short circuit (be it by "war cries [of capitalism] against the State, not only in the name of the market, but by virtue of its superior deterritorialization," or by the paranoiac projection of a global supergovernment required to master capitalistic flows): the problem of the relationship between the special systematicity of global capitalist accumulation and the States that, differently, unequally, if not contradictorily, take part in it. The main problem posed by the analogy with logical axiomatics, and around which the entire "Axiomatics and Present-Day Situation" section is organized at the end of the Plateau on State apparatuses relates to the plurality and heterogeneity of the "models" that satisfy or realize a similar axiomatic. Which supposes that it should be seen as a system of plastic structuring—*unequally* plastic, according to degrees of weakening or saturation (the boundaries of accumulation and realization of surplus value as immanent limits). In return, this opens the political problem of determining the constraints under which or to what point it imposes an isomorphy of models, requires or elicits a heterogeneity within this very isomorphy, and even needs a real polymorphy of its State models of realization.

These "problems" become singularly political when we think of modern States. 1. Are not all modern States isomorphic in relation to the capitalist axiomatic, to the point that the difference between democratic, totalitarian, liberal, and tyrannical States depends only on concrete variables, and on the worldwide distribution of those variables, which always undergo eventual readjustments? Even the so-called socialist States are isomorphic, to the extent that there is only one world market, the capitalist one. 2. Conversely, does not the world capitalist axiomatic tolerate a real polymorphy, or even a heteromorphy, of models, and for two reasons? On the one hand, capital as a general relation of production can very easily integrate concrete sectors or modes of production that are noncapitalist. But on the other hand, and this is the main point, the bureaucratic socialist States can themselves develop different modes of production that only conjugate with capitalism to form a set whose "power" exceeds that of the axiomatic itself [global war machine of "dissuasion"].[33]

In other words, the hypothesis of a capitalist axiomatic does not have as its objective a *modelizing* theory, but on the contrary a conceptual arrangement that allows deconstruction of the univocal representation of a model—of "economic development" or State form, of political regime or "economic policy"—It is absurd to say that all States "are equal" at present (given a capitalistic power that is supposedly indifferent to the sociopolitical contexts that arrange its relationships of production), or tend to be that way (by virtue of a supposed trend of capitalist globalization to homogenize the political and social forms reducing the differences between regimes, laws, and governmentality to surface differences); but it is inane to distinguish between "good" and "bad" States according to a politicist transposition of evolutionist economism, discriminating State forms that are "late" or "poorly adapted" to the promised nuptials by "development policies" between market economy, imperious valorization of capital, and liberal democracy—and "forgetting that polymorphy establishes strict complementarities between the Western democracies and the colonial or neocolonial tyrannies that they install or support in other regions."[34]

From there finally comes the junction between the hypothesis of the capitalist axiomatic and the historico-machinic category of "power of ecumenical englobing" (with the thesis according to which "social formations are defined by machinic processes (…) on which modes of production depend"): the real subsumption of social formations to the process of accumulation on a global scale *does not necessarily imply* the real subsumption of the social relations and modes of production of these formations themselves. For this reason, theories of "unequal development" can only escape the normative ideological representations of development by integrating issues of "development of underdevelopment" and by analyzing the inequality inherent in global capitalism not as delays or hold-overs of a linear curve of development, but as a production by the Centre of "archaisms with a present-day function" that can also combine with implantations of highly-developed capitalist sectors. This requires drawing up a table of correlations and correlated contradictory trends showing the differences that the ideologies of "economic development" and political "modernity" represent on a line of evolution, homogenization, or progressive harmonization (like the ideology of the "New Political Economy" that, at the time of *Capitalism and Schizophrenia*, was being developed, extending the "theory of modernization" which had success in the 1950s–1960s in the pretentious and mediocre style of Walt W. Rostow, and is now in line to impose itself as a justification of the drastic debt imposed on peripheral countries). Thus the hypothesis of a capitalist axiomatic is exposed in the end in the form of a "typology of modern States [joining] in this way a meta-economy," capable of exposing the lines of State-political differentiation *through which* global capitalism forms a system (or forms what Guattari would call an "Integrated Global Capitalism"). Once again, however, between the *isomorphy* of State models of realization (in virtue of the mode of production and the social relationship of capitalist production), their *heteromorphy* (in virtue of other relationships and modes of production, which are nonetheless subsumed by the capitalist environment and the constraints of a global integrated market), and their *polymorphy* (in virtue of capitalist relationships of production that maintain or even incite non-capitalist modes of production), the distinction remains academic as long as their signification in conjunction is not captured again. I would like to show how Deleuze and Guattari have these three aspects correspond to a/ the already clearly perceptible offensives of neo-liberal governments combining the deregulationism of commercial, monetary, and financial flows and the return to predatory techniques of primitive accumulation; b/ the real but ambiguous resistances that countries of "real socialism" or socialist governments of the Third World continue to oppose to the ecumenical englobing of capital; c/ the new forms of forced integration of countries on the periphery of the system of accumulation on a global scale beyond the relationships of dependence inherited from colonial subjection. This is the set of conjectures that underlies the "meta-economic" typology of contemporary States, or the three main tendencies that are registered in the potency and impotence of State capture, in the variable distributions of the two poles of sovereignty and the corresponding modalities of State violence, in the undecidables where State power trips and cedes the initiative. In Proposition XIV, they are the object of a "summary table of 'data,'" aimed at least at mapping the multiplicity of critical points or possible bifurcations—"for this reason, nothing is played out in advance."[35]

Isomorphy and Heterogeneity of Capitalist States—The Neo-Liberal Offensive on a Global Scale

The first tendency spotted by Deleuze and Guattari in the current axiomatic, the tendency to an *isomorphy* of socio-State forms of realization seems to express most directly the power of *real* englobing of the planetary environment by the geography of capital.[36] "One could cite not only the cold and concerted destruction of primitive societies but also the fall of the last despotic formations, for example, the Ottoman Empire, which met capitalist demands with too much resistance and inertia."[37] This tendency to isomorphism refers above all to a materialist genealogy and determination of the nation-State: "a group of producers in which labor and capital circulate freely, in other words, in which the homogeneity and competition of capital is effectuated, in principle without external obstacles."[38] In fact, if we identify the constituents of a nation in the combination "one land, one people" (by contrast "problem of the nation is aggravated in the two extreme cases of a land without a people and a people without a land"), the land "implies a certain deterritorialization of the territories (community land, imperial provinces, seigneurial domains, etc.)," like the *people* implies a "decoding of the population" (lineages and castes, clans and orders)—which was averted in preindustrial Europe precisely by the feudal organization of the countryside and the corporative organization of the cities:[39]

> The nation is constituted on the basis of these flows and is inseparable from the modern State that gives consistency to the corresponding land and people. It is the flow of naked labor that makes the people, just as it is the flow of Capital that makes the land and its industrial base. [...] It is in the form of the nation-state, with all its possible variations, that the State becomes the model of realization for the capitalist axiomatic. This is not at all to say that nations are appearances or ideological phenomena; on the contrary, they are the passional and living forms in which the qualitative homogeneity and the quantitative competition of abstract capital are first realized.[40]

It is essential, however, to distinguish this tendency to isomorphy from a process of *homogeneization*. Not only because of the concrete variables that obviously make variations in the State-social forms, nationalitarian constructions, and modes of "nationalization" of the State, but because of the complexity of this tendency, which itself includes two contradictory and coexisting tendencies, and which mean that the isomorphy tolerates and even engenders a great *heterogeneity* of States:

> The axioms of capitalism are obviously not theoretical proposi-
> tions, or ideological formulas, but operative statements that
> constitute the semiological form of Capital and that enter as com-
> ponent parts into assemblages of production, circulation, and
> consumption. The axioms are primary statements, which do not
> derive from or depend upon another statement. In this sense, a
> flow can be the object of one or several axioms (with the set of all
> axioms constituting the conjugation of the flows); but it can also
> lack any axioms of its own, its treatment being only a conse-
> quence of other axioms; finally, it can remain out of bounds,
> evolve without limits, be left in the state of an "untamed" varia-
> tion in the system. There is a tendency within capitalism
> continually to add more axioms. [...] A very general pole of the
> State, "social democracy," can be defined by this tendency to add,
> invent axioms in relation to spheres of investment and sources of
> profit [...] The opposite tendency is no less a part of capitalism:
> the tendency to withdraw, subtract axioms. One falls back on a
> very small number of axioms regulating the dominant flows,
> while the other flows are given a derivative, consequential status
> [...], or are left in an untamed state that does not preclude the
> brutal intervention of State power, quite the contrary. The
> "totalitarianism" pole of the State incarnates this tendency to

restrict the number of axioms [...].But one does not come without the other, either in two different but coexistent places or in two successive but closely linked moments; they always have a hold on each other, or are even contained in each other, constituting the same axiomatic.[41]

These two contradictory tendencies, towards the addition and towards the subtraction of axioms, are related to two fundamental factors that are closely linked.

1) First, while the tendency to isomorphism of national-capitalist States comes from their subsumption to the englobing of a global market, this subsumption itself takes on contrasting forms depending on the conditions of formation (or, on the contrary, of destruction) of an *integrated interior market* that goes along with the demands of the exterior market, and that calls on the State, in the articulation of the two, to displace the contradictions into class conflicts, social and political struggles, and international events that it incorporates in its institutions and its "governmentality." The historical sequences given as an illustration of this social-democratic trend to add axioms are more significant from this perspective: "After the end of World War I, the joint influence of the world depression and the Russian Revolution forced capitalism to multiply its axioms, to invent new ones dealing with the working class, employment, union organization, social institutions, the role of the State, the foreign and domestic markets. Keynesian economics and the New Deal were axiom laboratories. Examples of the creation of new axioms after the Second World War: the Marshall Plan, forms of assistance and lending, transformations in the monetary system."[42] From another angle, a second pole defines an opposite tendency, one to take away axioms, to deregulate flows of population, territory, and money, in favor of a few exclusive axioms that target the dominant

flows, the other flows—relative overpopulation, unprofitable equipment, or "disinvested" territory—receiving a "derivative, consequential status" or being "left in an untamed state" outside any system.[43] Exclusively promoting the external sector and industries focused on exporting raw materials or food, calling for foreign capital and over-indebtedness of the State, crushing the internal market, compressing wages, and restricting the fiscal levers of indirect redistribution of revenues: these are some of the methods that are on a path to be imposed systematically *through* the programs of "structural adjustment" of the IMF, by Western States under the hegemony of North American capital on "developing countries." I would also insist that Deleuze and Guattari's formulation deliberately leaves open the possibility of redeploying this tendency in the historical center of capitalist accumulation, to the extent that, in this conjuncture, or according to the changes in relationships of force between fractions of a partially transnationalized capitalist class, the conditions of exploitation and the sources of profit undergo a crushing and a *disintegration* of the interior market:[44] "isomorphy in no way implies homogeneity: there is isomorphy, but heterogeneity, between totalitarian and social democratic States wherever the mode of production is the same. […] *the isomorphy of the models*, with the two poles of addition and subtraction, depends on how the domestic and foreign markets are distributed in each case. […]a first bipolarity, applying to the States that are located at the center and are under the capitalist mode of production."[45] Following the capitalist-totalitarian pole, the only axioms retained at the limit deal with monetary and financial flows favorable to external commerce and to capturing externalized profits, while land and its equipment, society and its population itself, are no longer data taken up by specific axioms but become simple consequences dealt with on the margins like collateral damage.[46] "As for untamed evolutions, they appear among other places in the variations in the employment level, in the phenomena of exodus from the countryside, shanty-town-urbanization, etc.," in the margins of institutional regulations, and at the limit excluded from recognition and repressed from social perception itself, if necessary, delivered to the legal or para-legal repression of the State.

By calling this pole totalitarian, Deleuze and Guattari clearly distinguish themselves from the imposed use of this master signifier, which was generalized in the 1970s less in the service of critical analyses of real socialism than in favor of the always more arrogant benefit of anti-communist propaganda. When they identify this pole in libertarian ideology and in the neoliberal policies that started to be tested on a wider scale in the early 1970s, it is to conclude that it is inaccurate "to equate the bureaucratic socialist States with the totalitarian capitalist States,"[47] which for many sounded like a provocative oxymoron: "The totalitarian State is not a maximum State but rather, following Virilio's formulation, the minimum State of anarcho-capitalism (cf. Chile)."[48] Yet it underlines even better the point that our authors want to make: the correlation of two contradictory tendencies which, in function of strategies of capital and collective resistance, traverse and divide the capitalist policy required by constant readjustments of the capitalist axiomatic, "either in two different but coexistent places or in two successive but closely linked moments; they always have a hold on each other, or are even contained in each other, constituting the same axiomatic. A typical example would be present-day Brazil, with its ambiguous alternative 'totalitarianism-social democracy.'"[49]

2) This brings a second factor for thinking, on the systematic level of capitalist axiomatic and its extended reproduction, this distribution *and this entanglement* of two tendencies that traverse capitalist policies contradictorily. Concerning a completely different

situation, Samir Amin remarked that methods of primitive accumulation become more subsidiary the more the national bourgeoisie operates its profits in sectors grafted mainly on expanding the internal market, and only depend very indirectly on the external market.[50] The contradictory unity of tendencies to add and subtract axioms that Deleuze and Guattari describe express in capitalist policies the contradictory relationship that capitalist accumulation entertains with its own immanent limits:

> Capitalism is indeed an axiomatic, because it has no laws but immanent ones. It would like for us to believe that it confronts the limits of the Universe, the extreme limit of resources and energy. But all it confronts are its own limits (the periodic depreciation of existing capital); all it repels or displaces are its own limits (the formation of new capital, in new industries with a high profit rate). This is the history of oil and nuclear power. And it does both at once: capitalism confronts its own limits and simultaneously displaces them, setting them down again farther along. It could be said that the totalitarian tendency to restrict the number of axioms corresponds to the confrontation with the limits, whereas the social democratic tendency corresponds to the displacement of the limits.[51]

This poses a dual correlation: on the one hand, the addition of axioms and methods of expanded accumulation (displacement of immanent limits) relying on a generalization of wages and its integration, varying according to relationships of force and class breaks, in an institutional system combining the social State, "self-centered growth," development of internal consumption, and growth of public investment in equipment and services (infrastructures for land, urban areas, housing and transportation, health services, education, and more); on the other hand, between the subtraction of axioms and techniques of primitive accumulation (confronting obstacles to accumulation under the dual aspect of the tendency of profit rates to decline and the crisis of over-accumulation) where become involved methods of unproductive absorption or destruction of existing capital and depreciation of the value of the labor force, deregulation of wage conditions and de-institutionalization of "relative overpopulation," and techniques of "accumulation by spo-liation," by expropriation and forced deterritorialization, by privatization, and more. However, a third correlation is then super-posed on this dual correlation, one that relates to the economy of sovereign violence and its own bipolarity, which I presented in the first part of this book by highlighting its articulation with the dis-tinction primitive accumulation/expanded accumulation.[52] What is generally called "deregulation" often consists less in simple suppres-sions of norms and restrictive institutional arrangements than in their displacement to some flows at the exclusion of others that only receive a derivative treatment or are ejected from the system—which, as Deleuze and Guattari remind us, does not exclude violent repression of them, on the contrary: the suppression of an axiom returns potential to the "sovereign-paranoiac" regime, the aneco-nomic regime of State violence where the tendency to add axioms orients it to its "civic" economy, which does not simply mean legally limited but distributively targeted in terms of the flows differentially selected and integrated ("Even a social democracy adapted to the Third World surely does not undertake to integrate the whole poverty-stricken population into the domestic market; what it does, rather, is to effect the class rupture that will select the integratable ele-ments").[53] The essential point again here (and one that goes along with the previous analyses of the "archi-violence" of sovereignty), relates to how this contradictory bipolarization of capitalist politics and the correlative forms taken by sovereign violence applies to all of the combinations between these two poles, and the displacements from one to the other that the relationships of force between antagonistic classes impose.[54] We should keep these elements in mind when taking on the minority question in the next chapter.

Polymorphy, Neo-Imperialism, and Internal Colonization

The second essential polarity to determine the plurality of State models of realization supported by the capitalist axiomatic has an immediately geopolitical signification: "A second, West-East, bipolarity has been imposed on the States of the center, that of the capitalist States and the bureaucratic socialist States. Although this new distinction may share certain traits of the first (the so-called socialist States being capable of assimilation to the totalitarian States), the problem lies elsewhere. The numerous 'convergence' theories that attempt to demonstrate a certain homogenization of the States of the East and West are not very convincing. Even isomorphism is not applicable: there is a real heteromorphy, not only because the mode of production is not capitalist, but also because the relation of production is not Capital."[55] It is therefore under a different point of view than the States of "real socialism," having as its dominant relationship of production planning and not production for the market and putting value on capital, still constitute models of realization of the axiomatic of capital, in function of "the existence of a single external world market, which remains the deciding factor here, even above and beyond the relations of production from which it results." This confirms the entanglement in the same axiomatic of the power of *real* englobing to modes of *formal* englobing such that the *"socialist bureaucratic plan(e) takes* on a parasitic function in relation to the *plan(e) of capital*, which manifests a greater creativity, of the 'virus' type."[56]

If the heterogeneity of relationships of production "englobed" in the world market defined a heteromorphy of models of realization, Deleuze and Guattari distinguish a polymorphy of it, as correlate of a third bipolarity of the geography of capital that registers the data of dependence and unequal exchange, and particularly the transformations of differential forms of exploitation and appropriation of profits, through movements of decolonization and new forms of postcolonial domination. It means saying, in fact, that "the (shifting) distinction between the core and the periphery of the world-economy corresponds also to the geographical and politico-cultural distribution of strategies of exploitation."[57] In *Capitalism and Schizophrenia*, this polymorphy of Third World States in relation to the States of central capitalism is presented both as the result of colonial imperialism and as an "axiom of substitution for colonization"—or a variable set of axioms for which Deleuze and Guattari borrow the largest ones from the analyses of Samir Amin: a) the "distortion toward export activities (extraversion)," which does not result from the insufficiency of the domestic market, as standard theories of development would have it, applying a problematic appropriate for the "center" to the periphery, but from "the superiority of productivity of the center in all fields, which compels the periphery to confine itself to the role of complementary supplier of products to which natural advantage is relevant" (raw materials, agricultural and mineral products), crushing the possibilities of developing autocentric industries;[58] b) a specific distortion or hypertrophy of the tertiary sector, which the structures of demand and of productivity do not account for on their own, but which are the result of "the limitations and contradictions characteristic of peripheral development: insufficient industrialization and rising unemployment, reinforcing the position of land rent";[59] c) the "distortion in the periphery toward light *branches* of activity [...] along with the recourse to modern production technologies in these branches," which once again results from the international specialization of production; d) the chain of "disarticulations" that result from this triple distortion of the productive apparatus: adjustment of the orientation of peripheral production according to the needs of the center that prevents transmitting the benefits of economic progress of development poles to the entire economic body, the effects of central economic domination on the structures of commerce in the periphery, extreme inequalities in the distribution of productivity and revenues.[60]

These peripheral axioms carry out integration to the capitalist competition of the world market of postcolonial States of which the subsumption no longer passes through a directly political subjection, while continuing to ensure, for better or worse, the relative increase in rates of profit in the center. The tipping point to neo-imperialist structures of power is thus not only found in the transformations of relationships of political force on both sides of the newly conquered independences, but also in the tendencies to invert capitalist investments and the massively unilateral captures of profits:

> For it would be a great error to think that exports from the periphery originate primarily in traditional sectors or archaic territorialities: on the contrary, they come from modern industries and plantations that generate an immense surplus value, to a point where it is no longer the developed countries that supply the underdeveloped countries with capital, but quite the opposite.[61]
>
> Throughout a vast portion of the Third World, the general relation of production is capital—even throughout the entire Third World, in the sense that the socialized sector may utilize

that relation, adopting it in this case. But the mode of production is not necessarily capitalist, either in the so-called archaic or transitional forms, or in the most productive, highly industrialized sectors. This indeed represents a third case, included in the worldwide axiomatic: when capital acts as the relation of production but in noncapitalist modes of production.[62]

The three tendencies—to isomorphy, heteromorphy, and polymorphy—which were first indexed on the geography of capital inherited from the 19th and 20th centuries, seem to trace a relatively simple political-economic map: Center, West-East, North-South. Yet by the same token, the historical sequence for which Deleuze and Guattari identify the turning point, can be read both as a relative *fusion* of these three trends, and as an entanglement or *inclusion* of these differentiated spaces of the world-economy—which causes vacillations in the terminology in which it is uttered ("center"/ "periphery"; "developed countries"/"Third World"...).

1) In the first place, in fact, isomorphy, and its contradictory tendencies between social-democratic additions and neoliberal-authoritarian subtractions, no longer concern the Center alone, to the extent that "To a large extent, there is isomorphy between the United States and the bloodiest of the South American tyrannies (or between France, England, and West Germany and certain African States)."[63]

2) Second, the West-East axis of confrontation of blocs and the Center-Periphery axis of neo-imperialism, are in large part engaged by each other, not only in the justifications that the United States superpower finds, sometimes in one and sometimes in the other, to readjust its hegemony, but in the specific forms that the global war machine takes that was analyzed above (Chapter 4). This leads to Deleuze and Guattari's interest in the thesis developed since the

early 1970s by the theorists of National Defense: "the more equili-
brated things become at the center between the West and the East,
beginning with the equilibrium of overarmament, the more they
become unbalanced or "destabilized" from North to South and
destabilize the central equilibrium,"[64] a thesis for which we have
shown its immediacy for Deleuze especially with Reagan's renewal
of armament policies and the Pershing missile affair in 1983. More
generally, the picture of the global capitalist axiomatic in 1980
shows a plurality of trends, with issues that were still unpredictable
from the point of view of an eventual recomposition of the "world
order," of this potentialized power of war through the substitution for
"classical conflicts between States in the center (as well as peripheral
colonization)," of the "two great conflictual lines, between West and
East and North and South; these lines intersect and together cover
everything": "the overarmament of the West and East not only
leaves the reality of local wars entirely intact and gives them a new
force and new stakes; it not only founds the 'apocalyptic' possibility
of a direct confrontation along the two great axes; it also seems that
the war machine takes on a specific supplementary meaning: industrial, political, judicial, etc."[65] A meaning which is itself highly
overdetermined, where at least three series of factors are combined:

—the unprecedented dimensions of capitalist accumulation and
constant capital investment on a global scale, such that "the depreciation of existing capital and the formation of new capital assume
a rhythm and scale that necessarily take the route of a war machine,"
materialized in military-financial, technological, and industrial
complexes that are contiguous, and directly mobilized in "the redis-
tributions of the world necessary for the exploitation of maritime
and planetary resources",[66]

—the amount of the decoding of peripheral flows, aggravated
by their forced integration in the competition of the world market,

and giving a new meaning to "the oldest formula, which already obtained in the archaic empires under different conditions. The more the archaic empire overcoded the flows, the more it stimulated decoded flows that turned back against it and forced it to change. The more the decoded flows enter into a central axiomatic, the more they tend to escape to the periphery, to present problems that the axiomatic is incapable of resolving or controlling"—if not precisely by the mobilization of a global war machine projected with all the more violence that the objectives are less localizable, *both massified* and *molecularized*: flows of matter-energy, flows of population, flows of food, and urban flows ("the four main flows that torment the representatives of the world-economy or the axiomatic"), which are manifested in anomic forms of wild urbanization, of populations ravaged by famine, and forced migrations, but also in forms of resistance or response, more or less organized, State or para-State, liberating or nihilist;

—finally, a potential dual evolution of the global war machine itself, that Deleuze and Guattari often express as the correlation of a "macropolitics of security" and a "micropolitics of insecurity," or a combination of large-scale terror policies justified by maintaining peace and the "world order," and a fascinating policification drawing on the identity panic to which it contributes to the disorders of capitalist globalization.[67] This leads to the complex entanglements that we encountered in Chapter 4, circulating between the figure of an absolutized, theologized enemy, of Evil or the Antichrist, potentially transferable (from the line of confrontation of "blocs" to another "civilizational" line of conflict),[68] and the molecularized figure, essentially displaceable and reversible, of a non-qualified enemy "in conformity with the requirements of an axiomatic": "the 'unspecified enemy,' domestic or foreign (an individual, group, class, people, event, world)."[69]

3) Yet these evolutions, in third and final place, appear inseparable from a final entanglement of polarities disposed in the tableau of the capitalist axiomatic of the 13th Plateau: "the States of the center deal not only with the Third World, each of them has not only an external Third World, but there are internal Third Worlds that rise up within them and work them from the inside." The analyses developed by the theorists of dependence and the capitalist world-system are both reinforced and re-problematized by it, according to Deleuze and Guattari, both from the perspective of unequal geographies of circulation of capital, investments, and profits, as from the perspective of methods of exploitation and accumulation, and the regimes of violence that they mobilize. What Étienne Balibar recently proposed as a "generalized colonial hypothesis," based on an analysis of the imperialism of Rosa Luxembourg to make symmetry with the comparison that Marx made between "the exterminating methods of colonization [which] allowed an extension of the domination of capitalism in the 'peripheries' of its domain of origin, and those sometimes just as violent that were implemented to impose it in the 'center' of the world-economy,"[70] is expressed by Deleuze and Guattari in the following way in 1980:

> It could even be said in certain respects that the periphery and the center exchange determinations: a deterritorialization of the center, a decoding of the center in relation to national and territorial aggregates, cause the peripheral formations to become true centers of investment, while the central formations peripheralize. [...]The more the worldwide axiomatic installs high industry and highly industrialized agriculture at the periphery, provisionally reserving for the center so called postindustrial activities (automation, electronics, information technologies, the conquest of space, overarmament, etc.), the more it installs peripheral zones of

underdevelopment inside the center, internal Third Worlds, internal Souths. "Masses" of the population are abandoned to erratic work (subcontracting, temporary work, or work in the underground economy), and their official subsistence is assured only by State allocations and wages subject to interruption.[71]

This process of internal peripheralization or Third Worldization also has as its correlate—at the end of an historical sequence where labor struggles imposed a limitation on forms of overexploitation in the countries of central capitalism and wage conditions relatively integrated to the circuits of expanded accumulation, while the most brutal methods of overexploitation of the labor force and primitive accumulation were unleashed on the colonial peripheries—an inflection in the geographic distribution of circuits of expanded accumulation and the techniques of primitive accumulation, and in the correlative distribution of the two poles of State violence. To the point that it brings closer together, or even makes indistinguishable, the question of the polymorphy of peripheral States and the neoliberal-authoritarian tendency to subtraction from the "center" of axioms of work and territoriality. As if neoliberalism reinterpreted the lesson of Luxembourg in its own way: capital never finished its phase of "primitive" accumulation, or proletarization, of destruction of non-capitalist social relationships and of forced socialization of relationships of capital, of submission of socio-anthropological logics of collective territorialities to the contradictory logics of mobility and the fixation of the force of labor. Simply when capital starts to "recolonize its own center," the techniques of primitive accumulation are not only a way to prolong the expanded accumulation, they proceed on the contrary to a vast operation of depreciation of existing capital and devaluing of productive, scientific-technological, and human forces. Neoliberalism is in reality an archeo-liberalism, appropriate to the neo-archaism of capitalism itself.[72] It is a liberalism which, to mitigate the crises of accumulation, comes to treat capitalist societies, their populations, and their institutions, as if they were "pre-capitalist" societies. This gives it a special temporality, as well as the impermeability of its discourse to the crises that it contributes to starting, which refer to a capitalism that is always to come, finally released of its "archaic aspects," and its unending pre-modern age.

6

Becoming Minorities—Becoming Revolutionary

Macropolitics and Micropolitics:
Division in the Minoritarian Strategy

The importance given to minorities in *Capitalism and Schizophrenia* is both overly visible and cryptic. I wager that the reason is that the ways Deleuze and Guattari formulate it can enter into resonance with a problematic field that has become relatively common even for very different political thinking, while preserving a form of excess or radicalness that make these formulations at the limit, or taken literally, untenable. They are no less significant under one aspect or the other: it may even be the collusion that they operate that keeps them interesting today.

Under the first aspect, the fact is that Deleuze and Guattari's theory of minorities comes at the point of convergence and divergence between several currents of contemporary political thought. Whether they find support in the classic analyses of Arendt on national and Stateless minorities, on the critical historiography of *Subaltern Studies*, on the Foucaldian analysis of norms, on the question of the struggles for recognition taken up from Critical Theory, they each have their own way to problematize the status of the minority as the weak link condensing the primary tensions passing through contemporary nation-States, their institution of citizenship and the permanent struggles to maintain its rights, their mechanisms of regulation of social conflicts and of reproduction of economic, cultural, sexual, and racial inequalities. Recent work has taken the struggles of minorities to create conditions of equality and civil and political liberty as one of the decisive issues, if not the very place where the institution of citizenship is decided. "'Typical' carrier of the demand for rights in the city, symbol of its oscillation between exclusion and inclusion, between defending vested interests and potential universalization," minorities condense "the dialectic of inclusion and exclusion in the 'play' of citizenship, and the possibility to conceive of it not as much as a given status (from which certain "actors" benefit or not) as the very dynamic of this play, the stakes of the strategies it elicits through the space of society."[1] In a singular reversal, minorities have in sum come to give the major subject of modern political space, the People, its new name, and constitute, as "people of the people" or new "universal class," the real agent of "the invention of democracy" as infinite conquest of *aequa libertas*.

Such a theoretical investment, which tends to identify in certain minority struggles (even indistinctly in minority struggles— although the term "minority," detached from its properly "nationalitarian" use, has precisely become a floating signifier, and the problem is thus to know how we understand this "floatation") the place of a political subjectivation that is not only specific but *typical*, at the same time original and essential to the contemporary struggles of democratization, is obviously not without reflexive and critical effectiveness for political thought itself for as much as it associates its concepts with a horizon of autonomy and universality, of which the notion of minority seems to represent, in its very ambivalence, the dual privation: as oppressive minority of a majority subjected to a heteronomous power that separates it from its own demand for presupposed universality, or on the contrary, as a particular State under tutelage, or even (by shifting from Kantian utterances to sociologies of social normalization) as subjection of a community to its own particularity, to specific interests, to a particular identity, to a particular place of function in the social structure, to what Deleuze and Guattari call a "minority as system," or Rancière a "part" in the order of the "police," which nonetheless separates it from a political autonomy carried by an ideal of universality. Here we find tension characteristic of any thinking on politics as space of practices of emancipation and transformation, but pushed to a paradoxical extreme. Where the republican tradition taught us to distinguish heteronomy and autonomy, and to understand emancipation (leaving the state of minority) as the passage from one to the other in the unifying form of the sovereign people; there again where Marxist and socialist traditions learned to dialectalize heteronomy and autonomy in a process of emancipation carried by a universal class and conquered by the transformation of its heteronomic conditions of existence, the idea of a "minor political subject" seems to come before their coming together, as if their distance was eliminated in a problematic or perhaps untenable short-circuit, which also carries the suspicion of covering over, in an impossible theoretical form, a *void of the subject*. Unless things are perceived differently, and this paradoxical figure is given a symptomatic signification leaving the trace of a historical-conceptual crisis as much as a political one, opening the current situation to a field of multiple and conflicting interpretations; in other words, unless it is made into an analyzer of the aporia carved into the current situation by crises experienced historically by the major figures of the politics of democratization, of which this figure would be responsible for occupying their places, for better or worse—or *impossibly*.

From this point of view, it is significant that this question of the political subject has been the object of an intense work of reproblematization over three post-war decades, to the point that some of the current formulations can be understood, with different discursive referents, as the after-effect of their non-resolution or their impasses. This does not mean that the question is without a specific contemporary context, but it remains tied to the particularly complex global circumstances with which this research was faced, and on which we are still dependent today, albeit as inheritors of an encrypted will, which makes both its legacy and its losses unclear. Under these circumstances, the major paradigms of the political subject were combined, allied, and confronted, paradigms that were mobilized in the major cycles of collective struggle of the past two centuries: the republican figure of the people, or the figure of the people of the nation, which is itself inseparable from contradictory emancipatory and imperialist, democratic and fascist investments; the figure of the proletariat, but also that of the colonized; the emergence from these new figures of an essentially multiple and problematic political subject, "subaltern groups" and minorities. Under these circumstances as well, the discursive formations of social and political critique were deeply recomposed, with Marxists discursive formations at the fore, polarizing the modes of enunciation, representation, and problematization of social and political critique, of which the success is paradoxically indissociably linked with its multiple and conflictual, split and splitting heritages—these internal splits allowed the development of Marxist critiques of Marxism for almost a century—up to the point of explosion and dissemination making this self-referentiality of Marxism, even dissident, increasingly complicated.[7] In the aggravation of the crisis of the labor movement that began with the First World War and the defeat to fascism between the wars, it also made the identification of the subject of politics increasingly untenable despite the labor movement's belief that it could guarantee otherwise in the figure of a revolutionary proletariat constituted in the dialectic of mass movements and class antagonism.[3] This entire situation, as complex as it is undecided, that Deleuze and Guattari condensed in the almost compulsively repeated formula: "the people are missing"—I will return to this point.

Deleuze and Guattari's theory of minorities is one of the most eloquent testaments to this critical heritage because, while keeping its distance from both the melancholic interpretations and reactionary condemnation, it gives a particularly captivating formulation of it by bringing together *two propositions* held simultaneously, each as "excessive" as the other, and antinomical despite the apparent proximity of their utterance:

1) On the one hand, the proposition of a fundamental tendency of the contemporary situation: a "becoming-minoritarian of everybody," where new forms of political subjectivation and collective emancipation are decided, and even a "becoming-revolutionary of people" creating "the premises of a global movement," of which minorities "in the long run [...] promote compositions that do not pass by way of the capitalist economy any more than they do the State-form."[4] This is the formulation that is significantly found at the end of *Dialogues* and in the table of the global capitalist axiomatic of the 13th Plateau, which replays, while reversing it, the question of a universal class—"universal figure of [political] consciousness"— inscribing negativity within capitalist practices of power and its socio-State arrangements of realization, for which crises tend to "release" a revolutionary situation.

> What characterizes our situation is both beyond and on this side of the State. *Beyond* national States, the development of a world

market, the power of multinational companies, the outline of a "planetary" organization, the extension of capitalism to the whole social body, clearly forms a great abstract machine which over-codes the monetary, industrial and technological fluxes. [...] But the abstract machine, with its dysfunctions, is no more infallible than the national States which are not able to regulate them on their own territory and from one territory to another. The State no longer has at its disposal the political, institutional or even financial means which would enable it to fend off the social reper-cussions of the machine [...]. Enormous land slides are happening *on this side* of the State [...]. It is not surprising that all kinds of minority questions—linguistic, ethnic, regional, about sex, or youth—resurge not only as archaisms, but in up-to-date revolu-tionary forms which call once more into question in an entirely immanent manner both the global economy of the machine and the assemblages of national States. Instead of gambling on the eternal impossibility of the revolution and on the fascist return of a war-machine in general, why not think that *a new type of revo-lution is in the course of becoming possible*, and that all kinds of mutating, living machines conduct wars, are combined, and trace out a plane of consistence which undermines the plane of organi-zation of the World and the States? For, once again, the world and its States are no more masters of their plane than revolutionaries are condemned to the deformation of theirs. Everything is played in uncertain games, "front to front, back to back, back to front..." The question of the future of the revolution is a bad question because, in so far as it is asked, there are so many people who do not *become* revolutionaries, and this is exactly why it is done, to impede the question of the revolutionary-becoming of people, at every level, in every place.[5]

Against the old refrain of the poor success rate of past revolutions that was spread in the media space of the time, the concept of revolutionary-becoming attempts to join the bivalent instrumentalization of historical discourse in the face of emancipatory struggles. Not having history function as a discourse of authentication or disqualification of practical problems of revolutionary engagement, both existential and political; not seeking in it the prestige of grand teleological assurances or the vertigo of apocalyptical warnings on the horizon of the very word of revolution from the specter of "Totalitarianisms" (two ways of articulating historical discourse to a theology of guarantees); extracting it in sum from the endless back and forth between legitimation and delegitimation of popular struggles in the name of a "development plan" that would prefigure its destiny in the weft of history: this is what comes from distinguishing the history of revolutions from the "revolutionary-becomings" of people, becomings that can affect the collective subjectivity of unpredictable breaks, always singular in their emergence, sometimes connectable and generalizable in their effects, never reducible however to the historical linearities that would allow them to be inscribed in a univocal discourse of power or counter-power. This gesture also certainly targets, in conformance with the "minority strategy" that Deleuze and Guattari start to problematize in 1975–1977, to take by surprise the problem of the *norms of historicization* that all of the dominant ideologies (those of the bourgeoisie against the proletariat, national hegemonies against minorities, imperialist Nations against "peoples without history" in the colonies) have continued to impose on what could and could not be admitted, recognized, or simply signifiable and perceptible as "historical" action. Far from being a solely discursive and ideological question, the disjunction between becoming/history is indexed, as the previous quote shows, and increasingly clearly up to *A Thou-*

sand Plateaus, on a social and political efficacy marked by a relative decentering of social struggles in relation to the *State-national* axis as principle organizer of historical representation in general. It is precisely at this moment that the concept of becoming is grafted to the question of minorities initiated in the study of Kafka, and gives place to the conceptual hybridization of "becoming-minor," which seems to reverse the classic formula of emancipation and yet redefine its stakes.

Now—and this is the core of the problem from which we can follow the divergences in their reception since the 1990s—this moment is simultaneously the one, as this same quote also shows, where Deleuze and Guattari, developing their analysis of the axiomatic of "integrated global capitalism," determine that this decentering is not only and not primarily *the effect* of these new forms of struggle, but that it operates to the ambiguous benefit of the rise of new powers of capitalist accumulation that both profit and erode the mechanisms of social and economic intervention of States. From there, as we will see, the plurality of frontlines discerned by their problmeatization of minority struggles, at the same time as a bivalent position in relation to the State, oscillating between the radicalness of formulas ("abolish the State-form") and nuanced discernment on the reasons and manners of investing it ("this does not mean that struggle on the level of axioms is without importance, on the contrary…"). And this oscillation is all the more problematic, if we account for the fact that the distinction between revolutionary-becoming and the history of revolution inevitably internalizes a division internal to the very idea of revolution: between revolution as an historical concept and revolution as practical Idea. At least we could expect that this distinction calls in turn for a new understanding of their articulation (as the Marxist-Leninist concept of "revolutionary conjuncture"[6] proposed in its own way). Yet the formulations of Deleuze and Guattari in this regard oscillate again between unstable positions: either hardening the heterogeneity of the two poles, at the risk of making incomprehensible the fact that revolutionary-becoming animates a *politics*;[7] or by dialectalizing it, making the "result" of becoming in the historical thickness of societies the stakes of a "micropolitics" that can only indefinitely defer the question of thresholds of historical or macropolitical efficacy.[8]

2) These difficulties are not at all resolved but instead short-circuited by a second formulation of becoming-minoritarian that, far from projecting minorities to the forefront of a new universal class, covers the first statement with another one that is not only very different in its style but radically inverts its meaning. It is the theoretical matrix introduced by Deleuze in 1978 in his short text "Philosophie et minorité," then reworked with Guattari in the 4th, 10th, and 13th Plateaus: it formalizes a system of domination based on the majority/minority distinction seen from the perspective of a semiology of identity assignments, in other words, logical and semiotic operations through which a normative ensemble regulates the unequal inscription of practices and social multiplicities in "sub-sets" (minorities), both regimes of utterance and subjective positions in which groups and people are individualized, their interests and demands are articulated, and their belonging and identification are regulated.

> Majority implies a constant, of expression or content, like a standard meter against which it is evaluated. Suppose that the constant or standard is Man-White-male-adult-city dweller-speaking a standard language-European-average heterosexual (the Ulysses of Joyce or Ezra Pound). It is obvious that "man" is the majority, even if they are less numerous than mosquitoes, children, women, Blacks, peasants, homosexuals..., etc. Because they

appear twice, once in the constant and once in the variable from which the constant is taken. The majority supposes a state of power and domination, not the opposite [...]. Another determination than the constant will be considered minoritarian, by nature and no matter the number, in other words as a sub-system or outside the system. [...] Yet at this point, everything is revered. For the majority, to the extent that it is analytically understood in its abstract standard, is never no one, it is always Someone— Ulysses—while the minority is the becoming of everyone, their potential becoming to the extent that it deviates from the model. There is a majoritarian "fact" but it is the analytical fact of Someone, which is opposed to the becoming-minoritarian of everyone. For this reason, we must distinguish: majoritarian as homogenous and constant system, minorities as sub-systems, and minoritarian as potential and created, creative becoming.[9]

In its way, this second formulation also takes support from a certain circumstantial scouting: reversing the social-liberal representation of a governmentality capable of reorganizing its consensus around "liberal democracy" combining an apology of libertogeneous virtues of growth and the market, human-rights morality, and praise of the freedom of opinion freely manipulated by the mass media integrated in said market,[10] it synthesizes operations in virtue of which a "majority" as apparent reference or proclaimed recipient of a policy, supposes a relationship of domination which it allows in return to be organized as *hegemonic* domination. Yet it is also a question simultaneously of showing how this hegemony is reproduced in a circular structure that necessarily makes it an arrangement of minorization. On one side, this majoritarian referent has a content, precisely constructed by the hegemonization of particular contents corresponding to a given state of domination (in the lexicon borrowed here by Deleuze: some independent variables are extracted and raised to the status of constants); but in this content are subjectivated both those who are identified in (and that identify with) the majority and those who aren't and who cannot, but who (*precisely because there are not and cannot*) can identify themselves in a distinctive positivity which is the opposite of a privative identity. For this reason, the dual inscription of the constant (in the majority of which it defines the norm, in the minority in which it privatively defines the variable)[11] can be read in both ways: as an effect of the relationship of domination, expressed in the always *tautological* character of the criteria of the majoritarian;[12] but also as the means or the "language" in which the dominated can formulate their demands and even (as understood in the example of the majoritarian "the national Worker, qualified, male and over thirty-five"),[13] the means through which the dominant construct their hegemony at least partially in the language and the identifications of the dominated themselves.

What makes the plasticity of this arrangement, however, is at the same time what exposes it to imbalance if its logic is pushed to the end. First, the fact that a majority, while referring to a set for which, in the name of which, or in view of which policies are made, does not avoid defining in itself an empty universal, carries out both a passage to the logical limit and a concrete political technology. The passage to the limit is illustrated in the series often repeated by Deleuze and Guattari, with a few variants: Man-White-male-adult-salaried-"reasonable"-city dweller-speaking a standard language-European-heterosexual.... The list could virtually be continued to the point of ensuring that no one could be completely in conformance to it. Which opens the problem of fluctuating instrumentalizations of targeted criteria of discrimination in function of circumstances and political objectives, at the same time as that of the "intersection" of some of these criteria and a fusion of different corresponding relationships of domination. At the most general level, that the majority defines an empty universal, expresses the fact that norms fixed as majoritarian constants are less decreed so that one conforms to them than to measure those who do not conform to them, and to identify and categorize differentially the distances *between them* (and not simply between each other and the supposed identity fixed in the normative utterance). Following one of Foucault's lessons, normative utterances do not simply call for identification or conformance ("normalization"); they allow a recording of the different ways to behave in relation to this supposed interpellation (and that we also learn after the fact),[14] to identify the different rather than to make it identical, to measure and fixate the "deviance" in a reproducible space of division of the unequal, and to make its so-called "rectification" a means to produce new imputations of non-conformity, deviance, or "inadaptation." If, in this operation of inclusive exclusion, the majority is the analytical fact of *Someone*, the minority, constituted as "state" by this very operation, is the synthetic fact of "a few," whatever their number, gathered in a sub-system and made countable and quantifiable by the dominant norms. Several dialectics could then be established between the universal and the particular in this arrangement –including making those "outside the system" precisely because they are rejected to the frontier of constituted-recognized social states, the real placeholders of the majority or the only ones legitimately capable of representing its empty universality and give it their name.[15]

Yet precisely (and the distance from this second exposition of becoming-minoritarian from the first is the greatest here), the idea of becoming-minor or of a "minoritarian as creative and created potential," means that this arrangement of power cannot tend to closure without having the process escape it and destabilize it all the more as it seeks closure. In the first place, these minoritarian processes are not simply defined by deviance, but by the non-coded or non-regulated characteristics of the distances that they introduce in the distributive or differential positions, requiring place to be given to the non-categorizeable, the non-distributable, disturbing binary oppositions. They form a sticking point that prevents objective representation from closing in on itself, or the social system from coinciding with the structure of oppositional relations that make it a system of distinctive positions.[16] Between the "positions," there are still fully livable and manipulable *transpositional* subjective processes; *between* the "states" of identity, there are always objective becomings that can be thought and practiced positively.

The essential point relies on the specific effectiveness of these "trans-identificatory" minoritarian processes that weaken any hegemonic or majoritarian construction internally. It is clear that the question of language, from *Kafka. Toward a Minor Literature* to the Plateau "Postulates of Linguistics," constituted a privileged terrain for elaborating the becoming-minor, in light of the role of the construction of a linguistic unity in the independence struggles of national minorities, and more profoundly in light of the fact that the *national language* is the fundamental hegemony, the one that supports all of the others and which, more than the privileged instrument, forms the material element itself. In this element, Deleuze and Guattari have already analyzed the irreducible instability of any hegemonic construction.[17] This gives political stakes to their thoughts on bilingualism, on the play of "code switching" inherent in language practices, and finally the thesis of a multi-lingualism immanent to each language: the deconstruction of the epistemological unity of the object "language" carried out by Félix Guattari in *The Machinic Unconscious* and taken up the next year in the 4th

Plateau, leads us to conclude in return that linguistic unity is always *forced* by operations of power *impossibly* crushing collective arrangements of enunciation on a system of homogeneous expression.[18] "How many people today live in a language that is not their own? Or no longer, or not yet, even know their own and know poorly the major language that they are forced to serve? This is the problem of immigrants, and especially of their children, the problem of minorities, the problem of a minor literature, but also a problem for all of us: how to tear a minor literature away from its own language, allowing it to challenge the language and making it follow a sober revolutionary path?"[19] The becoming-minoritarian work simultaneously against the empty universal of the hegemonic norm and against the inclusive-excluding particularization of the minority as sub-system. At least, they can gain this dual efficacy if determined arrangements are able to implement their practical appropriation. The minor "machines of expression" are like this, of which Kafka offers an example on the level of literary enunciation; they occupy a position of minority weakening the normative constants of the majority from the inside, but simultaneously draw this minority itself into a transformation that removes it from its state of sub-system—which does not abolish its "deviance" but makes it dissipative, in other words, unlocalizeable, unmeasurable by the major rule of the measure of distances and the assignment of unequal identities.[20]

Then, in second place, not being particularizeable or universalizable, this process does not enter into the dialectic between the universal of the community and the distributive particularity of its parts or its places, but belongs more to a "heterogeneous" in the sense of Bataille, or even more to the Klossowskian "simulacra" from which Deleuze draws inspiration in 1967–1968 to reinterpret the critical point where the test of the selection of pretenders stumbles (here, pretenders to the "name of the people"). This heterogeneity is

not conceived of as remains or as piercing the horizon of totalization, as it is following a logic of "inclusive disjunction," which
affects any binary relationship between major subject/minor subjects with an essential disturbance. Thus it does not enter positively
into the construction of an antagonistic conflictuality or a counter-
hegemonic majority, not because it is outside it, but on the contrary
because it displaces alliances and compositions within it, using the
very manner by which assigned-recognized, majorized or minorized
identifications are affected by an other that they cannot discriminate
without including it.[21] Not only becoming-other but even more, as
shown in different perspectives by Étienne Balibar, Eduardo
Viveiros de Castro, *becoming-the-other*,[22] in a twist which seems to
announce Rancière's "heterology" of political subjectivity, *from a
disidentification and an impossible identification*, one in the other ("la
cause de l'autre").[23] From there comes the idea that the critical
efficacy of this process works simultaneously against the empty universal of the hegemonic norm and against the excluding-inclusive
particularization of a minority as sub-system. Becoming-minor is a
process that fundamentally affects *the "major" subject itself*, but no
longer at all like in the first formulation, under the effect of capitalistic decodings and additions and subtractions of socio-State
axioms that "regulate" the deregulations, but to the extent that the
minorities themselves are able to enter into a becoming-minor that
affects their own "variables."

> One reterritorializes, or allows oneself to be reterritorialized, on
> a minority as a state; but in a becoming, one is deterritorialized.
> Even blacks, as the Black Panthers said, must become-black.
> Even women must become-woman. Even Jews must become-
> Jewish (it certainly takes more than a state). But if this is the
> case, then becoming-Jewish necessarily affects the non-Jew as

much as the Jew. Becoming-woman necessarily affects men as much as women.[24]

Not that women, Jews, and Blacks have to become "what they are" but precisely the contrary: the problem of an "active micropolitics" is to create as many points of alterity both included in the subject and of which however the assumption on the self-referential mode (*us as* women, Jews, homosexuals) is impossible, in other words to construct as many series of points of view (necessarily *singular* and not "individual") that cannot be occupied without the subject occupying them undoing, transferring, and displacing the identity constructions in which it is nonetheless determined to recognize itself (it is the "strangification," the internal distanciation or disjunction that Deleuze would later call a "fabulation" of identities, or in reference to Klossowski, their *simulation*).

Passing from one formulation of becoming-minoritarian to another, without forcing a united thematization—between becoming-minoritarian as a tendency *imposed* by the current configuration of the capitalist axiomatic of States, and becoming-minoritarian as created and creative potential of "de-hegemonization"—or between the minoritarian *produced* by macropolitics and the minoritarian convocated by micropolitics—Deleuze and Guattari clearly seek to avoid a schema of negativity and negation of negation, in other words a teleology *conversion* that is supposed to reverse capitalist destructiveness into political creativity, exploitation and oppression into forces of liberation, or again minorization, as an arrangement of power and technique of subjection into becoming-minor as disidentification from the dominant order and repoliticization of a potentially antagonistic subjectivity. Nonetheless, they constantly superpose the two conceptual maps. When they distinguish a majority defined by dominant axioms, minorities segregated as unequally "integrated" sub-systems to institutional, statutory, or juridical recognition, and minorities rejected "outside the system (depending on the case)," this distribution is clearly congruent with the distinction within which are combined and divided the social-democratic and neoliberal-authoritarian tendencies of capitalist politics, between axioms treating dominant flows, derived propositions resulting from axioms, flows rejected or left in the "wild state." To the extent that the terms "too much" or "less than"—produced as excesses (decoded, deregulated, or "de-axiomatized" flows abandoned to the repressive violence of the State), or actively subtracted, self-removed from the hegemonic organization and the unequal play of inclusive exclusion (the process of "becoming minor," as interruption of identity assignments)—seem, in spite of (or because of?) their inverse valence, to be finally rearticulated in a pattern of negation and its replacement. Take for example the notable ambiguity in the final formulations of the 13th Plateau, when a final aspect of the analogy with the logical axiomatics reveals a problem of "undecidable propositions" *created* by the axiomatic itself and that it is nonetheless incapable of dealing with. There follows, but in a much more undecidable fashion than the authors tell us, the greatest exposition of the combined violence of capitalist destructiveness, State repression, and the "majoritarian" hatred in which it sometimes finds justification, and the lines of resistance where the dominant powers cede the initiative to a "power" of response and bifurcation capable of breaking them:

> The situation seems inextricable because the axiomatic never ceases to create all of these problems, while at the same time its axioms, even multiplied, deny it the means of resolving them (for example, the circulation and distribution that would make it possible to feed the world). Even a social democracy adapted to

the Third World surely does not undertake to integrate the whole poverty-stricken population into the domestic market; what it does, rather, is to effect the class rupture that will select the integratable elements. And the States of the center deal not only with the Third World, each of them has not only an external Third World, but there are internal Third Worlds that rise up within them and work them from the inside. [...] The totalitarian tendency to abandon axioms of employment and the social democratic tendency to multiply statutes can combine here, but always in order to effect class ruptures. The opposition between the axiomatic and the flows it does not succeed in mastering becomes all the more accentuated.[25]

What defines a minority, then, is not the number but the relations internal to the number. A minority can be numerous, or even infinite; so can a majority. What distinguishes them is that in the case of a majority the relation internal to the number constitutes a set that may be finite or infinite, but is always denumerable, whereas the minority is defined as a nondenumerable set, however many elements it may have. [...]The axiomatic manipulates only denumerable sets, even infinite ones, whereas the minorities constitute "fuzzy," nondenumerable, nonaxiomizable sets [...].What is proper to the minority is to assert a power of the nondenumerable, even if that minority is composed of a single member. That is the formula for multiplicities.[26]

All of these difficulties, having direct repercussions on the practical-political problem of struggles against the global capitalist axiomatic and its different socio-State models of realization, can be illuminated by the symptomatic reading already mentioned. This reading will allow us in particular to test the hypothesis that through a series of returns and inversions, Deleuze and Guattari's concept of minorities comes to occupy the place of of the Marxist concept of revolutionary proletariat, and that it internalizes at the same time some presuppositions and some problematic nodes. It is therefore, among others, a possible formulation of the always more avoided difficulty, in these circumstances, to maintain the identification of the subject of emancipation that Marxism believed it could guarantee, and at the same time, the difficulty of thinking in the void carved out by its retreat. Yet I think it is equally useful for illuminating the divergences in the later interpretations of Deleuze and Guattari, and of which the oscillation can be found far beyond these two authors, between on the one hand the representations of a disseminated, eclipsed subject, almost unlocalizable (the anonymous instance of Rancière's "sans-parts" constitutes a brilliant illustration of this case), and on the other the representations of a new universal subject (the figure of the "multitude" forged by Negri and Hardt by offering undoubtedly the most emblematic version in its evocative force), all sorts of communication capable of being established between these two poles to bear witness communally of the power of a similar problematic dismissal.

Minorization and Proletarization in the Contemporary Capitalist Axiomatic: Social-Liberal Governmentality

To understand the effects of circulation between the two formulations of "becoming-minoritarian" mentioned above, it is of course necessary to keep the explicit yet above all conceptual distinction between the becoming-minoritarian as "created and creative potential," and minorities as "states," subsystems made minor by a system of power that constitutes them as such. We cannot overlook, however, the fact that the first is difficult to understand without reference to the second, unless minorities undergo an heroic idealization and there is an underestimation in return of the trials of heteronomy, fragility, and contingency that the authors of *Capitalism and Schizophrenia* often make understood in their conception of becoming. From this point of view again, the minoritarian strategy of Deleuze and Guattari, and the notion of becoming-minoritarian that condenses its expectations, risks being both theoretically unintelligible and politically empty, if not nihilistic, if they are not inscribed in the cartography in conjunction with the global capitalist axiomatic. On this basis, we can test the hypothesis that minoritarian struggles take the relay of class struggle in Deleuze and Guattari's analysis: this does not mean that they supplant it but rather that they extend it by complexifying its coordinates, by transforming its modes of realization, but also by internalizing some of its presuppositions and certain difficulties. As we have seen, it is in this finding of circumstances that "minorities," a floating signifier *par excellence*, are nonetheless perceived as a central referent of the modes of governmentality of integrated global capitalism. It thus gives an effective and macropolitical, reason for the scope that the question of minorities takes in Deleuze and Guattari, but also the dissemination of its motif in political thinking that never endeavors to subsume its multiplicity under an objective or subjective principle of identification, like a state or a class. It also allows us to shed light on the thematization, beyond the example of Kafka that motivates its first formulations, of the specific conflictuality of minorities, which leads Deleuze and Guattari to highlight in the multiplication of minoritarian groups the index of a revolutionary subjectivation, on a global scale.

Firstly, the factors related to the constitution of minorities are not fundamentally different from the factors of proletarianization. When Deleuze and Guattari write that "the power of minority, of particularity, finds its figure or its universal consciousness in the proletariat,"[27] it is in the first place because their concept of minority redraws the demarcating line of the base of Marxist communism and utopian communism. We find here a refusal to consider the socioeconomic structure's forces of rupture independently of the contradictory dynamics by which the structure sustains these forces within itself, and by which it at least partially conditions their forms of crystallization and effectuation. This is why they index their locating of becoming-minoritarian on the systematic dynamics of worldwide capitalism, which proceed *de facto* to their real generalization. Adhering to the geo-economic and geopolitical axes of capital accumulation within relations of unequal dependence between "Center" and "Peripheries," the following are considered by Deleuze and Guattari the principal factors which engender minoritarian sets: decodings of alimentary flows generating famine, decodings of populational and urban flows through the dismantling of indigenous habitats and urbanizations, and decodings of flows of matter-energy generating political and monetary instability. In accordance with the transformations of relations between constant capital and variable capital in the countries of the Center, the following lead to the formation of "peripheral" zones of underdevelopment within the countries of the Center itself: the development of a "floating" and precarious labor force of which "official subsistence is assured only by State allocations and wages subject to interruption," and the development of an "intensive surplus labor that no longer even takes the route of labor but goes through the modes of life, the collective forms of expression, the means of communication, circulation and consumption and so on. These sorts of "internal Third Worlds" or "internal Souths" foment many new struggles in all the linguistic, ethnic, regional, sexist, juvenile domains, but such struggles are always overdetermined by the systemic inequality of the IMC.[28]

The global capitalist system "minorizes" as much as it proletarianizes. The difference between the two points of view will therefore need to be further examined. The Marxist notion of the proletariat entails *at least*: its position within the structure of production, determined by its dispossession of the means of production and its insertion into the process of production as a pure, abstract labor force; the living conditions of the working population of big industry, which involve not only the homogenization of human misery, but populational concentration and the appearance of forms of cooperation which produce, within the "pores" of industrial sites, unheard of forms of solidarity, of relationships and collective consciousness; the power of *becoming* of that which thus tends to be constituted as a class, or following the expression of Etienne Balibar, its transitional value. While considering the surprising rarity within *Das Kapital* of the notion of the proletariat—a notion which nevertheless condensed until then for Marx all the implications of the "point of view of class"—Balibar remarks: "Everything happened as if the proletariat as such had nothing to do with the positive function that the exploited labor force carries out in the sphere of production, in so far as 'productive force' above all else; as if it had nothing to do with the formation of value, the transformation of surplus labor into surplus value, the metamorphosis of 'living work' into 'capital.'"[29] In a strikingly similar vein, Deleuze and Guattari's notion of minority seems firstly to involve a *signified* that remains problematic, and secondly to indicate nothing other than the transitional vector of a substratum which is fundamentally unstable and even unassignable (the "becoming-minoritarian of everybody"). However, no effacement of the *signifier* results; on the contrary, the signifier's proliferation is found at all levels of the analysis between 1975 and 1980, a proliferation which seems to challenge every attempt to reassemble their instances and occurrences into a unitary subjective, organizational, or strategic form.

This is because minorities are nothing other than "proletarianized" masses, but they are masses *inasmuch as they are immediately formed within* institutional, social, juridical and ideological structures of national States. Dissociated from a strictly economic determination of the proletariat as well as from a strictly sociological determination of the working class, the concept of minority records the State's process of socialization, that is to say, the process through which State power is incorporated into the social and institutional structures of the capitalist formation. We could thus call "minorization" that internal distance, in the process of proletarianization, between that which is expropriated of all social power throughout the structure of production, and that which is partially (and unequally) reintegrated into the liberal State-form, through social and political rights, statutory and symbolic recognitions, organs of representation and delegation. From which come a few corollaries:

1) The notion of minority consequently involves an irreducible multiplicity, which is neither soluble in the sketch of a contradiction between capital and labor, nor in the supposed homogeneity of workers' conditions. The minoritarian sets recall, in their very constitution, the variability of national frameworks and of State apparatuses which manage these sets, which partially integrate them, and which are immediately confronted in them with multiplicity: the variability of States' positions within the international division of labor and the unequal integration of their interior market into the global market; the variability of political structures and regimes fluctuating between social-democratic and totalitarian poles, namely between institutional and juridical integration of minorities as "subsystems," and exclusion "outside the system" of minorities subsequently abandoned to repressive State violence; the

correlative variability of the forms and degrees of development of minoritarian struggles; the variability of the types of political manipulation of minorities, be it to repeat the classical process of introducing competition between producers and sowing dissension into the working class, or the displacement of social and political conflicts onto "cultural" norms, which are more or less naturalized and apparently without immediate relation with the norms of economic exploitation (place of residence, ethnicity, linguistic or religious criteria, generational relations, sexual conduct, etc.). Yet the conflicts thus displaced onto the cultural terrain pose in turn sundry problems for the State.[32]

2) We can then understand in which way Deleuze and Guattari can superpose the two conceptual maps: the bipolarity of capitalist governments in the addition/subtraction of axioms (and the decoded flows that connect them or on the contrary deregulate and reject them "outside the system"); the majority/minority bipolarity (and the case of "becoming-minoritarian" that escapes both the major and minor as sub-system). A state of minority cannot be analyzed as a "state" that can be described with invariants or indicators of constants, in other words by projecting on it a stability that removes its very minorization. It is analyzed as a curve of variation, opened by a structure of inclusive exclusion between extreme situations that polarize it, between a tendency to inclusion in circuits of demand and social and political recognition, and a maximal exclusion that, at the limit, no longer includes anything, but deports or exterminates (populations minorized outside the system, subjected to State police violence, and potentially without any connection to the axiomatic and reduced to the status of "human waste") [33] Understanding this structure of exclusive inclusion thus implies understanding not only the chiasmus that defines it (and the political responses that it makes possible within social

and political institutions), but a spectrum of variations, shifts between situations that are not separated by any unequivocal frontier. This orients Deleuze and Guattari's analysis towards identifying the structural and circumstantial factors that make one modality of segregation pass into another or threaten to conjugate them according to removal of population and employment axioms or monetary and territorial axioms (social marginalization, spatial and cultural reclusion, exclusion from economic and political relationships), and which make possible or impossible the rise to these extremes. Within these factors, the struggles engaged in by organizations representing minorities within institutions of national and international public policy are essential and problematic, and in any case never exempt from the difficulties encountered by "struggles for recognition." These struggles are amphibological by nature, as suggested by the formalization of arrangements of minorization: the representative authorities must contribute to forging the identity of what they represent, or more exactly substitute one regime of identification for others; and they cannot be effective except by doing it in the regimes of utterances of the State authorities which they address, at the cost of a reduction of complexity—varying from one organization to another, and therefore inscribed in the political and strategic divergences of these organizations between each other—of the practices of collective existence involved. The reduction of this contrast, as we know, has only ever known one historical solution, as soon as a "minority" could establish itself as "nationalitarian" minority: the creation of a State, the Statification of the nation, and the nationalization of communities by social, linguistic, and cultural "ideological apparatuses" determining these communities to recognize their identity and their political unity in "their" State. Yet everywhere else:

It is hard to see what an Amazon-State would be, a women's State, or a State of erratic workers, a State of the "refusal" of work. If minorities do not constitute viable States culturally, politically, economically, it is because the State-form is not appropriate to them, nor the axiomatic of capital, nor the corresponding culture. We have often seen capitalism maintain and organize inviable States, according to its needs, and for the precise purpose of crushing minorities.[34]

3) Finally, the problem privileged in the last part of the 13th Plateau on the removal of the axioms of employment and deregulation of salary conditions touches on what was the nodal operator of the construction of a majority consensus in the post-war, social-capitalist States. It thus leaves open the possibility of understanding the difference between "becoming-proletarian" and "becoming-minoritarian" as a *difference internal to the proletariat itself*. It also allows us to confront Deleuze and Guattari's minoritarian strategy with the more recent debates on the "biopolitics of capital" or its "law of population" through which Marx highlighted the problem of "relative surplus population" caused by the structural contradictions of capital accumulation and exploitation of the labor force. For Marx, the proper of capitalist domination is not to proletarize but to *differentiate* the populations that it proletarizes. The expanded reproduction of capital does not occur without proletarizing an excess in relation to the force of labor that it can effectively "consume" in function of the existing capital, the sources of accumulation, and the rates of exploitation of surplus labor. What Marx calls relative surplus population, at the same time proletarized and external to the salary relationship, included in the labor market (which it even helps form) and excluded from labor (by the devalorization of labor force, the disqualification of know-how, and

structural unemployment) is the basic determination of inclusive exclusion as it comes into play in the bipolarity of capitalist States between a "social-democratic tendency" (adding axioms) and a "totalitarian tendency" (removing axioms). It is often said, as Deleuze and Guattari do, that minority struggles cannot simply be identified with the struggles of labor against capital. This is obvious, since the State first recruits its minorities in relative surplus population and segments them. Minorization is not to be confused with proletarization, but with its internal differentiation between the population subjected to the relationship with capital and the "supernumerary" population, which therefore poses specific problems of subsumption. For this reason, minorities are always caught to some extent in the process of economic and social expropriation of proletarization, inseparable from its diverse combinations of destructions and cultural and territorial "survivals." Yet this is also why they can in some cases maintain a certain degree of autonomy in their codes, or take as a mark of autonomy the coding—ethnic, religious, linguistic, etc.—in which the State "recognizes" them as "subsets."

This systematic result of relative surplus population directly affects the treatment of minorities because it touches on the articulation between the combinations of addition and subtraction of axioms of capitalist governmentalities, the specific economy of State violence that informs the structure of minorizaiton (between integration in "subsets" and exclusion "outside the system") and the unequal social, and geographic distribution of methods of expanded accumulation and primitive accumulation. In fact, the "*surplus-population*" differential does not operate in the same way, and its "relative" aspect does not have the same meaning, depending on the dynamics that command a) European primitive accumulation (preliminary proletarization), b) the primitive accumulation reproduced by historical accumulation as engine of the expanded reproduction of capital on a global scale (colonization), and c) the primitive accumulation internalized as engine of the involved reproduction of capital in its initial peripheral center (interior peripheralization or colonization). Marx has been critiqued for distinguishing primitive accumulation and accumulation proper as two successive historical phases, instead of analyzing their articulation as a permanent condition of the expanded reproduction of capital. However, this distinction positioned him better to distinguish different forms of surplus population, and the corresponding functions of State power, for which Deleuze and Guattari's thesis of internal peripheralization requires us to rethink in the current context of imbrication. In primitive accumulation,[35] the liberation of the two basic factors of an economic structure dominated by the accumulation of capital (formation of money-capital as independent investment power; formation of a "naked" labor force by expropriation and de-socialization of immediate producers) is not effectuated without a direct and constant intervention of State power in varying combinations of legal violence and brute repression (expropriation of small farmers, privatization of common goods, anti-vagabondage legislation and repression, etc.). Moreover, this intervention is necessary to *force* the combination of these two factors by the violent production of a surplus population as preliminary condition to the establishment of a labor market.[36] Yet to the extent that relationships of production are not mounted, this "accumulation" of proletarized mass becomes part of this surplus population. The latter can therefore be equally called relative and absolute: relative retrospectively, or by anticipatory recurrence in function of still non-existent socioeconomic relationships, it is an absolutely excessive surplus population, absolutely unexploitable, absolutely exposed to a violence of repression that is itself unproductive, and thus virtually exterminating (history of "bloody legislation" against supernumerary masses). This is so much the case that one should say that the "supernumerary" is first in relation to the rule of numeration, in other words in relation to the social relation that makes human multiplicities countable.[37]

As soon as this combination "takes root," however, and that the new relationships of production themselves directly determine the conditions of their own reproduction, we have seen what follows: not a disappearance of State violence but the transformation of its economy. Its direct violence is incorporated in relationships of production that it contributed to establishing and recodes the non-incorporated remainder in relationships of law that guarantee them under the authority of a State. This violence thus becomes structural, materialized and as if naturalized in the "normal" order of social relations; it no longer has to manifest itself brutally except under exceptional circumstances and earns a surplus legitimacy from only being exercised "exceptionally."[38] The crucial point is that surplus population becomes an *organic* piece of this incorporation of the genealogical violence of capital in the social relationships of production. It conditions the existence of a labor market that seems to only exercise its own, endogenous constraints on individuals, substituting for external State constraints the silent pressure of the supernumerary. This is why it is included in the rule of law, while concentrating the oscillations of State power between inclusion and exclusion, between addition and subtraction of axioms, and the corresponding modalities of State violence. The main strategies of capitalist governmentality are distributed according to this situation, according to their way of regulating the *"surplus*-population" differential: social-liberal strategies are inclined to treat relative surplus population as populations integrated in the relationships of production and to count them in the corresponding social institutions (constituting minorities as subsystems, giving a part to the "sans-part"); neoliberal strategies aspire to treat integrated populations as relative surplus populations and to destroy social institutions, according to the delirium of only ever dealing with capital and the enactment of this delirium in the elimination of what is not codeable in "human capital." One is no more cynical than the other, as cynicism is an immanent dimension of the structure itself,[39] as shown in the new form taken by the supernumerary.

> But under these conditions, the capitalist axiomatic continually produces and reproduces what the war machine tries to exterminate. Even the organization of famine multiplies the starving as much as it kills them. [...] However relentless the killing, it is relatively difficult to liquidate a people or a group, even in the Third World, once it has enough connections with elements of the axiomatic.[40]

In a sense, everything seems to change, in relation to primitive accumulation, as soon as the relationship of production is set up: both the nature of the population/surplus population differential and the meaning of relative and absolute. When the relationship of production constitutes the presupposition of its own cycle of expanded accumulation, surplus population is thus determined by this relationship itself, by the rhythm and scale of its destruction of non-capitalist social relations, and by its capacity to consume labor force. The indistinctness between relative and absolute thus takes on an objective or actual meaning in function of the real generalization of capital, which tends to become exclusive of any other social relationship: such that populations "relatively" excluded from this social relationship, or that no longer present enough connections with the axiomatic to be exploited, tend just as well to join in an absolute exclusion (not the "reserve industrial army but the "dead weight of its reserve"). If expanded accumulation is carried by a tendency to *saturation,* then primitive accumulation tends towards emptying,[41] the equivalents of which are rarely seen outside of colonial enterprises that begin, not by exploiting the indigenous populations, but first by emptying it, even if it means importing populations to exploit later.[42] Or more in conformance with the demands of an axiomatic: *a tendency to let emptiness happen* depending on the axioms retained and on their simple "natural" consequence (famine, climate or epidemiological disaster). When the internal peripheralization finally tends to remake the capitalist West a space of primitive accumulation, capital does not recolonize its former center without taking the form of a strange desire for a *tabula rasa*—a "depopulation of the people" while making the "earth uninhabitable"[43]—which restarts the great emptying, but this time at the heart of over-accumulation, which does not make it less violent, whether it takes again the form of forced emigration or the slow and invisible death of people in "instance of disappearance" in the middle of our streets.

Autonomy and Universality in Minoritarian Struggles: Blocks of Alliances and Becoming-Revolutionary

A final difference between becoming minoritarian and "becoming-proletariat" concerns the axiom put forward since *The Communist Manifesto*: the idea of a trend towards simplification of the antagonism supposed to oppose, increasingly clearly and inevitably, "two great classes directly facing each other," bourgeoisie and proletariat.[44] If the notion of minorities reactivates for Deleuze and Guattari the problem of the relation between the capitalist social machine and the politicizing of forces capable of shattering it, this very notion does not at all seem to guarantee a unified base, or a potentially unifiable subject, such as an objectively determinable class in which the possibility of a collective awareness and the work of its political construction could be localized. This is a difficulty which is above all political, and is the correlate of the one just mentioned which expressed (and constantly risked being concealed by) the thesis of the underlying simplification of the antagonism: in a way, this thesis clearly expressed the necessity of the construction of a proletarian politics outside of the State, while worker struggles forced the bourgeoisie to be recomposed as a class inside of the State. And yet, this thesis simultaneously tended to misjudge that same necessity. Indeed, complemented in Marxism by an underestimation of capitalism's inventiveness and the suppleness of institutional and State frameworks capable of developing the capitalist relations of production, it led to the conception of the relevant theoretical and practical problems as fated to be spontaneously resolved by the infallible historic evolution of the mode of production.[45] The multiplication of the functions of capital and the interests that they determine, the complexification of the processes of production, circulation, and consumption, the increase in State interventions within capitalist social relations and modes of distribution of social wealth, and then State internalization in breaks and compositions of class, reformulate the decisive problem of an autonomous politics of revolutionary movement: the invention of original forms of organization, but also of culture, thought and practices, capable of maintaining the asymmetrical character of conflict, and thus of creating within the revolutionary process the immanent conditions of a politics which would not be modelled on the forms of bourgeois politics or the practices of capitalist State power. In discussing the theory of the war machine, I mentioned these issues, which were at the heart of Guattari's reflections on the *institutional creativity* within the labor movement as early as the 1960s. Deleuze and Guattari do not leave them behind, while leaving the formulas sufficiently unstable to indicate that the problem goes beyond theoretical prescriptions:

> The question of a revolution has never been utopian spontaneity versus State organization. When we challenge the model of the State apparatus or of the party organization which is modelled on the conquest of that apparatus, we do not, however, fall into the grotesque alternatives: either that of appealing to a state of nature, to a spontaneous dynamic, or that of becoming the self-styled lucid thinker of an impossible revolution, whose very impossibility is such a source of pleasure. The question has always been organizational, not at all ideological: is an organization possible which is not modelled on the apparatus of the State, even to prefigure the State to come? Perhaps a war-machine with its lines of flight?[46]

Not only do minoritarian struggles encounter these problems in turn, but they confront them in an even more direct fashion, precisely because the minoritarian sets are immediately constituted in the socio-institutional tissue of the State, immediately part and partisan of its contradictory tendencies (social-democrats/neoliberal-authoritarians) and the working-class struggles that affect its combinations. The problem of the political autonomy of a new revolutionary movement is even more crucial for Deleuze and Guattari, since it condenses their evaluation of the ambivalent success of the worker movement. On the one hand, it succeeded in imposing a class duality and social antagonisms which brought the proletariat out of its state of minority, in the specific sense of a subsystem integrated into the new "industrial system," as the Saint-Simonians would say. On the other hand, it proved itself less and less capable of calling into question its own class identity (and its "universal class" identity, destining it to establish a transitional new hegemony), whereas the political and union apparatuses, which were supposed to materially incarnate it, tended to be incorporated into the State-form as organs of conflict regulation within the social State, or as "driving belts" within the domination of a totalitarian bureaucracy.[47] This is the source of Deleuze and Guattari's interest in Operaismo (Workerism) and in particular Mario Tronti's "strategy of refusal," wagering on the antecedence of worker's resistance to the strategies and "planning" of capital organized in the context of a Fordist State which, organizing the working proletariat itself as a class-function of capital, risked less to open the space for a "class struggle without classes" (of which minoritarian struggles would still be a figure) than, on the contrary, that of a working class without struggle.[48]

Yet Deleuze and Guattari see in it a further reason to maintain the distinction between minoritarian strategy and revolutionary strategy working to reverse a hegemony by the construction of an alternative hegemony, not without highlighting at the same time the irreducible limits of the struggles of minorities internal to institutional, juridical, and political structures of the State.[49] The first part of this assessment seems to be motivated by a libertarian impulse and the second part appears to reactivate familiar critiques of Parliamentarianism and reformism. Deleuze and Guattari's analysis is, however, more complex because it engages the internal contradictions of the modern State in that it develops within its national framework the capitalistic relations of production required by an enlarged accumulation and reproduction process, which passes through a worldwide division of labor and a transnationalization of capital movements. As simultaneously instruments of capital valorization and the management of systematic disequilibria and crises, the State institutions concentrate within themselves all the contradictions of the process of accumulation. They also negotiate for better or for worse its social repercussions according to both the degree of socialization of their political, economic and juridical apparatuses and the level of corresponding social struggles. For as much as the minoritarian groups are themselves taken up in the variable combinations of institutional integration and repression, and for as much as they take part in these contradictions internal to the State, their struggles cannot fail to take place inside of it. "Their tactics necessarily go that route": "this is not to say that the struggle on the level of the axioms is without importance; on the contrary, it is determining (at the most diverse levels: women's struggle for the vote, for abortion, for jobs; the struggle of the regions for autonomy; the struggle of the Third World; the struggle of the oppressed masses and minorities in the East or West...)."[50] And what is more, these struggles inside of the juridical, political and economic institutions of States are not only tactically inevitable but *strategically necessary*. They are necessary to generate pressure and to influence the conditions in which the State develops, within its own order and its own power, the relations of production of global capitalist accumulation (contrary to the mystifying representation of a capitalist system which simply and purely transcends States). These struggles interior to the institutions of the State are necessary to exacerbate the distance between the constraints of global accumulation and the impotence of States to "regulate" their repercussions, whether those be economic, social, cultural, ecological (contrary to the no less mystifying representation of an omnipotent technocracy contributing to the simplifying reduction of every struggle within the State to a "recuperation" which could only be avoided through some isolated regional struggles renouncing all global strategy and all exterior support).[51] Since so many ideological readings have falsified this point, I would underline that there is no sense from this point of view in *opposing* minority struggles and the struggles of the working class, which are all the more necessary in that they are faced with the same difficulties (the problem is instead to know what forms these struggles can take or take again, when the working class, if not by tendency the salaried classes, tends to be re-minoritized by the subtraction of the axioms of employment and the de-institutionalization of relative surplus population):

> It would be an error to take a disinterested stance toward struggle on the level of the axioms. It is sometimes thought that every axiom, in capitalism or in one of its States, constitutes a "recuperation." But this disenchanted concept is not a good one. The constant readjustments of the capitalist axiomatic, in other words, the additions (the enunciation of new axioms) and the withdrawals (the creation of exclusive axioms), are the object of struggles in no way confined to the technocracy. Everywhere, the workers' struggles overspill the framework of the capitalist enterprises, which imply for the most part derivative propositions. The struggles bear directly upon the axioms that preside over the State's public spending, or that even concern a specific international organization (for example, a multinational corporation can at will plan the liquidation of a factory inside a country). [...] But the pressure of the living flows, and of the problems they pose and impose, must be exerted inside the axiomatic, as much in order to fight the totalitarian reductions as to anticipate and precipitate the additions, to orient them and prevent their technocratic perversion.[52]

The "local struggles" evoked here are explicitly distinguished from sectorial struggles that "imply for the most part derivative propositions" and of which the limits come directly, in Deleuze and Guattari's terms, from *the respective independence of the axioms [...]* that comes from the divisions and sectors of the capitalist mode of production," and the socio-technological and economic structurings of the functions of capital, revealing in their dynamic imbalance that "the difference and independence of the axioms in no way compromise the consistency of the overall axiomatic."[53] While "local struggles," as illustrated in the examples given in these pages, "directly target national and international axioms, at the precise point of their insertion in the field of immanence" (a multinational, according to the now common example, planning the liquidation of a production site in a country…), revealing the stubborn particularity that capitalist policies are opposed with in places where they seek to simply draw the consequences of their axioms: "However modest the demand, it always constitutes a point that the axiomatic cannot tolerate: when people demand to formulate their problems themselves, and to determine at least the particular conditions under which they can receive a more general solution (hold to the *Particular* as an innovative form)."[54] Far from being secondary, this point is at the center of the diagnosis that Deleuze and Guattari make, in 1984, that French society was entering its twilight years, the symptom of which was its repression of May 1968.[55] To the exogenous factors (the offensives of international capital against the franc) and endogenous factors (the evolution of internal power relationships within the Socialist Party in favor of its social-liberal wing) generally called on to explain the "turn to rigor" in the spring of 1983, Deleuze and Guattari add a first principle without which the preceding factors would not have such binding effect: the renunciation, *as early as 1981*, of including working-class demonstration and initiatives in social change when it was necessary for "society [to] be capable of forming collective arrangements corresponding to the new subjectivity, in such a way that it wants change" and without which any "real 'reconversion'" would be stifled before it began. It is precisely at the level of this institutional and organizational creativity implied by popular mobilization ("hold the *Particular* as innovative form") that is played out—created, displaced, reified, or reworked the differential between spontaneity and organization that the debates within the Third International had finished by cementing into a binary alternative, and that there can be a practical approach to the problem of the remanence and fixation that compromise revolutionary transformation in the very agents who claim to lead it.[56] The *nolle prosequi* of May 1968 diagnosed in 1984 does not indicate the failure of its effects but on the contrary the failure to inscribe these effects in practical, discursive, theoretical, or organizational traces through processes of institutionalization which would have been the only way to support the rearrangements of political subjectivity required by the event. This non-pursuit is accompanied by a foreclosure of the subjective-institutional problem, which could leave no other alternative than between the fantasy of an omnipotent technocracy "which would implement from above the necessary economic reconversion" on the one hand, and on the other, subjects made vulnerable and relegated to "controlled 'situations of abandon,'" with no other solution than to give themselves up to "American-style wild capitalism," or to seize on the tired, old institutional solutions of Family, Religion, and Nation that feed the reactionary obsession of Order and the hysteria of Identities.[57]

But then, *in this very movement* where they operate within State apparatuses and their institutions, these struggles reveal themselves simultaneously as "the index of another, coexistent combat" which, directly or indirectly, puts into question the global capitalist axiomatic itself to the extent that they confront the obstacles that their function of "effectuation" imposes on State politics:

> It is always astounding to see the same story repeated: the modesty of the minorities' initial demands, coupled with the impotence of the axiomatic to resolve the slightest corresponding problem. In

short, the struggle around axioms is most important when it manifests, itself opens, the gap between two types of propositions, propositions of flow and propositions of axioms. [...]The issue is not at all anarchy versus organization, nor even centralism versus decentralization, but a calculus or conception of the problems of nondenumerable sets, against the axiomatic of denumerable sets. Such a calculus may have its own compositions, organizations, even centralizations; nevertheless, it proceeds not via the States or the axiomatic process but via a pure becoming of minorities.[58]

At this second, simultaneous front, according to Deleuze and Guattari, the autonomy of a revolutionary politics of minorities passes primarily through a critique of the two "cuts" or two boundaries by which the capitalist State codes its social groups in the form of a nation, the basic axiom or "the very operation of a collective subjectification,"[59] which minorities always more or less internalize but under necessarily conflicting conditions: a) a *national/extra-national boundary*, which tends to make minorities (usually immigrant minorities, but also potentially every minority, whatever their criteria of segregation) *interior foreigners* or even "internal enemies" (a trend that we can expect to increase, according to Deleuze and Guattari's analysis of the changes in capitalists of the "center" by the factors of "third-worldization" or internal peripheralization); b) an *individual/collective* boundary, which inscribes in the structure of the "major" national subjectivity a private-public division which is particularly problematic regarding the subjective position of minorities (but also accompanies the methods of neutralization of public space analyzed in "control societies").[60] The isolation and thus the "communitarianization" of minoritarian struggles proceed through these two boundaries. They form the double bind of a State strategy of differential and unequal integration into the national community and identity. They permit the State to confine their demands to the private sphere as only relevant to strictly individual problems, or else to tolerate their collective impact and political significance on the condition that they do not begin to connect to international coordinates or other minoritarian groups.

If the actual becoming of the world determines the emergence of "a universal figure of minoritarian consciousness as the becoming of everybody," and if this raises problems that the hypothetical construction of no other hegemony would be capable by itself of resolving, these problems are *a fortiori* barred in advance when burying oneself inside of one's minority, one's particularism, which is only a breeding ground for marginalism. "It is certainly not by using a minor language as a dialect, by regionalizing or ghettoizing, that one becomes revolutionary; rather, by using a number of minority elements, by connecting, conjugating them, one invents a specific, unforeseen, autonomous becoming,"[61]—a becoming which then passes necessarily through transversal connections between various struggles, in a national and international space. This is a strategic line and also a criterion of evaluation. Minorities are certainly not revolutionary in themselves. Yet the problem remains that of an evaluation *immanent* to the very struggles they engage in, to the practical style of these struggles, to the modes of existence which they suppose, to the problems which they enunciate and the demands which they make (or to the utterances which they more or less consciously interiorize). For Deleuze and Guattari, the base criterion of such an evaluation is their variable aptitude to join with other struggles, to connect their problems to others which may be very different regarding interests and group identities—"a constructivism, a "diagrammatism," operating by the determination of the conditions of the problem and by transversal links between problems: it opposes both the automation of the capitalist axioms and bureaucratic programming."[62] In all these ways, the true effect of minoritarian struggles in the actual conjuncture—namely at the moment when Deleuze and Guattari can affirm that "our age is becoming that of minorities" and that this tendency of the present reopens "the question of the becoming-revolutionary of people, at every level, in every place"—is not communitarianism, according to an already republicanized conception of minorities throughout a universal incarnated in the *État de droit* or Rule of law. It is rather a *new internationalism* which excludes the State-form. Its task would be to construct a "minoritarian universal" that would express both *practices of universality* which are more effectively real than the universality of the national-capitalist State, and a composition of power at least as powerful, confronted with the capitalist system, as the historic worker movement.

Here, as we know, lies the problem. Or rather, "the minoritarian becoming as universal figure of consciousness" or of political subjectivation: can it claim more than to name generically the immense practical-political problems that have not stopped causing difficulties for the last forty years?[63] At the very least, the revolutionary workers' movement could claim, even at the price of countless self-delusions, a real underlying universality, correlative with the historic movement of the concentration of capital resuscitating from itself its most profound negativity: a new collective subject, a bringer of a universal interest, a precursor of a society itself universal, liberated from private property as principle of particularization and antagonistic division of the social field. It is certain that minorities must politically work their own particularities—not renounce the "particular" element to the extent that it animates a mode of construction of social, economic or political problems, capable of joining in their technocratic administration by the class fractions holding social-State institutions which in many cases means working politically against their "particularism" such as it is managed by these institutions. They undoubtedly have to fight against the double boundary, being both interior (private/public) and exterior (national/international), which allows the functioning of the national coding of minoritarian groups.[64] Yet it is in function of other social and political practices and institutions that the sense of a "minoritarian strategy" is determined in Deleuze and Guattari, carving a separate path in relation to the collective identifications instituted (whether the principle is found in cultural values, economic interests, behavioral norms, or even cultural policies), without however reinvesting the synecdochal scheme that commanded the subjectivation of the democratization struggles since the "bourgeois" revolutions: the Third Estate of Sieyès, assuming all the tasks useful to society, but held itself for nothing and aspiring to be something; the industrial proletariat, *eigentlos*, carrying a universal interest by its very exclusion from private property distributing the particular interests of bourgeois society; the uncounted part of the "sans-parts" carrying without title the unconditionality of equality, taking for themselves the empty name of the community by politicizing the dispute over what is excluded from it...

This double distance, the fragile path between these two positions with which it coexists, explains that becoming-minoritarian is finally identified with a problem of *alliance* and composition of alliances. This problem relates as much to the relationships between majority and minorities as to the relationships of minorities between each other (but the two problems are connected if we take into account the fact that minorization as a technology of power always implies a hierarchization—and relationships of power—*between minorities*).[65]

With the problem of conceiving of a "minoritarian universal" which would be constructed by and within a revolutionary process taking up the contradictions of the current capitalist world, and that yet does not entertain the fantasy of the messianic universality of a new subject, the theory of "blocks of alliances" leads us to think of a practice of intensive universality, one that does not refer to the universality of an interest or a common identity but a co-transformation. When Deleuze and Guattari write that a minority has to become-minoritarian ("it certainly takes more than a state"), they see it as a way to form simultaneously an "agent" or an "active medium" through which another subject "enters a becoming-minoritarian that rends him from his major identity"[66] (which the thesis of internal peripherization also leads us to understand on the level of international relations, from the perspective of a "de-Westernization" of the historical center of capitalist globalization). Active medium, the minority becomes by the same token a vanishing mediator since it implies "two simultaneous movements, one by which a term (the subject) is withdrawn from the majority, and another by which a term (the medium or agent) rises up from the minority. There is an asymmetrical and indissociable block of becoming, a block of alliance.[67] As the heterogenous matrix of political subjectivation, I have already suggested the affinity of this double-becoming with what Rancière developed a few years later in the node of disidentification in relation to points of hegemonified points of identification and an impossible identification with the uncounted Other. For Deleuze and Guattari, however, the power of an "uncountable" capable of calling into question the axioms on which the count of the majority is based, the counting of its minorized "subsystems," the miscounting of those "outside the system," implies a practice of alliance of which the possibility does not *result* from the disidentification from assigned identities (majoritarian or minoritarian), but on the contrary conditions and provokes it, which prevents circumscribing the dispute of the minorized sans-parts without questioning the incidences it is capable of producing on the majoritarian order and those who are subjectivated there. We could also ask, from this point of view, whether the matrix of a block of alliance is not underlying a certain view of a "simplification of antagonism," in the form of a reduction of identificatory possibilities *between which* these double-becomings become urgent and necessary. Yet that would lead, by the same token, and by extending the stakes of micropolitics beyond its first formulations in Deleuze and Guattari, to questioning the reactions that a majority can oppose to its own becoming-minor, without misjudging its ambivalence, resistance, and even extreme violence.

It would only be another way of signifying that, if it is by the multiplication of these "blocks of alliances" or a double becoming that the "becoming-minoritarian of everyone" can occur as a *political construction*, its process does not refer more to the emerging spontaneities of "life" than to the opportunistic awakenings of "History." Perhaps this point only remains obscure because of two theoretical errors which compromise the politics of minorities for Deleuze and Guattari. They are two *political* errors precisely because they result from an overly "theorizing" vision of their thought. The first is speculating *abstractly* on "the" becoming, outside of the couplings of always contextualized becomings which make of them problems of collective experimentation capable of rendering identity positions *in reality abstract*. The second is the error of (theoretically) making the multiple a given, in being or in a transcendental structure, while it is *to be made* (practically) and is only effectively constructed by these dynamic couplings, in these connections of asymmetrical becomings. "Before being, there is politics,"[60] and before ontology, there is strategy. The constructions of alliances decide both the type of multiplicity that are promoted and the practices of identity which are invented or reproduced.

Certainly we must then give up the assumption that a collective consciousness could only have as possible content a common identity (the identity of "objective interests," problems or conditions), to accede to a universal consciousness having for content a community of interdependent transformations capable of modifying in their turn the very form of the universal. Then we must consider a universality of a process of relational inventions, and not of an identity of subsumption; a universality which is not projected forward in a maximum of identitary integration, but which is programmed and reshuffled in a maximum of transversal connections between heterogeneous systems; rather than a socio-logical universal as category or class, a tactical and strategic universal as an indefinite dynamic system of practice of alliance, where the alliance proceeds neither through integration of terms into a superior identity that homogenizes them, nor through mutual reinforcement of differential identities, but through the blocks of asymmetrical becomings where a term may become other thanks to the becoming-other of another term which is itself connected to an *nth* in an open series. No longer an extensive and quantifiable universality, but on the contrary an intensive and unquantifiable universality, in the sense that subjects become in common in a process where their identitary anchorages tend to take on a plasticity that makes them manipulable and transformable. From this point of view, becoming is a practices of *transference,* and it lodges in the heart of the problem of political organization a question of institutional transference that directly connects with the radically constructivist conception of autonomy required by a new minoritarian internationalism.[69] *Minorities of all countries, are you becoming...?* Excessive formulas, we said. I will conclude with the symptomatic evidence in this "excess."

Conclusion

Micropolitics Did Not Take Place

In the last chapter, I highlighted the way in which Deleuze and Guattari's concept of the minoritarian reinterpreted the figure of the proletariat, which is none other than the Marxist and socialist concept of becoming-revolutionary, through a series of transformations. Yet this figure is not the only one involved. It is nonetheless remarkable that the theme of minorities combines multiple temporalities and geographies, through the examples mentioned and the analysis of cases retained by Deleuze and Guattari, allowing their conjunctions and conflicts to communicate. The first given, as general as it is patent, is clearly the constitution of minorities within the ideological form of the *Nation*, within historical processes that themselves vary from the construction of *national subjectivities*, of which minorities are a correlative and recurrent effect:[1] "Not only are [nations] constituted in an active struggle against the imperial or evolved systems, the feudal systems, and the autonomous cities, but they crush their own 'minorities,' in other words, minoritarian phenomena that could be termed 'nationalitarian,' which work from within and if need be turn to the old codes to find a greater degree of freedom. The constituents of the nation are a land and a people."[2] And a people is subjected to the status of minority first by depriving it of its land, no less than its language, by treating it as a land empty of people,[3] no less than a dead or folkloric language. Yet these very nationalitarian phenomena, produced or "counter-produced" by nationalist constructions, make a return when the nation-State, through the formation of a transnational bourgeoisie and the antagonistic divisions that fragment the capitalist class itself, sees the *hegemonic* function of the nation return, making it available once again for independentist demands,[4] but also capable of giving in to the hystericization of identity in a compensatory and reactive way.

Partially covering this first stratum, a specific value should be given to the fact that the question of minorities is introduced in their study of Kafka, a study that resituates his literary work in a precisely determined context, one for which the developments and after-effects allow it to communicate with heterogeneous times, including our own. Deleuze and Guattari read the minor "machines of expression" as an *analytical process* that succeeded in capturing the still unrepresentable forces of the near future in the social field, and in exposing the arrangements of utterance and collective positions of desire that emerged from the Great War, the radicalization of European nationalisms, the new forms of bureaucratic power, the changes in capitalism across the Atlantic....[5] In this very way, the labor of the work is also that of a schizoanalysis or a stratigraphy of European subjectivity. First involved, of course, are the social and historical coordinates with which Kafka's writing is directly engaged: shifting borders and migratory movements related to the history of imperialism, to the dismemberment of the last two multinational empires on the continent, to the movements of annexation and creation of States, to territorial reworkings and displacements of populations resulting from the War of 1914. Given the portrait of the global capitalist axiomatics and the tendential, geo-economic, and geopolitical mutations that our authors find in it, the problem of minorities as they first describe it in the context of Kafka also works as a symptom of the return of a repressed, inscribing European subjectivity in the critical closing of a historical sequence that began with the decentering of the world-economy to US power, the construction of the Soviet bloc and the geopolitical bipolarization of the world-economy, and the tenacity of colonial domination already contested from every side. What returns are the conditions that opened this sequence and gave rise simultaneously to the production of the "problem of minorities" *in its immediately European dimensions*: when at the end of the First World War, the condition of minority was Europeanized by the way in which the major victorious or defeated powers determined the conditions of a pacified European system and made minorities the laboratory of new practices of mass subjection, from measures withdrawing rights to pure and simple denaturalization and deportation.[6] There is the return of the unending after-effect that systematization of the State-national form offer itself on the European continent: establishing the minority as an organic piece of a continental nomos founded on the territorial and identitarian articulation of the State(=)nation, the structural inability of this system to go without the techniques of minorization that are part and parcel of this articulation, the chronic need to reactivate economic rivalries and intra-continental policies to monetize them as well as the working class struggles and demands within each State. We know the scope of the signifying batteries that crystallized under these conditions, starting with the signifier "minority" itself, its rapid inflation in the legal vocabulary of international law, but also its inscription in a series of new cuts and connections (internal immigrant/stateless, internal enemy/foreign worker, colonization/proletarization…) within which minorization as an arrangement of power was redefined. And there is nothing about them which can lead us to believe that they no longer exist for us as well. In her analysis of these conditions, Arendt makes this crucial remark in passing: "The national liberation movements of the East were revolutionary in much the same way as the workers' movements in the West; both represented the 'unhistorical' strata of Europe's population and both strove to secure recognition and participation in public affairs. Since the object was to conserve the European status quo, the granting of national self-determination and sovereignty to all European peoples seemed indeed inevitable; the alternative would have been to condemn them ruthlessly to the status of colonial peoples (something the pan-movements had always proposed) and to introduce colonial methods into European affairs."[7] *Fluctuatio animi* in the new nomos of the Earth: as if States had hesitated between two solutions, two ways of concluding their *Pax Europa*: either generalized minorization or an intra-continental colonization. Since the second had led to triggering the war, the victorious powers opted for generalization of the nation-State to the entire continent, systematizing the subordination of the institutions of citizenship to the principle of nationality, and "inclusively excluding" from the new States almost a third of their populations that were officially recognized as being in an exceptional situation, placed under the special protection of international organizations powerless to have it respected in the very name of the principle of national sovereignty from which the state of minority came. To preserve the status quo, European powers adopted a method that made the status quo just as impossible as the other, making this impossibility even more explosive than ever. It made minority statuses perpetual in the European political system, opened the field of inexpiable national conflicts in the new States created in the East, called on social-democratic and nationalist alliances to repress labor rebellions in the West, prepared—where alliances revealed themselves to be insufficient—to unleash fascist organizations to complete the task, *and also introduced colonial methods* into European affairs, beginning with measures of subjection and semi-citizenship already tested in the colonies, partial rights for national minorities, and a permanent state of exception for stateless minorities. Each new failure in the working class construction of European citizenship, like the one Deleuze and Guattari were concerned about in 1977–1978 in seeing this hypothetical construction crushed by the formation of a police-judicial space cemented around the interests of the dominant economic powers,[8] could already appear to be a new way to prepare European States to reproduce their techniques of segregation and repression inherited from this complex of internal colonization, treating populations in turn as colonized of exiles, national minorities and stateless, internal immigrants or without a country.

Deleuze and Guattari may see minorities as the nodal reference of contemporary capitalist policies because this reference combines multiples scenes, which has the pitfall, as we have seen, that the minority strategy, the vectorization of theoretical-practical problems— of political subjectivation and conscientization, of strategic organization and programming—carried by the minority signifier, condense a multiplicity of fronts that cannot be reduced to a simple political line. Close to the analyses of Hannah Arendt on minorities as a "permanent institution" of the European nation-State system,[9] reinterpreting the analyses of William Benjamin as well on the "aesthetic" construction of a national people by fascism and more generally the contradictory historical investments of the Nation as an operation of collective subjection,[10] identifying the internalization of mechanisms of colonial domination in the countries of advanced capitalism, and opening at the same time a questioning of its effects on intra continental relationships of force, on the modes of antagonistic subjection but also the micro-fascisms and anti-minoritarian tensions made possible by this "internal peripheralization," Deleuze and Guattari propose a formula that condenses this plurality of genealogical paths of emergence of the becoming-minoritarian as a paradoxically dominant mode (*indominant?*) of subjection of emancipatory conflicts, in a context where the "names of the people"—Nation, Proletariat, Colonized—have become floating, if not unavailable: "*The people are missing.*" The people are missing and it is under the conditions where they are missing that minorities are determined to occupy their place or invent other places. The highly overdetermined aspect of this formula, which can take on heterogenic and even antinomic meanings, and is therefore one that no theoretical decision can decide on *a priori*, will become clearer by unfolding briefly, and to conclude, the multiplicity of internal scenes that populate and dramatize it.

The people are missing... First, this expression has a history that increases its resonances and meanings. Deleuze and Guattari sometimes attribute it to Kafka while borrowing it from Paul Klee at the Jena conference in January 1924 where he was describing the post-revolutionary period of Bauhaus of the years 1919–1922, in particular the problems posed by the project of "the union of art and people" in a *Gesamtkunstwerk*. The expression is inseparable from its date and from the context of utterance that imprints it in a historical scene painted with hope and blood: the Revolution of 1917, the possibility of its spread to the country with the strongest labor movement in Europe, the November Revolution and the brief Republic of Councils violently repressed by the SPD armed with the *Freikorps*. From there, this expression refers to an indissociably aesthetic and political problem present throughout the 19th century, Romanticism, the period of Wagner's anarchist sympathies and his first theories of the *gemeinsame Kunstwerk der Zukunft*, the common work of art of the future, from which Gropius borrowed the canonical expressions in the *Bauhaus Manifesto* in 1919, shortly before it was instrumentalized by the German fascists. From there, the people is missing, not only because the revolutionary proletariat was bloodily repressed, but because the people was irreversibly divided in the history of antagonistic ideological-political investments of its concept, while the total work of art that was supposed to unify a collective subject anticipating in it an action to come, soon brings the project for art of the masses to serve the proletarian and international construction of the "total person" in the ideological bosom of national revolution, vital community, and race regeneration.[11]

This is already enough to make the initial expression somewhat ambiguous, leaving the recognition of the minoritarian as political subjectivation to be understood in two quite different ways. "The people is missing" could mean that it is only present through a particular insistence that only applies to it, for the unconditional equality or political universality of which it is the name: by a minority that takes the place of the people in its absence, which is equivalent to this people not given and thus, even in impotence and oppression, gives it its presence by recalling its necessity in its absence. Thus, "The moment the master, or the colonizer, proclaims 'There have never been people here,' the missing people are a becoming, they invent themselves, in shanty towns and camps, or in ghettos, in new conditions of struggle to which a necessarily political art must contribute."[12] However, it can also mean the opposite, that the minoritarian is what takes the place of this absence itself, which makes present not the missing people, but the lack itself, making this *lack in person* an act of resistance against the forces that project the image of the existence of this current people or one to come, for which we cannot proclaim the full presence without already enclosing the elimination of minorities. Such that through its obstinate reiteration from book to book, the "expression" starts to resonate in the Lacanian sense in which Deleuze uses it for example in Bartleby's sentence *I would prefer not to. The people is missing…*, an expression saved from disaster, on the edge of collapse, and of which only its insistence would still face every claim to constitute a subject of utterance representing the whole.

That minorities can be seen as centers of a political subjectivity capable of instantiating the People in its absence, therefore, in that it only exists to be reaffirmed by a place-holder that cannot, however, be identified with it or appropriate its name, is no doubt what makes it a privileged analyzer for Deleuze and Guattari for the historical-conceptual aporia of contemporary political subjectivation, at the same time as the decisive operator of the recompositions of emancipatory politics. Not that this makes their forms and issues more predictable. The reading Étienne Balibar has proposed of Deleuze and Guattari's "minority strategy," in the framework of an updating of what he calls "the antinomy of anti-State civility" seems to me to be perfectly well-founded from this point of view.[13] The question of the rise to "extreme objective and subjective violence" remains on its horizon, because it's always a question of questioning the limits of the political field from the difficulties there are in assigning to politics conditions of possibility that do not include its conditions of impossibility. For this reason, I looked to discern different ways to illimiting violence or to give rise to its aneconomic figures in *Capitalism and Schizophrenia*, taking the materialism of "machinic processes" as a guide. Yet it also connects with a fundamental intuition of Deleuze and Guattari's thinking on politics, according to which the contingence and finiteness of politics are irreducible, or rather constantly put back into play, because it is submitted to something heterogeneous, under the dependence of an authority that, from another place than the one where political practice can take hold, exposes it constantly to a *contingency of contingency* itself. To put it another way: this authority constantly displaces the conditions of politics, can transform them but also destroy them at the limit, even though it is not uninscribable in the order of political rationalities where it produces these effects, even though it cannot be translated into practical syllogisms of means and ends, can be proportional to tactical calculations and strategic anticipations, axiomatizeable in instituting rights and duties and in the instruments of regulation of historic relationships of force.

To problematize this authority, theoretically but also practically, Deleuze and Guattari propose at one time the concept of "desiring process" (or schizophrenic desire), followed by that of "becoming-minoritarian." Both are forged in the insistent interrogation of historical fascism and the permanent mechanisms of influence of a mass micro-fascism in the post-war, national-capitalist States. This leads to the importance of the "between-the-wars tropism" of Deleuze and Guattari's thought on politics and the State through-out the book. In their work together, they always saw fascism as a nodal aporia of politics: the inability to gain an aptitude to manipulate the unconscious crystallizations of collective identifica-tions, in the urgency of conditions marked by a manipulation of the unconscious on a mass scale through which political space itself was destroyed. This is the problem Deleuze and Guattari brought out in the inaugural concerns of Reich's Freudian-Marxism, in light of which the theoretical and practical claims of both Freudianism and Marxism should have been tested: the problem of mechanisms of collective identification and finally of the place one is ready to give in political analysis to the work of fantasy, the imagination of institutional and "historical-global" identifications, including in their extreme forms of depersonalization or on the contrary of hystericalization and delirium of identities (although to put it correctly, extreme forms communicate, singularly in periods of eco-nomic and political crisis where the competition between States, their populations, and their territories is exacerbated). Yet this would also deepen the practical implications, and ask again the fundamental problem of a politics of emancipation appointing and being appointed to the autonomy of its subject: the problem of the heteronomy of this politics itself, which never fully masters its own conditions. Once again, this takes the problem to its "excess" limit: the limit of an unpoliticalizable, heterogeneous authority, this other stage of the unconscious where the impasses and crises that traverse its agents are symptomatically inscribed. These symptoms, theorized as "desiring machines" then as "becoming," incapable of integration in a political, strategic, or even ethical-social rationality in the sense of a Hegelian *Sittlichkeit*, can however return abruptly on the level of the relationship with the body and language, art and sexuality, space and history, forming traces of self-heterogeneity of the subjects of political intervention: this calls for the construction of an analytical space *sui generis*, one that allows for points of reference to be arranged while warding off the disasters risked by the ambition to take absolute hold over them. Deleuze and Guattari would thus bring the instance of the minoritarian, or this "complex" within which a resistance is subjectivized and collectivized, into the most muddled proximity with the violence which it confronts. A complex that is expressed profoundly in this passage from Faulkner's *Intruder in the Dust*, where the situation of southern Whites after the Civil War applies just as well to all Whites, men and women, rich and poor, urban and rural: "we are in the position of the German after 1933 who had no other alternative between being either a Nazi or a Jew" or "to avoid ending up a fascist there was no other choice but to become-black."[14] A new "formula" that can only obviously stand on its own, but that is already of the nature of opening this scene to factors that, under certain conditions, can lead to the condensation and contradictory simultaneity of a reduction suffered by indentificatory processes, a forced disidentification, and an impossible identification. This analytical scene, which Deleuze and Guattari began to thematize as a "schizo-analysis," then as a "micropolitical analysis" of becoming-minoritarian, make them not only the first "Lacanian-Marxists" which later ones, with Žižek at their head, have so far avoided confronting seriously, but also the first thinkers of "impolitics" in the post-war sequence, whose dialogs with Derrida, Esposito, and Balibar remain to be developed.

It cannot be overlooked, then, that the two major texts by Deleuze on the minoritarian are texts focusing on artistic practices: with Guattari in 1975, Kafka's writing machine and the problem of minor literatures for Jewish Czech writers in the late Austro-Hungarian Empire; then in the early 1980s on Third World cinema, in the analyses of *The Time-Image* on the place for a politics of minoritarian cinema in decolonization struggles and "postcolonial" conflicts.[15] In each case, the problem is to define as minoritarian, not the pretext to an "aestheticization" of political problems, but on the contrary, the problematic instance due to which a certain *minoritarian politics* must be defined, calling on the forces and means of art to *analyze* (since it is all, once again, definitively a question of transference) the indentificatory modalities of groups, introduce some "play," a *distance* for disidentifications and new identifications, where the space of political subjectivation tends to close on itself, and the political practice of abolishing itself from the inside. For this reason, the Deleuzian analysis of minoritarian cinema gives importance to the idea of a creative "story-telling" capable of bringing about a redistribution of possible identifications, by wagering on moments of undecidability between "fiction" and "reality" (when "real" people start fictionalizing the identities imposed on them or those they reject), reversibility of imagination and reality or the collusion of myths and history, to reconstruct a surface of circulation through a series of "states" played or identities *simulated*, and reopen a process of political subjectivation that had been blocked until then. A *wager*: including the fabrication of identities in this process also involves undecidable effects, related to the political manipulation of the chains of violence and counter-violence that it can open.[16] These analyses of Kafka and on minority cinema at least suggest that the heteronomy of the subject of politics, or this heterogeneous instance working the imagination of identifications and disidentifications directly in reality, in the domain of political practices, necessarily confronts the *theoretical practice* itself, in turn, in its own heteronomy. In other words, the critical processes of subjectivation, in that they call for investigating the heteronomous conditions of constructing and transforming collective identities, cannot be thought philosophically without the philosophical concept and its discursiveness being confronted in turn with the alterity that confers on them their materiality. Thus the most decisive steps for theory, here and elsewhere, can often take place in non-theoretical arenas: history, but also art and the unconscious. Under the constraints and urgency of macropolitical struggles, these arenas are needed, each time, to open the analytical space welcoming these "impolitical" symptoms, where we find at play, *at the same time*, revolutionary subjectivity and the collapse of the very possibility of politics: *face to face, back to back, back to face…*

Notes

Introduction

1. See, on the contrary, the important work carried out by the team at the review *Chimères*, as well as *Multitudes*, 34, 2008/3: *L'effet-Guattari*.

2. Gilles Deleuze and Félix Guattari, *Anti-Oedipus* (Minneapolis: University of Minnesota Press, 1983) [*AO*]; and Gilles Deleuze and Félix Guattari, *A Thousand Plateaus* (Minneapolis: University of Minnesota Press, 1987) [*TP*].

3. Isabelle Garo, *Foucault, Deleuze, Althusser & Marx—La politique dans la philosophie* (Paris : Éditions Demopolis, 2011) Chapter 1, and Chapter 3 on Deleuze.

4. See, for example, Stéphane Legrand, *Les Normes chez Foucault* (Paris: PUF, 2007); and Andrea Cavazzini, *Crise du marxisme et critique de l'État. Le dernier combat d'Althusser* (Reims: Le Clou dans le Fer, 2009).

5. Deleuze and Guattari diagnosed it early on: see "May 68 did not Take Place" (1984) in *Gilles Deleuze, Two Regimes of Madness. Texts and Interviews 1975–1995* (Boston: MIT Press/Semiotexte, 2007).

6. Isabelle Garo, *Foucault, Deleuze, Althusser & Marx*, op. cit., 49–58.

7. For a first presentation of this hypothesis, see Guillaume Sibertin-Blanc, "D'une conjuncture l'autre: Guattari et Deleuze après-coup," *Actuel Marx*, 52: Deleuze/Guattari (Paris: PUF, 2nd semester 2012), 28–47.

8. See Gérard Duménil and Dominique Lévy, "Le coup de 1979—Le choc de 2000," *Cahiers de critique communiste*, 2003: *Mondialisation et impérialisme*, 15–19.

9. See Chapter 5 in reference to *AO*, 222–262; and *TP*, 453–473.

10. See Chapter 2.

1. Historical Materialism and Schizoanalysis of the Form-State

1. *AO*, 217–222.

2. On Félix Guattari's development of this notion since the beginning of the 1960s, see *Psychanalyse et transversalité* (Paris: La Découverte, 2003 (1972)).

3. *AO*, 206, 213, 221.

4. At least, this is the reading I proposed in *Deleuze et l'Anti-Oedipe. La production du désir* (Paris: PUF, 2010).

5. Marshall Sahlins, *Stone Age Economics*. (New York: Aldine de Gruyter, 1972). The French translation published by Gallimard in 1976 has a preface by Pierre Clastres, "L'économie primitive."

6. Pierre Clastres, *Society Against the State* (New York: Zone Books, 1987). Clastrian anthropology, and the critique of Marxism that it intended are not discussed directly until the 12th and 13th Plateaus, and remain lateral references in *Anti-Oedipus*, which focuses more on Africanist terrain, especially in relation to the question of sacred royalty, the question of segmentarity made classic by British political anthropology, and Marxist anthropology sensitive to the structural questions of the Althusserians, in particular Emmanuel Terray: see Antoine Janvier, "De la réciprocité des échanges aux dettes d'alliance: *L'Anti-Œdipe* et l'économie poli- tique des sociétés 'primitives,'" *Actuel Marx* 52, 82–107; and Igor Krtolica, "Note sur Althusser chez les 'sauvages,'" *Archives du GRM* 27.11.2007 (http://www.europhilosophie.eu/recherche/IMG/pdf/Note_Igor_GRM.pdf)

7. Clastres, *Society Against the State*, 167.

8. *TP*, 359.

9. *TP*, 427–428.

10. Leroi-Gourhan, *Gesture and Speech*, 171. "While we may expect to discover evi- dence of ever older semiurbanized units going back to the very beginnings of proto-agriculture, the first city will probably never be found."

11. Braudel, *The Structures of Everyday Life*, 484. In reference to Jane Jacobs, *The Economy of Cities* (New York: Random House, 1969), and for the Anatolian digs, to the syntheses of James Mellaart, *Çatal Hüyük. A Neolithic Town in Anatolia* (New York: McGraw Hill, 1967) and *Villes primitives d'Asie Mineure*, French translation by Antoinette Zundel-Bernard (Paris/Brussels: Sequoia-Elsevier, 1969).

12. *TP*, 427.

13. This point has been made perfectly explicit, from another perspective, by Vladimir Milisavljevic, "Une violence qui se présuppose: la question de la violence de Benjamin à Deleuze et Guattari" *Actuel Marx* 52, 78–91.

14. *TP*, 385 and 427.

15. On the theoretical debates between Marxist anthropologists and historians, the repercussions of which can be read in *Anti-Oedipus*, see Ferenc Tökei, *Sur le mode de production asiatique* (Budapest: Akadémiai Kiadó, 1966), 10–16; and Maurice Godelier, "La Notion de 'mode de production asiatique' et les schémas marxistes d'évolution des sociétés," in CERM, *Sur le "mode de production asiatique"* (Paris: Éditions Sociales, 1969), 47–100.

16. Karl August Wittfogel, *Le Despotisme oriental* (Paris: Minuit, 1964 [1957]).

17. *AO*, 196–198.

18. *AO*, 199.

19. *AO*, 219, note.

20. *AO*, 139–140 and 152–153.

21. *AO*, 198.

22. *AO*, 220.

23. See Jean-Pierre Vernant, *Les Origines de la pensée grecque* (Paris : PUF, 1962), 31, on the collapse of the Mycenaean palatial system.

24. "The emergence of the State brought about the great typological division between Savage and Civilized man; it created the unbridgeable gulf whereby everything was changed, because time became History." Pierre Clastres, *Society Against the State*, 200.

25. *AO*, 217–219.

26. Friedrich Nietzsche, *On the Genealogy of Morality*, translated by Carol Diethe (Cambridge: Cambridge University Press, 1994), 58. (Second Essay, §17.) On this unusual connection of Nietzsche and the Asiatic mode of production, see also Gilles Deleuze, "Nomad Thought," in *Desert Islands and Other Texts* (Cambridge, MA: Semiotexte/MIT Press, 2004).

27. See Sibertin-Blanc, *Deleuze et l'Anti-Œdipe*, 118–123.

28. See chapters 2, 4, and 5.

29. See chapters 5 and 6.

30. See *AO*, 191–200 et seq. in reference to Karl Marx, *Grundrisse*, (New York: Penguin Books, 1993), 220–222; and to Elias Canetti, *Crowds and Power* (New York: Farrar, Strauss and Giroud, 1984), 412–418. Remember that the idea of "natural or divine presupposition" introduced by Marx to analyze the pre-capitalist forms of appropriation of social production becomes for Deleuze and Guattari (beyond the "body of the despot" which only forms one symbolic-imaginary instance among others) an instance common to "all types of society as a constant of social reproduction" (*AO*, 11)—the analysis of its figures and its varying place in social relationships extending Étienne Balibar's indications in favor of a structural re-theorization of fetishism, of which the case of fetishism of commodities privileged by Marxist tradition is only a particular case: see Étienne Balibar "Les Concepts fondamentaux du matérialisme historique," in Louis Althusser et al., *Lire le Capital* (Paris: Puf 1996 (1965)), 442–453 and 509–519; Sibertin-Blanc, *Deleuze et l'Anti-Œdipe*, 50–54.

31. Jacques Derrida, "Force of Law," tr. Mary Quaintance, in *Deconstruction and the Possibility of Justice*, edited by Drucilla Cornell, Michael Rosenfeld, and David Gray Carlson (New York: Routledge, 1992), 3–67; and Étienne Balibar, *Violence et civilité* (Paris: Galilée, 2010).

32. Ibn Battuta, *Voyages*, t. II, *De la Mecque aux steppes russes*, tr. C. Defremery, B.R. Sanguinetti (Paris : Maspero, 1982 (1858)); see Elias Canetti, *Crowds and Power*, 424–426.

33. *TP*, 448–449.

2. Capture: For a Concept of Primitive Accumulation of State Power

1. *TP*, 360.

2. According to the specific meaning given to the notion of decoding: that which escapes the extra-economic codes governing the reproduction of a social structure, and even more, that which questions or destroys codes.

3. I will return to these points in the third part.

4. In fact, the chapter "Geophilosophy" of *What is Philosophy?* takes up this framework, with new inflections, and in a much more lapidary way, without substantially modifying the conceptual architecture developed in Propositions XI, XII, and XIII of the 13th Plateau.

5. *TP*, 435–437.

6. Gilles Deleuze, *Spinoza: Practical Philosophy*, (San Francisco: City Lights, 2001), 95.

7. See *TP*, 12th Plateau, Proposition IX (and Chapter 4 here).

8. See *TP*, 13th Plateau, Propositions XIII and XIV (and Chapter 5 here).

9. See *TP*, 565 note 12 ("primitive war remains subordinated to these preventive mechanisms and does not become autonomous as a machine, even when it comprises a specialized body" and 429.

10. *TP*, 360. On the polarization power of urban formations (as opposed to State formations), see *TP*, 431–435. These analyses follow the question of the history of capital, its urban and State developments, and the development of its modern threshold when it takes on the power of a formation of "encompassing": see *TP*, 435–437, 451–454, 460 *et seq.* and Part 3 below.

11. On the conflicts ("race for speed") between the city and the States in the development of capitalistic power from the 15th to the 18th centuries, see Fernand Braudel, *La Dynamique du capitalisme* (Paris: Garnier-Flammarion, 1988), 20–21 and 34–37, and *Civilisation matérielle, économie et capitalisme*, tome 1, 547–637, from which Deleuze and Guattari drew the idea of a category of power specific to urban formations ("polarization").

12. Jean-Pierre Vernant, *The Origins of Greek Thought*.

13. Fernand Braudel, *La Dynamique du capitalisme*, 34–35

14. Fernand Braudel, *Civilisation matérielle, économie et capitalisme*, tome 1, 583. See François Fouquet and Lion Murard, *Les équipements du pouvoir* (Paris: U.G.E., 1973), 79–106.

15. Fernand Braudel, *Civilisation matérielle, économie et capitalisme*, tome 1, 591.

16. On the concept of limit in *Anti-Oedipus*, and the distinction between "real," "relative," and "absolute" limits, see Guillaume Sibertin-Blanc, *Deleuze et l'Anti-Oedipe*, 61–77 and 88 *et seq.*

17. The two processes of the "nomad war machine" and "ecumenical englobing" present even more functioning of the limit (as localization in an unlimited "smooth space," and as saturation of an "axiomatic"): they will each be examined for themselves, respectively, in the next two sections.

18. *TP*, 447.

19. *TP*, 431.

20. *AO*, 195. "The death of the primitive system always comes from without; history is the history of contingencies and encounters. [...]But this death that comes from without is also that which was rising from within [...].It is not always easy to know if one is considering a primitive community that is repressing an endogenous tendency, or one that is regaining its cohesion as best it can after a terrible exogenous adventure." The result is once again the impossibility of a relationship of *evolution* between the categories of "Savages" and "Barbarians" in the universal history of *Anti-Oedipus*.

21. Luc De Heusch, "L'inversion de la dette (propos sur les royautés sacrées africaines)," in Miguel Abensour, *L'esprit des lois sauvages* (Paris : Seuil, 1987), 41

22. *TP*, 430. See also *TP*, 210–212.

23. See Eduardo Viveiros de Castro, *Métaphysiques cannibales* (Paris : PUF, 2009), in particular pages 121–129 and 147–149 where two transformations of Native American shamanism, one of which signals an anti-State prophetism and the other a pro-State priesthood: the author notes how this disjunction converges with the 5th Plateau.

24. *TP*, 419.

25. In analyzing the spatiotemporal organization of activities among the Nuer, Evans-Pritchard underlined this serial itinerancy that inscribes each territorial segment into a succession, keeps territories non-coexistent, and prevents a direct comparison between different segments. Evans-Pritchard, *The Nuer* (Oxford: Clarendon Press, 1940). French translation by Louis Evrard (Paris: Gallimard, 1968), pages 125–127. For a no less exemplary case of productive activities

determined by "constantly varying" codes, see *TP*, 491–492, once again in reference to Marshall Sahlins.

26. Lévi-Strauss remarked on this in *Race and History* (Paris: UNESCO, 1952) in pages 45–47.

27. *TP*, 440–441.

28. The model of analysis can be found here in the Marxist idea of absolute rent, based on the special characteristics of land property: see *TP*, 567, note 31. In his return to the question of "rent or monopoly," David Harvey extends the thesis of Deleuze and Guattari (although Harvey does not refer to it).

29. *TP*, 442.

30. On the concept of "finite blocks of debt" in *Anti-Oedipus*, taking the reverse reading of the consecrated Lévi-Strauss reading of practices of gifts and counter-gifts, taking inspiration as much from a Nietzschean interpretation of Mauss as Edmund Leach's classic study of the Kachin, and reopening the program of a critique of political economy in function of different *political*-economic regimes of the debitor-creditor relationship: see Antoine Janvier, "De la réciprocité des échanges aux dettes d'alliance."

31. *TP*, 440. "beforehand, there may be exchange granaries, granaries specifically for exchange purposes, but there is no stock in the strict sense. Exchange does not assume a preexistent stock, it assumes only a certain 'elasticity.'"

32. Michel Foucault, *Lectures on the Will to Know. Lectures at the Collège de France 1970–1971* (New York: Picador 2014). These analyses and their use by Deleuze and Guattari were recently reactivated in an opportune way by Maurizio Lazzarato, *La Fabrique de l'homme endetté. Essai sur la condition néolibérale* (Paris: Amsterdam, 2011), 57–69.

33. *TP*, 568 (note 33) and already in *AO*, 196–197 in reference to Edouard Will, *Korinthiaka: recherches sur l'histoire et la civilization de Corinthe des origins aux guerres médiques* (Paris: Editions de Boccard, 1955), 470.

34. *TP*, 429.

35. *AO*, 197 in reference to Étienne Balazs' study on the role of imperial power under the Tang Dynasty in a highly overcoded monetary system: *La Bureaucratie celeste* (Paris: Gallimard, 1968), chapter XIII "La naissance du capitalism en Chine," 299–300.

36. *TP*, 443.

37. *TP*, 446.

38. See the two symmetrical openings of the 12th and 13th Plateaus.

39. *TP*, 427 and 460 ("there is a unique moment, in the sense of a coupling of forces, and this moment of the State is capture, bond, knot, nexum, magical capture. Must we speak of a second pole, which would operate instead by pact and contract? Is this not instead that other force, with capture as the unique moment of coupling?").

40. Take, for example, the case analyzed by Clastres ("Sorrows of the Savage Warrior" in *Archaeology of Violence*) of an intersecting dynamic of two ascensions to the extreme: that of the risks taken in the assault and that of the prestige earned with success, which makes a place of power (threshold) discernable while at the same time warding off its constant occupation—the warrior only increasing his or her prestige by devoting him or herself to certain death (limit). Our authors note the analogy with an arrangement observed in the sociology of gangs, where the rules for rising to leadership are taken from the mechanisms of elimination and exclusion (depending on age, a "promotion" forcing one to leave the group for the professional underworld, or according to a logic of deadly one-upmanship similar to the one analyzed by Clastres): *TP*, 380.

41. *TP*, 450. [Translator's note: Here the use of "coup" plays on the meaning of *un coup* in French as "a blow or strike" and its use in the expressions *d'un coup* ("all at once") and *réussir un coup* ("succeed at something," "pull something off").]

42. *TP*, 425.

43. Pierre Noailles, *Fas et jus. Études sur le droit romain* (Paris : Belles Lettres, 1948), 100–101 and 114 et sq; Georges Dumézil, *Mitra-Varuna. An Essay on Two Indo-European Representations of Sovereignty* (New York : Zone Books, 1988), 95–114; and Louis Gernet, *Droit et pré-droit en Grèce ancienne* (Paris : Garnier-Flammarion, 1976), 105, 115, and especially 141–142. Deleuze and Guattari allude to these debates in *TP*, 449–450.

44. Dumézil, *Mythes et dieux des Indo-européens* (Paris : Flammarion, 1992), 147 and 183. See *TP*, 423–425.

45. See Gernet, *Droit et pré-droit en Grèce archaïque*, 132–133 and 141–142.

46. Dumézil highlights this point in *Mitra-Varuna*, 91–92, 119–120, and 172. Uranos "does not fight and has no weapon. No mention is made of any resistance to his violence, and, yet, at least some of his victims are said to be 'without rivals for their stature and their strength.' This is as if to say that resistance to Uranos is inconceivable [...]. When he takes the initiative, 'he binds' and that is it."

47. This concept of "absolute peace," which should be brought into the contemporary debates on the idea of a "just war" revived by American foreign policy, as well as the analyses of Carl Schmitt who attempted the first reexamination of it in light of 20th century history, returns in Deleuze and Guattari's thinking about the contemporary economy of violence at the end of the 1970s. I will look at this point in Part Two.

48. Karl Marx, *Capital: Volume 1: A Critique of Political Economy*, translated by Ben Fowkes (New York: Vintage, 1977).

49. "[The capitalist] does not only 'deduct' or 'rob,' but forces the *production of surplus value*, therefore the deducting only helps to produce […]. But all this does not make 'capital profit' into a '*constitutive element* of value, but only proves that in the value not '*constituted*' by the labor of the capitalist, there is a portion which he can appropriate 'legally,' i.e. without infringing the rights corresponding to commodity-exchange." Karl Marx, *Marx: Later Political Writings* (Cambridge: Cambridge University Press, 1996), 232.

50. *TP*, 447.

51. *TP*, 447.

52. *TP*, 447–448.

53. Karl Marx, *Capital*, Book 1, 8, Chapter 28.

54. See Louis Althusser, "Marx dans ses limites" (1978) in *Écrits philosophiques et politiques*, 1 (Paris : Stock/IMEC, 1994), 461–463 ; and the commentary by Julien Pallotta, "La violence dans la théorie de l'État de Louis Althusser," in Guillaume Sibertin-Blanc (dir.), *Violence: Anthropologie, politique, philosophie* (Toulouse: Éditions EuroPhilosophie, 2009), which is based on the reshaping of these questions by Étienne Balibar in *La Crainte des masses* (Paris: Galilée, 1997), 408 *et seq.*

55. All of these questions are discussed in the last part of the 13th Plateau ("*Proposition XIV: Axiomatic and Current Situation*"): see Chapters 5 and 6 here.

3. Nomadology: Hypothesis of the War Machine

1. *TP*, 230, 360, 417, 426.

2. For more details on the use of Clastres and Dumézil in the 12th Plateau on the anti-State war function, see Sibertin-Blanc, "Mécanismes guerriers et généalogie de la guerre: l'hypothèse de la machine de guerre' de Deleuze et Guattari," *Aterion*, 3 (Lyon: E.N.S. L-SH, September 2005), 277–299. (http://asterion.revues.org/document425.html).

3. "Until now […] revolutionary parties have constituted themselves as embryonic State apparatuses, instead of forming war-machines irreducible to such apparatuses," Gilles Deleuze, *Desert Islands and Other Texts, 1953–1974* (New York: Semiotext(e), 2004), 276.

4. *TP*, 472–473.

5. René Grousset, *The Empire of the Steppes*. Translated by Naomi Walford. (Rutgers, NJ: Rutgers University Press, 1970). See Chapter 1 and on Genghis Khan, pages 189–248.

6. Mikhail Gryaznov, *The Ancient Civilization of South Siberia* (London: Barrie & Jenkins, 1969).

7. See Jean-Loup Amselle, *Retrovolutions. Essais sur les primitivismes contemporains* (Paris : Stock, 2010).

8. See Michel Foucault, *The Thought from Outside* (New York: Zone Books, 1989). On desert space, see in particular the two texts on the nomadic period of the Jewish people, which are echoed in the 5th Plateau, Maurice Blanchot, "Prophetic Speech," *The Book to Come* (Stanford: Stanford University Press, 2003), 79–85 and "Being Jewish," *The Infinite Conversation* (Minneapolis, MN: University of Minnesota Press, 1993), 123–129.

9. The readiness to reproach them for it is thus null and void (Jean-Loup Amselle, *L'Occident décroché. Enquête sur le postcolonialisme* (Paris: Stock, 2008) 21–22). For a more informed, and much more rigorous and inventive use of Deleuze and Guattari's "nomadology" in cultural anthropology, see the work of Barbara Glowczewski, in particular *Les Rêveurs du desert* (Arles: Actes Sud, 1996); "Guattari et l'anthropologie: aborigènes et territoires exitentiels," *Multitudes* 2008/3, n. 34, 84–94; and with Jessica de Largy Healy, *Pistes de Rêves. Voyage en terres aborigènes* (Paris: Éditions du Chêne, 2005).

10. See for example the treatment of the legendary theme of "nomadic thieves of children" *TP*, 392–393.

11. See Part I.

12. *TP*, 23.

13. *TP*, 354. On the use of signs and the problems raised by nomad writing, see *TP*, 402.

14. Schmitt, *The Nomos of the Earth*, 82. Schmitt notes that the first two cases were combined in the "Great Invasions" (61–62) such that the upheaval of political-territorial structures to which they lead in the nomos of the Roman Empire should be redescribed: not only "great migrations," but "a series of major land-appropriations" founding a new order of coexistence between territorialized powers.

15. Schmitt, *The Nomos of the Earth*, 51.

16. *TP*, 360–361: "It is in terms not of independence, but of coexistence and competition *in a perpetual field of interaction*, that we must conceive of exteriority and interiority, war machines of metamorphosis and State apparatuses of identity […].The same field circumscribes its interiority in States, but describes its exteriority in what escapes States or stands against States."

17. *TP*, 422.

18. See *Rig Veda*, VI, 47, quoted in Dumézil, *The Destiny of the Warrior* (Chicago: University of Chicago Press, 1970) ("He loves no more the men he loved aforetime:

he turns and moves away allied with others. [...] In every figure he hath been the mode: this is his only form for us to look on. Indra moves multiform by his illusions; for his Bay Steeds are yoked, ten times a hundred."—Translation by Ralph T.H. Griffith (1896))

19. *TP*, 360–361.

20. *TP*, 420.

21. Gilles Deleuze, *Negotiations* (New York: Columbia University Press, 1990), 172.

22. *TP*, 422–423. The prototypical importance of Genghis Khan-style civilization in Deleuze and Guattari's "nomadology" illustrates the always polyvocal or overdetermined aspect of the examples chosen. Why does the "dramatization" of the philosophical concept of nomadism pass through two privileged historical sequences (two sequences that are in some ways related, at least in their effects)—the Crusades on the one hand, and on the other the sequence that extends from Genghis Khan's invasions to the fall of the Mongol civilization—if not because they touch directly on the debates surrounding the world-economy and on the Euro-centrism of the primacy traditionally given since Smith and Marx to the discovery of America and the East Indian routes to explain the rise of the capitalist bourgeoisie, to the detriment of the "world systems" that dominated before the 16th century, the question of the decline of Chinese power, the fragmentation of the Sino-Arab trade network after the "collapse of the Mongols" to the emergence of new trade connections from Europe to the Orient (in particular through the "captures" of the Crusades)? See, for example, Jacques Gernet, *Le Monde chinois* (Paris: Armand Colin, 1972), 305–306 and Janet Abu-Lughod, *Before European Hegemony. The World System A.D. 1250–1350* (New York: Oxford University Press, 1989).

23. *TP*, 422–423.

24. Gilles Deleuze, *Difference and Repetition*, 35–37. ("A distribution of this type proceeds by fixed and proportional determinations which may be assimilated to 'properties' or limited territories within representation. The agrarian question may well have been very important for this organization of judgment as the faculty which distinguishes parts...").

25. Ibid., 36.

26. Emmanuel Laroche, *Histoire de la racine NEM en Grec ancien* (Paris: Klincksieck, 1949) ; see Gilles Deleuze, *Difference and Repetition*, 36, note 6; *TP*, 380, note 51 ; and Carl Schmitt, "Appropriation/Distribution/Production: Toward a Proper Formulation of Basic Questions of Any Social and Economic Order"(1953), translated by G. L. Ulmen from *Verfassungsrechtliche Aufsatze aus den Jahren 1924–1954: Materialien zu einer Vassungslehre* (Berlin: Dunker & Humblot, 1973), 489–501.

27. See Carl Schmitt, *The Nomos of the Earth*, 68–70, on the Aristotelian interpretation of Solon's reforms, the division of land, and the abolition of debt. See also Jacques Rancière, *Aux bords de la politique* (Paris: La Fabrique, 1998), 26–36.

28. *TP*, 410.

29. This is precisely, according to Laroche, one of the archaic meanings of "nomos" from nomadic culture: graze in the active sense—"who makes graze, nomad"—or as means—"who grazes, wanderer" (Emmanuel Laroche, *Histoire de la racine NEM*, 121). It marks the opposition between two semantic values: of "repartition" and "distribution." The second remains the *telos* internal to the Schmittian "nomos of the Earth"; Deleuze on the contrary (following Laroche, *Ibid.*, 256) favors the idea of repartition: the nomos is not the division and distribution of the land for people (objective repartition supposing capture objectivizing the land), but the repartition of people, animals, things, and events on an undivided, open, unlimited space (repartition on un-objectivizible and un-attributable land).

30. See *TP*, 380–382 and 493–494 (in reference to Anny Milovanoff, "La seconde peau du nomade," *Nouvelles littératures*, 2646 (July 27, 1978) on the Larbaa nomads on the border of the Algerian Sahara).

31. Carl Schmitt, "Appropriation/Distribution/Production."

32. Joshua 11:23 cited in Carl Schmitt, *The Nomos of the Earth*, 81. Schmitt refers to this passage again in a 1963 text forming a seventh corollary in the appendix to his 1950 work, as well as to Numbers 34:13 on the division by drawn lots between the different tribes of Israel.

33. "The ties to mythological sources of jurisprudential thinking are much deeper than those to geography. [...] In mythical language, the earth became known as the mother of law. This signifies a threefold root of law and justice.. [...] the earth is bound to law in three ways. She contains law within herself, as a reward of labor; she manifests law upon herself, as fixed boundaries; and she sustains law above herself, as a public sign of order. Law is bound to the earth and related to the earth. This is what the poet means when he speaks of the infinitely just earth: *justissima tellus*" Carl Schmitt, *The Nomos of the Earth*, 38, 41–42.

34. Gilles Deleuze and Félix Guattari, *What is Philosophy*, 85–86.

35. Carl Schmitt, *The Nomos of the Earth*, 42–43.

36. Carl Schmitt, *Theory of the Partisan*, 13–14 and 49.

37. *TP*, 363.

38. Following a long-standing theme (it can be found for example in the Revolutionary period in the blockade project of Bertrand Barère, *La Liberté des Mers ou le Gouvernement anglais dévoilé* (February 19, 1798).

39. On the subtlety of perceptive semiotics in the high seas, the question of high-sea navigation methods by striation (by means of astronomy and geography) but also "pre-astronomical" procedures of empirical and complex nomadic navigation, see *TP*, 479–480 and the references to Pierre Chaunu: on the relationship of these

themes with the central problem of the global history of the decline of Chinese and Arab navigation between the 13th and 17th centuries, see *TP*, 386–387.

40. See Carl Schmitt, *The Nomos of the Earth*, 50–56 and 309–323; *Theory of the Partisan*, 13–15; "L'ordre du monde après la Deuxième Guerre mondiale" (1962) in *La Guerre civile mondiale*, 66–70. See *TP*, "Of the Refrain."

41. See the exemplary case of the *fleet in being*, *TP*, 387 and the quote from Virilio, 387, note 65 ("The fleet in being… is the permanent presence in the sea of an invisible fleet able to strike no matter where and no matter when […]. The fleet in being creates … the notion of displacement without destination in space and time… The strategic submarine has no need to go anywhere in particular; it is content, while controlling the sea, to remain Invisible"); and perhaps even more significant (bearing witness to a maritime investment of terrestrial space, and of a technical capture of smooth space by a State), the case of the tank, invented when trench warfare was bogged down and craters made the field of operations impracticable, the war of movement initially based on mobile artillery was reversed into a complete, forced immobility. The solution of the British was to have "reconstituted a kind of maritime or smooth space on land" (*TP*, 560, note 76) and "superimposed naval tactics on land warfare" to *re-mobilize war* (the construction of "land cruisers" was assigned to the Bureau of Naval Designs); see J. F. C. Fuller, *Armament and History*, (Boston: Da Capo Press, 1998), 137ff; and William Mc Neill, *The Pursuit of Power: Technology, Armed Force, and Society since A.D. 1000* (Chicago: University of Chicago Press, 1982), 334–336.

42. *TP*, 386.

43. *TP*, 499–500 ("how the forces at work within space continually striate it, and how in the course of its striation it develops other forces and emits new smooth spaces").

44. On guerilla, see in particular *TP*, 387, 416–417, 422–423. However, this theme also has a diffuse presence in many other contexts, even unexpected ones (such as the problem of turbulent movement in the history of hydraulics (*TP*, 489–490). See also the magnificent text on the *Seven Pillars of Wisdom* "The Shame and the Glory: T.E. Lawrence" in *Essays Critical and Clinical*, 115–125. Paying attention to the historical context of Deleuze and Guattari's reflection, Marco Rampazzo Bazzan has proposed a fine explication of the problems raised by "urban guerilla" in the Red Army Faction in light of the smooth space/striated space dialectic: Marco Ramapazzo Bazzan, "La machine de guerre comme analyseur des théorisations de la guérilla urbaine en R.F.A. depuis le 2 juin 1967" in Vladimir Milisavljevic and Guillaume Sibertin-Blanc, *Deleuze et la violence* (Toulouse/Belgrade: Europhilosophie-Institut de Philosophie et de Théorie sociale, 2012), 79–100.

45. See Barthélémy Courmont and Darko Ribnikar, *Les guerres asymétriques* (Paris: Iris/PUF, 2002), 26–29 and 43, who remind us that the dissymmetrical logic, under these different aspects, " generally involves States."

46. See in particular *TP*, 395–397 (on the concept of "counterattack") and 422.

47. On the combination "war continued on the strategic level"/"impetuousness in tactical operations," see Mao Zedong, "Strategic Problems of China's Revolutionary War" (Beijing, 1936), republished in Gérard Chaliand, *The Art of War in World History: From Antiquity to the Nuclear Age* (Berkeley, CA: University of California Press, 1994), 976–988.

48. On this precept, the absence of defensive position, and the opposition between war of contact and war of detachment, see the unequaled pages of T.E. Lawrence, *Seven Pillars of Wisdom*, 172–173 ("We were to contain the enemy by the silent threat of a vast unknown desert not disclosing ourselves until the moment of attack.") See also the ordering of the tactical reasons of revolutionary war in Mao Zedong, "Strategic Problems of China's Revolutionary War," 984.

49. On the importance, not of "being superior at the critical point and moment of attack," but of mastering critical points, preserving decisions on what is critical, such that only one critical point could, in the end, suffice, see T.E. Lawrence, *Seven Pillars of Wisdom*, 183 and Mao Zedong, "Strategic Problems of China's Revolutionary War," 977.

50. See, on the contrary, the main counter-insurgency methods prescribed for the War in Vietnam by the presidential advisor Robert Thompson, *Defeating Communist Insurgency: Experiences in Malaysia and Vietnam* (London: Chatto & WIndus, 1966).

51. T.E. Lawrence, *Seven Pillars of Wisdom*, 181–182.

52. There is even the irony that the Israeli army "used" the analyses of Deleuze and Guattari or the SiItuationists to redefine its methods of intervention in the Occupied Territories: see the short, captivating work by Eyal Weizman, *A travers les murs. L'architecture de la nouvelle guerre urbaine* (Paris: La fabrique, 2008).

53. Remember that smooth space became a major property of what Deleuze described at the end of the 1980s, in an often-discussed text on "societies of control" (*Negotiations*).

54. Taking lessons from the wars in Indochina and Algeria in a work that has become a classic of counter-insurgency manual, Colonel Roger Trinquier contests the idea that to defeat a guerilla "it is enough to use its own weapons against it" and "oppose guerilla with counter-guerilla" (*La guerre moderne* (Paris: La Table ronde, 1961)).

55. On the opposition between Che Guevara and Mao on this point, see Barthélémy Courmont and Darko Ribnikar, *Les guerres asymétiques* (Paris: IRIS/PUF, 2002), 35–37. On this problem during the Spanish Civil War, see the texts and statements of Buenaventura Durruti recorded by André Prudhommeaux, *Catalogne 36–37* and *Cahiers de Terre libre* (1937) republished in Daniel Guérin, *Ni Dieu ni Maître. Anthologie de l'anachisme* (1970) (Paris: La Découverte, 1999), tome II, 320–344.

56. T.E. Lawrence, *Seven Pillars of Wisdom*, 86–87.

57. Gilles Deleuze and Félix Guattari, *What is Philosophy?*, 85.

58. On the theme of "open spaces" from 1943 and on the post-war international scene, see Jean-François Kervégan, "Carl Schmitt et 'l'unité du monde,'" *Revista de Filosophia*, 13 (July–December 1996), 99–114.

59. Deleuze, "Nietzsche and Saint Paul, Lawrence and John of Patmos" in *Essays Critical and Clinical*, 45–46.

60. This logic is implemented, in a practical state, in all of the analyses of the 12th Plateau; however, it is specifically thematized in Proposition VIII (*TP*, 404–415). Here, I am using in particular the synthesized typological presentation on pages 381–382 and 409–410.

61. This affinity is explained at the end of the *Treatise on Nomadology*, illustrating it on the anthropological-historical level, in relation to the extraction of minerals and forging weapons, by the close interactions between nomad peoples of Asia and metallurgists: *TP*, 411–412.

62. *TP*, 380.

63. *Idem.* Deleuze and Guattari immediately add: "Nomads and migrants can mix in many ways, or form a common aggregate; their causes and conditions are no less distinct for that," even when these causes and conditions are fulfilled, successively or simultaneously, in a group or a single person, then migrant and nomad are under two distinct relationships.

64. *TP*, 409.

65. *TP*, 409–410.

66. On serial itinerancy and its relationship to the process of anticipation-warding off, see *TP*, 236 and 450.

67. *TP*, 410.

68. *TP*, 410.

69. See Deleuze, *Essays Critical and Clinical*, 63.

70. *TP*, 380.

71. *TP*, 385–386.

72. *TP*, 385–386.

73. *TP*, 386.

74. This entire logic of territorialization should be further confronted with the issues of geographic materialism of David Harvey, starting with the opposition between the "capitalist logic" and "territorial logic" of power, which is more binary

and, in the end, ambiguous. The accumulation of capital, as Harvey himself emphasizes, is always territorialized, such that the problem is rather to determine the different modalities of territorialization of capitalist accumulation, taking into account how "capital" is a metamorphic relationship passing through heterogeneous forms (industrial, banking, financial, etc.), which are incommensurable or non-convertible without the intervention of specialized institutions that themselves refer, as Harvey also shows, to forms of power related to distinct modes of territorialization and deterritorialization (States, cities, regions, or "open spaces"...), which cannot be subsumed under a single "territorial logic or politics of power."

4. The Formula and the Hypothesis: State Appropriation and Genealogy of War Power

1. Claus von Clausewitz, *On War* (Princeton, N. J.: Princeton University Press, 1976) Book I, ch. I, §24.

2. *TP*, 418.

3. *TP*, 419–420. In Book VIII, Clausewitz returns to his distinction between a pure concept of war and real war, and reformulates the problems of the factors that condition or on the contrary oppose the political-historical application of the concept and, at the frequently reached limit, "can become so preponderant that they reduce war to [...] armed neutrality or [...] a threatening posture in support of negotiation."; "But what is now the non-conducting medium which hinders the complete discharge? Why is the philosophical conception not satisfied? That medium consists in the number of interests, forces, and circumstances of various kinds, in the existence of the State, which are affected by the War, and through the infinite ramifications of which the logical consequence cannot be carried out as it would on the simple threads of a few conclusions; in this labyrinth it sticks fast." (*On War*, Book VIII).

4. Clausewitz, *On War*, B. VIII ch. 3B.

5. *Ibid.*

6. *Ibid.*, B. I ch. 2, and B. VIII ch. 6A–B.

7. *Ibid.*, B. I ch. 1 §3.

8. *Ibid.*, B. VIII ch. 2.

9. *TP*, 354–355.

10. Clausewitz, *On War*, B. I ch. 1; B. VIII ch. 2 and ch. 6B. See also Chapter 16 of Book III dedicated to strategy.

11. *TP*, 421.

12. *TP*, 354.

13. Gilles Deleuze, *Difference and Repetition*, 135, 154.

14. Clausewitz, *On War*, B. I, ch. 2. ("the destruction of the enemy forces," means "they must be put in such a condition that they can no longer carry on the fight").

15. *Ibid.*, B. I ch. 4 §3.

16. *TP*, 420.

17. Clausewitz, *On War*, B. I ch. 1 §24.

18. *Ibid.*, B. IV ch. 11; B. VIII ch. 1.

19. *TP*, 416.

20. Therefore, I cannot follow Michael Hardt's proposal to substitute the expression "smooth machine" for "war machine" to lift the equivocalness of the latter expression (Michael Hardt, "Reading Notes on Deleuze and Guattari—Capitalism and Schizophrenia," "http://people.duke.edu/~hardt/mp5.htm). As a purely verbal gesture, it has little chance of reducing the *effective* ambivalence denoted in the expression retained by Deleuze and Guattari, but only to reinforce misunderstanding of it, the very one that allows a comfortable substitution of the axiological valorization for a problematizing approach to the concept. They are very careful to avoid summary identifications, of the war machine and the process of emancipation, or of smooth space and the space of liberation, to the extent that they conclude the 12th Plateau with this very warning.

21. *TP*, 417.

22. *TP*, 418.

23. *TP*, 418–419.

24. *TP*, 418.

25. René Grousset, *L'Empire des steppes*, 495–496.

26. *TP*, 351–352, 424–427. On the distinction between the encastment of the war machine and its *appropriation*, see *TP*, 419 and 425.

27. See Part I above: "Archi-Violence."

28. See *Armées et fiscalité dans le monde antique* (Paris: CNRS, 1977), in particular, Edmond Van't Dack, "Sur l'évolution des institutions militaires lagides," and Guillaume Cardascia, "Armée et fiscalité dans la Babylonie achéménide" (on the institution of *hatru*) ; see *AO*, 198–197 and *TP*, 442–443.

29. Norbert Elias, *The Court Society* (New York: Pantheon, 1983 (1933)), Chapter 5.

30. See above, Chapter 2.

31. Clausewitz, *On War*, B. VIII, ch. 3B.

32. *AO*, 221–222, 251–259.

33. *TP*, 419.

34. *TP*, 368; See M. Foucault, *Surveiller et punir* (Paris: Gallimard, 1993(1975)) 166–175, 190–199, 230.

35. *TP*, 421.

36. Erich von Ludendorff, *Der totale Krieg* (München: Ludendorffs Verlag, 1935).

37. We should remember that *The Total War* (*Der totale Krieg*) presents itself as much as a collection of considerations addressed in warning of a coming conflict as a critical analysis of the political and military strategy adopted by the German authorities during the First World War.

38. Walter Benjamin, "Theories of German Fascism: On the Collection of Essays *War and Warrior*, edited by Ernst Jünger" *New German Critique*, No. 17, Special Walter Benjamin Issue (Spring, 1979), pp. 120–128. (For these "trailblazers of the *Wehrmacht*," "the uniform represents their highest end, most desired by all their heartstrings, and that the circumstances under which one dons the uniform are of little importance by comparison.")

39. *Ibid.*, 126.

40. On the correlation between *partial* mobilization and the "special reason of State" inherited from absolute monarchy and the decisions of the sovereign, see Ernst Jünger, *Total Mobilization* (1930), French translation by Henri Plard and Marc De Launay, *Recherches*, 32/33 (Spetember 1978). Jünger presents in contrast the different processes that are combined in the tendency to total mobilization, enrollment of the entire population, maximum requisition, and the unlimited use of all credit "to keep the machine running," the absorption of "armed action" in "the much broader representation [of war] as a giant labor process." "In order to deploy energies of such proportion [...] this is a mobilization [*Rustung*] that requires extension to the deepest marrow, life's finest nerve. Its realization is the task of total mobilization: an act which, as if through a single grasp of the control panel, conveys the extensively branched and densely veined power supply of modern life towards the great current of martial energy." Deleuze and Guattari show a clear interest for Jünger and refer in particular to *Der Arbeiter, Herrschaft und Gestalt* (1932): see *TP*, 403 and 425.

41. Walter Benjamin, "Theories of German Fascism," 128.

42. See Clausewitz, *On War*, ch. 17 "Bonaparte's audacity and luck have cast the old accepted practices to the winds. Major powers were shattered with virtually a single blow. The stubborn resistance of the Spaniards [...] showed what can be accomplished by arming a people and by insurrection. [...] All these cases have shown what an enormous contribution the heart and temper of a nation can make to the sum total of its politics, war potential, and fighting strength. Now that governments have become conscious of these resources, we cannot expect them to remain unused in the future, whether the war is fought in self-defense or in order to satisfy intense ambition."

43. Erich von Ludendorff, *Der totale Krieg*. See Raymond Aron opposing Ludendorff and Lenin on this question in particular: *Penser la guerre, Clausewitz*, t. 1: *L'âge planétaire* (Paris: Gallimard, 1976), 57–68.

44. *TP*, 421.

45. Raymond Aron, *Penser la guerre*, 58–61, 128.

46. See, for example, Thomas Lindenmann, "Ludendorff et la guerre totale. Une approche 'perceptuelle,'" in François Géré and Thierry Widemann (dir.), *La guerre totale* (Paris: Economica, 2001), 24–29.

47. *TP*, 230. See *TP*, 214.

48. See Johann Chapoutot, *Le National-socialisme et l'Antiquité* (Paris: PUF, 2008).

49. *TP*, 489. On the thesis of the National-Socialist State as a suicidal State, see Paul Virilio, *L'insécurité du territoire* (Paris: Galilée, 1993 (1976)), 25–52; and Michel Foucault, *Society Must Be Defended. Lectures at the Collège de France, 1975–1976* (New York: Picador, 1997).

50. See Hannah Arendt, *The Origins of Totalitarianism*, III: *Totalitarianism* (New York: Harcourt, 1958 (1951)) ch.1 §1 and on "movement" as unlimited process.

51. Deleuze and Guattari insist on this point: the Nazi war machine and its destruction, even its self-destruction, far from being blind were explicitly anticipated and even "promised" to the German people by the dignitaries and ideologues of the regime (*TP*, 230–231). See Joachim Fest, *Inside Hitler's Bunker: The Last Days of the Third Reich* (New York: Farrar, Strauss and Giroux, 2004 (2002)).

52. *TP*, 421.

53. *TP*, 467.

54. *TP*, 461–466. See below, Chapter 5.

55. *TP*, 466. Under these new conditions, a *privatization* (or a partial externalization delegating it to mercenary enterprises) of police and military violence becomes possible and necessary.

56. See Karl Marx, *Das Kapital. Book III* (1894) Section III, Conclusions; *AO*, 230–231; and *TP*, 463.

57. *TP*, 492.

58. *TP*, 345.

59. *TP*, 466.

60. *TP*, 467.

61. See Gilles Deleuze and Jean-Pierre Bamberger, "Pacifism Today," *Two Regimes of Madness*, 222–232.

62. Paul Virilio, *L'Insécurité du territoire*, 99.

63. *Ibid.*, 238–239.

64. *Ibid.*, 231–232. (Virilio relies here on the statements of General François Maurin, "Pérennité et nécessité de la defense," *Revue de la défense nationale*, 7, July 1973).

65. See Michael Hardt and Tony Negri, *Multitude. War and Democracy in the Age of Empire* (New York: Penguin Books, 2005) who note, according to a Schmittian as much as a Deluze-Guattari inspiration, that the registers of the "war against terrorism," but also the "war on poverty," etc. have taken us "from metaphorical and rhetorical invocations of war to real wars against indefinite, immaterial enemies"—in conformance with the regime of domination that Deleuze and Guattari call "axiomatic." Hardt and Negri connect it to the indetermination of the spatial and temporal limits of war, the growing entanglement of international relations and internal politics, of which the domains tend be combined, the transformation of the concepts of belligerent and hostility, and the reactivation of the concept of "just war."

66. *TP*, 471; and Deleuze, *Essays Critical and Clinical*, 45–46.

67. Guy Brossollet, *Essai sur la non-bataille* (Paris: Belin, 1975), 15.

68. See Deleuze, "Spoilers of Peace," *Two Regimes of Madness*, 161.

69. On this question: a/ Gilles Deleuze and Félix Guattari, "Europe the Wrong Way," *Two Regimes of Madness*, 148–150, in response to the Klaus Croissant Affair and "the possibility that Europe as a whole will fall under the kind of control being called for by Germany" and the "police, legal and "information" model" put in place by the emergency laws in the name of the struggle against terrorism (*Ibid*, 149–150); b/ Gilles Deleuze, *Cinema 2: The Time Image* (Minneapolis: University of Minnesota Press, 1989) on the transformations of "information" or media power from *Mabuse* by Lang to Sidney Lumet or Robert Altman; c/ Gilles Deleuze, "Postscript on Control Societies," *Negotiations*, 177 et seq.

70. I take the liberty to refer here to the cartography that has already been done between *A Thousand Plateaus* and the contextual interventions of the 1976–1984 years in my doctoral thesis, *Politique et Clinique. Recherche sur la philosophie pratique de Gilles Deleuze*. Doctoral thesis, December 2008, University Lille 3, 898–917. (http://documents.univ-lille3.fr/files/pub/www/recherche/theses/SIBERTIN_BLANC_GUILLAUME.pdf).

71. Michel Foucault, *Society Must Be Defended*, January 7 and 21, 1976 lessons; and *Discipline and Punish* (New York: Pantheon Books, 1978).

72. Carl Schmitt, *The Concept of the Political*, 66–67.

73. See Étienne Balibar, "Le moment philosophique determine par la guerre dans la politique: Lénine 1914–1916," in Phillippe Soulez (dir.), *Les Philosophes et la guerre de 14* (Saint-Denis: Presses Universitaires de Vincennes, 1988), 105–120

"Fin de la politique ou politique sans fin? Marx et l'aporie de la 'politique communiste,'" presentation to the working group of Pierre Macherey, "La Philosophie au
sens large," Université Lille 3, December 17, 2008; and *Violence et civilité*, Chapters "Gewalt" and "Variations post-clausewiziennes."

74. This is the very determination of the "nomad war machine" from the formal
point of view of "power": "war machines have *a power of metamorphosis*, which of
course allows them to be captured by States, but also to resist that capture and rise
up again in other forms" (*TP*, 437); that for which "*the war machine has an extremely
variable relation to war itself* [and] is not uniformly defined." (*TP*, 422): in other
words, this relationship is in final instance dependent on circumstances.

75. On Lenin's dual struggle against the social-chauvinists rallying to Sacred
Unions and against the pacifists, see Georges Haupt, "Guerre et revolution chez
Lénine," *Revue française de science politique* year 21, 2, 1971.

76. *TP*, 472–473.

5. The Axiomatic of Capital: States and Accumulation on a Global Scale

1. See Guillaume Sibertin-Blanc, *Deleuze et l'Anti-Œdipe*, 62–67.

2. *AO*, 153 and 177.

3. The critique of structuralism in *Anti-Oedipus* should not be confused with the
one started by Guattari in the 1960s (see *Psychoanalysis and Transversality*,
"Machine and Structure"), which takes as a double target the orthodox versions of
Levi-Strauss' anthropology and Lacanian psychoanalysis, with a liquidation of
every structural problematization of the critique of political economy and the
analysis of the capitalist mode of production.

4. See *AO*, Chapter III, in particular sections 1, 5, 9, 10, and 11.

5. See *AO*, 136–140, 146, 153, 224–226, 245 et seq., in reference to Louis
Althusser, et al., *Reading Capital*: in particular Étienne Balibar, "The Basic Concepts of Historical Materialism,"223 et seq.

6. On the decoding of the body by "privatization of organs" or dissolution of
"collective investments of organs," of which only the destruction makes something
like a "productive" body possible, see *AO*, 141–144, 210–211, 247…: the appearance
of a "private man" as support for a labor force to which he can be attached as owner,
user, or one who cedes its use to another supposes a series of processes of *desocialization* of the relationship to the body and the values of use of its forces and its parts.

7. "It is beneath the blows of private property, then of commodity production, that
the State witnesses its decline. Land enters into the sphere of private property and
into that of commodities. *Classes* appear, inasmuch as the dominant classes are no
longer merged with the State apparatus, but are distinct determinations that make
use of this transformed apparatus. At first situated adjacent to communal property,
then entering into the latter's composition or conditioning it, then becoming more

and more a determining force, private property brings about an internalization of the creditor-debtor relation in the relations of opposed classes." (*AO*, 218).

8. See *AO*, 217–218, 222–223, in reference in particular to Karl Marx, Karl Marx, "Reply to Milkhailovski" (Nov., 1877), in Karl Marx and Friedrich Engels, *Basic Writings on Politics and Philosophy* (Garden City N.Y.: Doubleday, 1959); and again in 1980, *TP*, 452–453: "The situation is that the pressure of the flows draws capitalism in negative outline, but for it to be realized there must be a whole *integral of decoded flows*, a whole *generalized conjunction* that overspills and overturns the preceding apparatuses [...] *a general axiomatic of decoded flows*."

9. *AO*, 223–224.

10. *AO*, 244: "Civilization is defined by the decoding and the deterritorialization of flows *in capitalist production*. Any method will do for ensuring this universal decoding: the privatization brought to bear on property, goods, and the means of production, but also on the organs of "private man" himself; the abstraction of monetary quantities, but also the abstraction of the quantity of labor." (My emphasis)

11. *AO*, 257.

12. *AO*, 247–252 et seq.

13. *AO*, 170 and 248, citing Lauren and Paul Bohannan, *The Tiv of Central Nigeria* (London: International African Institute, 1953). In a similar context, see Maurice Godelier, *Rationalité et irrationalité en économie* (Paris: Maspero, 1966), 274–275, analyzing the "monetary" system of the Siane within a system of categorization of "goods" that makes them unexchangeable.

14. *AO*, 247–248, in reference to Étienne Balibar "The Fundamental Concepts of Historical Materialism." Here, however, Deleuze and Guattari try to articulate in one formulation two different cases: the one suggested by Marx in the "Pre-Capitalist Economic Formations" (on the subject of "primitive communes" but also "Asian" production) where the conditions of exploitation of surplus labor make it so that the product is "immediately" appropriated to a third instance (leading to, as noted in Chapter 1, the idea of a structural reproblematization of fetishism as underlying a "natural or divine presupposition" of social production, following the conceptual series *body of land/body of the despot/body of capital*); and the case mentioned by Marx in *Capital* Book III, 6, Chapter 24 on feudal servitude, where the qualitative and temporal difference between labor and surplus labor imposes "extra-economic reasons, whatever their nature, to oblige them to perform labor for the sake of the property owner."

15. The indirect influence of Louis Althusser's analysis of "The Object of Capital" (*Reading Capital*) will be recognized here. Althusser constructs an anti-economist reading of the Marxist concept of surplus value from a symptom analysis of absence from the discourse of political economy of its *name*, with surplus value only being recognized-misrecognized in its only economic "forms of existence" (profit, interest, land income, as "derived forms").

16. Deleuze and Guattari borrow from the differential relationship (and from its 17th century interpretation) a/ the notion of a relationship that does not depend on the variable values of its terms, but that on the contrary itself constitutes the terms that it places in relationship while determining the limits of variation of their values (capital and labor do not exist, no more than "constant capital" and "variable capital," outside of their conjunction, which determines them differentially as such); b/ a relationship that envelops an unlimited internal tendency, one without a resolving quotient, and of which one of the possible attractions is the reabsorption of one of the terms in an "infinitely small" quantity (either the tendency to a falling rate of profit itself or one of its parameters that Marx expressed sometimes by borrowing from the differential relationship model: the development of productivity and the organic composition of capital in view of which "the value-creating power of the individual labour capacity is an infinitesimal, vanishing magnitude" (Karl Marx, *Grundrisse*, 694); c/ a relationship, in the end, which envelops of differential of *power* between the two magnitudes considered, which makes them *incommensurable* like the incommensurability internal to money between money of exchange and money of credit, or between its functions in the division of revenue and in the financing of accumulation (thus it is insufficient to define capitalist illimitation through the commensurability of the merchandise-form alone, without taking into account the relationships of force between labor and capital). All of these points are developed in *AO*, 226–230.

17. *AO*, 227–230, 245, 260.

18. Karl Marx, *Capital*, B. III., p. 350–354.

19. *AO*, 230–231.

20. *AO*, 251–252. On the role of the State in the reproduction of labor force and money as "special merchandise," Deleuze and Guattari rely in particular on the work of Suzanne de Brunhoff relating to problems of reproduction of general equivalency and the convertability of currencies, but also the development of the insurance system and State management of relative overpopulation. On the dual character of the capitalist State that results from it, both "external and immanent," see the synthesis by Suzanne de Brunhoff, *État et capital* (Paris: PUF, 1973).

21. See *AO*, 235 in reference to Paul Baran and Paul Sweezy, *Monopoly Capital: An Essay on the American Economic and Social Order* (New York: Monthly Review Press, 1966), chapters 7 and 8 on the role of non-productive State spending in absorbing surplus, by the civil government and militarism.

22. See *TP*, 435–437, 453–456, 460–473. "We define social formations by *machinic processes* and not by modes of production (these on the contrary depend on the processes)" (*TP*, 435).

23. For a later return to these debates which sheds light on the stakes after the fact, see the dossier in *Sociologie et société*, vol. XXII/1, April 1990 dedicated to "Theories of Transition" and the subsequent dialogue between Gunder Frank and Wallerstein (Andre Gunder Frank, "De quelles transitions et de quells modes de production

s'agit-il dans le système mondial reel? Commentaire sur l'article de Wallerstein"; and Immanuel Wallerstein, "Système mondial contre système-monde: le dérapage conceptuel de Frank," in *Sociologie et société*, vol. XXII/2, October 1990, 207–222.

24. Thus the possibility of a continuist thesis like the one finally defended by Gunder Frank ("history reveals that a *same global, economic, and inter-State historical system has existed for at least five thousand years...*"), on the observation that all of the "proto-capitalist" elements that can be identified at the end of "feudal" Europe (capital, money, profits, merchants, salaried labor, entrepreneurship, investments, technology, etc.) and even the structural or "systematic" characteristics (structure of concentration of capital, formation of a bipolarized center-periphery system, etc.) "also characterize the economy and the political system of the Antique and even archaic world" (Andre Gunder Frank, "De quelles transitions et de quells modes de production s'agit-il dans le système mondial reel?", 210 et seq.

25. *TP*, 435.

26. *TP*, 435–436.

27. *TP*, 454. This distinction between two forms of englobing is not without similarity to the one proposed by Wallerstein between a mosaic of "mini-systems" connected by more or less intense and regular commercial exchanges, or even "world empires" caught in cycles of partial integration and relatively shared economic rhythms, and a "world system" bearing witness to a synchronization of economic rhythms, of a systematic structuring of a set of inter-State relations, and in the case of the "modern world system" ("the capitalist world economy"), of a rearticulation of a trade network based on an axial division of labor drawing on highly integrated processes of production.

28. See David Harvey, *The New Imperialism* (Oxford: Oxford University Press, 2003), 47–48.

29. *TP*, 454.

30. *TP*, 447, 461 notes 40 and 60–61.

31. *TP*, 455. This problem of the politics internal to scientific fields is central to Guattari's work in the 1970s (see in particular *Molecular Revolution* (New York: Penguin, 1984). On the political conflicts internal to scientific practices following lines of division between "theorematic" and "problematic," nomologic and experimental, or axiomatic and intuitionist approaches, see *TP*, 361–374 and the Plateau "Postulates of Linguistics," which draws in large part on chapters 2 and 3 of Félix Guattari, *The Machinic Unconscious* (New York: Semiotext(e), 2010).

32. *TP*, 461.

33. *TP*, 455. In reference to Robert Blanché, *L'axiomatique* (Paris: PUF, 1955), §12 on the plurality, for a single axiomatic, of "different realizations, which can be borrowed from realms of thought very distant from the initial one"; page 47 et seq. for the definition of the *isomorphy* of models of realization constituting "different

interpretations" of a single axiomatique; §15 on the polymorphy of models of realization in a non-saturated system ("since non-saturation precisely means the possibility of one or more bifurcations"); and §26 on the possibility of polymorphic models even in a saturated axiomatic system.

34. *TP*, 456, 466; and *What is Philosophy?*, 103.

35. *TP*, 461 et seq.

36. *TP*, 436. "To the extent that capitalism constitutes an axiomatic (production for the market), all States and all social formations tend to become isomorphic in their capacity as models of realization: there is but one centered world market[...]. Worldwide organization thus ceases to pass "between" heterogeneous formations since it assures the isomorphy of those formations."

37. *TP*, 436.

38. *TP*, 455.

39. *TP*, 453. See Karl Marx, *Capital*, Book 1, Section VIII, Chapter XXXI ("The Genesis of the Industrial Capitalist"): "The money capital formed by means of usury and commerce was prevented from turning into industrial capital in the country by the feudal constitution, in the towns by the guild organization. These fetters vanished with the dissolution of feudal society, with the expropriation and partial eviction of the country population."

40. *TP*, 456.

41. *TP*, 461–463.

42. *TP*, 462.

43. *TP*, 462.

44. See below the problem of "interior peripherization": what Europe was becoming according to Deleuze-and-Guattari.

45. *TP*, 464.

46. *TP*, 462.

47. *TP*, 456.

48. From which comes, simultaneously, the distinction of the totalitarian capitalist State, as experimented in the neo-liberal laboratories of Latin American dictatorships, and the national-socialist "fascist" State: *TP*, 462.

49. *TP*, 463.

50. Samir Amin, *L'Accumulation à l'échelle mondiale* (Dakar-Paris: IFAN/Anthropos, 1970), 365.

51. *TP*, 462.

52. See above, Chapter 2, "Capture: For a Concept of Primitive Accumulation of State Power"

53. *TP*, 468.

54. *TP*, 462.

55. *TP*, 464.

56. *TP*, 465.

57. Étienne Balibar, "From Class Struggle to Classless Struggle?" in Étienne Balibar and Immanuel Wallerstein, *Race, Nation, Class. Ambiguous Identities* (New York: Verso, 2011), 177. ("Contrary to the illusions of development, which suppose that inequalities represent merely a lagging behind that will gradually be made up, the valorization of capital in the world-economy implies that practically *all historical forms of exploitation should be used simultaneously...*").

58. Samir Amin, *Accumulation on a World Scale*, 391.

59. *Ibid*, 391 (while this hypertrophy in the center translates "the difficulties of realizing the surplus value which are inherent in the advanced monopoly phase," it constitutes in itself in the periphery "a brake on accumulation").

60. *Ibid*, 393.

61. *AO*, 231.

62. *TP*, 465. Deleuze and Guattari already disqualify what would become the neo-liberal credo of the New International Economy" of Paul Krugman, attempting to justify the deregulation of capitalist and financial flows by a new international division of labor which would lead growth in the South into a vicious circle through unqualified jobs and replacing lost jobs with de-industrialization in the North with the development of qualified jobs in the "knowledge economy" or "service economy."

63. *TP*, 465.

64. *TP*, 468.

65. *TP*, 466.

66. *TP*, 466.

67. See, in particular, *TP*, 216–217, 468–469.

68. See Gilles Deleuze, "Nietzsche and Saint Paul, Lawrence and John of Patmos," *Essays Critical and Clinical* (1978); and the series of interventions on Palestine in *Two Regimes of Madness*: "Spoilers of Peace"(1978), 161–163; "The Indians of Palestine"(1982), 194–200; "The Importance of Being Arafat" (1984), 241–245; and "Stones" (1988), 338–339.

69. *TP*, 467.

70. Etienne Balibar, *Violence and Civility: On the Limits of Political Philosophy* (New York: Columbia University Press, 2015), 91 et seq. ("once capitalism has finished conquering, dividing up, and colonizing the world in the geographic sense (thus becoming 'planetary') it begins to recolonize it or to colonize its own 'core.'") See also, Etienne Balibar, "réflexions sur la crise européenne en cours," "http://www.gauchemip.org/spip.php?article13620"http://www.gauchemip.org/spip.php?article136 20 (no page numbers); and Pierre Sauvêtre, "Minoriser l'Europe pour sortir du post-colonialisme intérieur, » in *Lignes*, 34, February 2011, 145–160, which takes this "general colonial hypothesis" and shows its contemporaneity in the case of the Romas in Europe by combining the analyses of Balibar and Deleuze-Guattari.

71. *TP*, 468–469; see already in 1972 *AO*, 231. For an emblematic case of internal peripherization, see the analysis of Emmanuel Terray on the exploitation of immigrant workers in Europe in terms of "delocalization in place," in Emmanuel Terray et al., *Sans-papiers: l'archaïsme fatal* (Paris: la Découverte, 1999), 9–34. Alain François, in taking up Terray's analysis, shows how the presentation of the capitalist axiomatic in the 13th Plateau is already confronting the neoliberal order that was only systematized over the subsequent decades ("Capitalisme et sans-papiers," in Antoine Pickels et al., *A la lumière des sans-papiers* (Brussels: Éditions Complexe, 2001), 109–125.

72. On the different mechanisms through which neoliberal policies have maintained the new cycle of "accumulation through dispossession" over the past forty years since the 1973 crisis, see David Harvey, *The New Imperialism*, 145 et seq.

6. Becoming Minorities—Becoming Revolutionary

1. Étienne Balibar, "Droit au territoire," Preface to Enrica Rigo, *Europa di confine. Transformazioni della cittadinanza nell'Unione allargata* (Rome : Meltemi Editore, 2007).

2. See the writing of Louis Althusser in the late 1970s ("Enfin la crise du marxisme!", "Le marxisme comme théorie 'finie,'" etc.) and the analyses of Andrea Cavazzini, *Crise du marxisme et critique de l'État. Le dernier combat d'Althusser* (Reims: Le Clou dans le Fer, 2009).

3. "There's no longer any image of proletarians around of which [*sic*] it's just a matter of becoming conscious."Gilles Deleuze, "Control and Becoming," *Negotiations*, 173.

4. *TP*, 470.

5. Gilles Deleuze and Claire Parnet, *Dialogues* (New York : The Athlone Press, 1987), 146–147.

6. Guillaume Sibertin-Blanc, "D'une conjuncture l'autre: Guattari et Deleuze après-coup."

7. *TP*, 295–296: "History is made only by those who oppose history (not by those who insert themselves into it, or even reshape it). […] it always goes down in History but never comes from it."

8. See Gilles Deleuze, *Negotiations*, 175–176; and Gilles Deleuze and Félix Guattari, *What is Philosophy?*, 107.

9. Gilles Deleuze, "Philosophie et minorité," *Critique*, 369, February 1978, 154–155; taken up and modified in *TP*, 105. See also, *TP*, 291–293 and 469–470; and Gilles Deleuze, "Un manifeste en moins" in Carmelo Bene and Gilles Deleuze, *Superpositions* (Paris: Minuit, 1979), 124–125.

10. A decade later, Deleuze and Guattari would paint a bitter portrait: *What is Philosophy?*, 101–103, and on the function of opinion in the construction of a majority of consensus, 145–146 ("The essence of opinion is will to majority and already speaks in the name of a majority[…]").

11. *TP*, 293.

12. *TP*, 471.

13. *TP*, 469.

14. *Anti-Oedipus* named this operation "paralogism of displacement" (*AO*, 114–115).

15. See in this sense the reinterpretation suggested by Ernesto Laclau of Rancière's "*sans-parts*," in the framework (which transforms if not inverts its political significa- tion) of a "hegemonic logic": *On Populist Reason* (New York: Verso Books, 2007).; and the suggestive reading of Laclau by Slavoj Žižek, *The Ticklish Subject: The Absent Centre of Political Ontology* (New York: Verso Books, 2000), 182–187.

16. On the "binary machines," see Félix Guattari, *The Machinic Unconscious*, and *TP*, 7th, 9th, and 10th Plateaus.

17. On the internal polyglossia of Kafka's German, its territorial, political, and even geopolitical dimensions, as well as its semantic and syntactical dimensions, see Gilles Deleuze and Félix Guattari, *Kafka. Toward a Minor Literature* (Minneapolis, MN: University of Minnesota Press, 1986), 18–27; and *TP*, 101 et seq.

18. On these questions, see Jean-Jacques Lecercle, *A Marxist Philosophy of Language* (New York : Historical Materialism, 2009); Antoine Janvier and Julien Pieron, "'Pos- tulats de la linguistique' et politique de la langue: Benveniste, Labov, Ducrot," *Dissensus*, 3, February 2010, 138–163 ; and Guillaume Sibertin-Blanc, "Politique du style et minorization : de la sociolinguistique à la pragmatique de l'expression," in Adnen Jdey (dir.), *Les Styles de Deleuze* (Brussels : Les Impressions Nouvelles, 2011).

19. Gilles Deleuze and Félix Guattari, *Kafka. Toward a Minor Literature*, 19.

20. See Deleuze's preface to Guy Hocquenghem, *L'Après-Mai des Faunes* in *Desert Islands*, 284–288.

21. "Anything at all can do the job, but it always turns out to be a political affair. Becoming-minoritarian is a political affair and necessitates a labor of power (*puis- sance*), an active micropolitics. This is the opposite of macropolitics, and even of

History, in which it is a question of knowing how to win or obtain a majority."
(*TP*, 292).

22. See Étienne Balibar, *Violence and Civility*, 3rd Conference; and Eduardo Viveiros de Castro, *Cannibal Metaphysics*.

23. See Jacques Rancière, *La Mésentente* (Paris: Galilée, 1995), 89–90; and especially "La cause de l'autre," *Lignes*, 30, February 1997: *Algérie-France: Regards* croisés, 41–42. See the reconstruction of Kafka's "problem of expression" from the different linguistic impossibilities (which are at the same time points of subjectivity and politicaly untenable identification) from which the creative result of the literary process is determined, both stylistically and politically: see *Kafka, Toward a Minor Literature*, 16–22; *Cinema 2: The Time-Image*, Chapter 8, section 3; and Guillaume Sibertin-Blanc, "Politique du style et minoration chez Deleuze," 193–198.

24. *TP*, 291.

25. *TP*, 468–469.

26. *TP*, 469–470.

27. *TP*, 472.

28. *TP*, 468–9.

29. Étienne Balibar, *La crainte des masses* (Paris: Galilée, 1997, 223).

30. *TP*, 461–2.

31. *TP*, 462–3.

32. *AO*, 257–8.

33. See Bertrand Ogilvie, *L'Homme jetable. Essai sur l'exterminisme et la violence extreme* (Paris: Amsterdam, 2012).

34. *TP*, 472.

35. See Chapter 2: Capture and Sovereignty: State Economy and Aneconomy of Violence.

36. Karl Marx, *Capital*, Book 1, 873–877, 927–930.

37. *TP*, 470–471.

38. *TP*, 447–448; see Chapter 2.

39. See *AO*, 225, 238–239, 268–269.

40. *TP*, 471–472.

41. Karl Marx, *Capital*, Book 1, 848: "The continual emigration to the towns, the continual formation of a surplus population in the countryside through the concentration of farms, the conversion of arable land into pasture, the introduction of

machinery, etc., are things which go hand in hand with the continual eviction of the agricultural population by the destruction of their cottages. [...] The creation of dense knots of humanity in scattered little villages and small country towns corresponds to the forcible draining of men from the surface of the land."

42. This was the case of Native Americans in North America, for which Elias Sanbar suggested an analogy with Palestine: see Gilles Deleuze, "The Importance of Being Arafat," 241; and Gilles Deleuze and Elias Sanbar, "Indians of Palestine," 197–198: "[E.S.] The Zionist movement mobilized the Jewish community in Palestine not with the idea that the Palestinians would one day leave, but with the idea that the country was 'empty.' [...] if this disappearance was going to succeed, from the outset they had to act as though it had already happened, by "never seeing" the existence of the Other, who was nonetheless unmistakably present. Emptying the territory, if it were to succeed, had to begin by emptying 'the Other' from the head of the colonizer."

43. *TP*, 345–346.

44. Karl Marx and Friedrich Engels, *The Communist Manifesto*, (Radford, VA: Wilder Publications, 2007), 8.

45. On these questions, see Étienne Balibar, *La crainte des masses*, Chapters "La relève de l'idéalisme" and "Le proletariat insaissisable."

46. Gilles Deleuze and Claire Parnet, *Dialogues*, 145. On the problem of the organization of institutional creativity in Guattari, see in particular "Causality, Subjectivity, History" (1966–1968) in Félix Guattari, *Psychoanalysis and Transversality* (New York: Semiotext(e), 2015).

47. *AO*, 255–257.

48. *TP*, 472–473. And Gilles Deleuze, *Foucault*, 74. See also Étienne Balibar, "La lutte de classes sans classes?" in Éitenne Balibar and Immanuel Wallerstein, *Race, Nation, Class*.

49. *TP*, 470–471.

50. *TP*, 470–471.

51. See *TP*, 456. And Gilles Deleuze and Claire Parnet, *Dialogues*, 145–146.

52. *TP*, 463–464.

53. *TP*, 465.

54. *TP*, 471.

55. See Guillaume Sibertin-Blanc, "D'une conjecture l'autre: Guattari et Deleuze après-coup," *Actuel Marx*, 52, 28–47.

56. See Gilles Deleuze, *Foucault*, 95.

57. Gilles Deleuze and Félix Guattari, "May '68 Did Not Take Place," *Two Regimes of Madness*, 233–236.

58. *TP*, 471.

59. *TP*, 456.

60. The minoritarian, as Deleuze and Guattari note in *Kafka*, is indicated precisely by the impossibility of internalizing these divisions, if not in particularly difficult and contradictory conditions. Thus the individual/collective cut: precisely because it is in an unstable, marginal, or precarious state in relation to the conditions of life and the rights of "major" subjects, everything that comes in the eyes of the latter from "the individual concern (familial, marital, and so on) joins with other no less individual concerns, the social milieu serving as a mere environment or a background," takes on the contrary for the minoritarian an *immediately* collective, social, and political scope (*Kafka*, 17). As early as 1974, Deleuze revealed a similar problem in his preface to Guy Hocquenghem' *L'Après-midi des Faunes*, in *Desert Islands*, 284–288. These two works perform the concept of "paralogism of application (*rabattement*)" forged in *Anti-Oedipus*, 275 et seq,; see Guillaume Sibertin-Blanc, *Deleuze et l'Anti-Oedipe*, 96–103.

61. *TP*, 106.

62. *TP*, 473.

63. See for example the way that thinkers like Chandra Mohanty and Judith Butler have reformulated the question of the "conditions of possibility of an international feminist coalition" holding at a distance the "falsely homogenous conception" of conditions of oppression and demands produced by Western feminists. Butler indicates the instability that affects the asking of the question itself: on the one hand, "We could disagree on the status and character of modernity and yet find ourselves joined in asserting and defending the rights of indigenous women to health care, reproductive technology, decent wages, physical protection, cultural rights, freedom of assembly." These "universal" demands do not fail to be diffracted in encountering the fact that "an international coalition of feminist activists and thinkers [...] will have to accept the array of sometimes incommensurable epistemological and political beliefs and modes and means of agency that bring us into activism" (Judith Butler, *Precarious Life: The Powers of Mourning and Violence* (New York: Verso, 2004), 48).

64. Gilles Deleuze and Claire Parnet, *Dialogues*, 174–175.

65. This question was at the heart of the new "dramaturgy of power" at the time, as seen in the work of Michel Deutsch, Franz Xaver Kroetz, or Jean-Paul Wenzel, and throughout Reiner Werner Fassbinder, who made what Marieluise FLeisser called the *druck nach unten* one of the main motifs of his work. On this entire sequence, see Armelle Talbot, *Théâtres du pouvoir, théâtres du quotidian.Retour sur les dramaturgies des années 1970* (Louvain-La-Neuve: Études théâtrales, 43, 2008), in particular, 83–90.

66. *TP*, 291.

67. *Idem.*

68. *TP*, 203.

69. *TP*, 106.

Conclusion

1. *TP*, 458.

2. *TP*, 456.

3. See Guillaume Sibertin-Blanc, "Peuple et territoire: Deleuze lecteur de la *Revue des Études Palestiniennes*," in Catherine Mayaux (dir.), *Écrivains et intellectuels français face au monde arabe* (Paris: Honoré Champion, 2011), 251–260.

4. *TP*, 470: "everywhere we look we see the conditions for a worldwide movement: the minorities recreate "nationalitarian" phenomena that the nation-states had been charged with controlling and quashing."

5. Gilles Deleuze and Félix Guattari, *Kafka. Toward a Minor Literature.* (Minneapolis: University of Minnesota Press, 1986) 27 et sq., 41–42, 56–57, 82–85.

6. Hannah Arendt, *Imperialism* (New York: Mariner Books, 1968), 147 et seq.

7. *Ibid*, 151.

8. Deleuze et Guattari, "Le pire moyen de faire l'Europe," *op. cit.*

9. Hannah Arendt, *Imperialism*, *op. cit.*, 149 *et. seq.*

10. *TP*, 456. See Gilles Deleuze, *Cinema 2.The Time-Image*, 146–150, 151–167, 207–215.

11. On all of these question, totalization as an indissociably aesthetic and political problem starting with Romanticism, the different destinies of the land/people break, the Wagnerian moment and its ambiguities, and the evolution of Paul Klee himself, see *TP*, 338–342; on the historical crisis of the project of revolutionary art as art of the masses, in correlation with the irreversible crisis of a concept full of people, see the discussion of the theses of Walter Benjamin and Siegfried Kracauer in Gilles Deleuze, *Cinema 2. The Time-Image*, op. cit., Chapter 7, section 1 and Chapter 10, section 1.

12. Gilles Deleuze, Cinema 2. The Time-Image, *op. cit.*, 209.

13. Étienne Balibar, *Violence et civilité*, *op. cit.*, 187.

14. Cited in *TP*, 292, note 81.

15. See Gilles Deleuze, *Cinema 2. The Time-Image*, 144–150.

16. See the analyses of the films of Glauber Rocha and the indirect references to Franz Fanon in *Cinema 2. The Time-Image*, *op. cit.*, Chapter 8, section 3.